China's Belt and Road
The Initiative and Its Financial Focus

Series on China's Belt and Road Initiative

Print ISSN: 2591-7730
Online ISSN: 2591-7749

Series Editors: ZHENG Yongnian *(National University of Singapore, Sinapore)*
Kerry BROWN *(King's College London, UK)*
WANG Yiwei *(Renmin University of China, China)*
LIU Weidong *(Chinese Academy of Sciences, China)*

This book series showcases the most up-to-date and significant research on China's Belt and Road Initiative (BRI) by leading scholars from inside and outside China. It presents a panoramic view on the BRI, from the perspectives of China's domestic policy, China's foreign investment, international relations, cultural cooperation and historical inheritance. As the first English book series on the BRI, this series offers a valuable English-language resource for researchers, policymakers, professionals and students to better understand the challenges and opportunities brought by the BRI.

Published:

Vol. 2 *China's Belt and Road: The Initiative and Its Financial Focus*
by YU Xugang, Cristiano RIZZI, Mario TETTAMANTI,
Fabio E. ZICCARDI and GUO Li

Vol. 1 *The Political Economy of China's Belt and Road Initiative*
by ZOU Lei
translated by ZHANG Zhiping

China's Belt and Road
The Initiative and Its Financial Focus

YU Xugang
Dentons Law Offices, China

Cristiano RIZZI
Link to Beijing Consulting Partnership Enterprise, China

Mario TETTAMANTI
Link to Beijing Consulting Partnership Enterprise, China

Fabio E. ZICCARDI
Milan University, Italy

GUO Li
Peking University, China

World Scientific

NEW JERSEY · LONDON · SINGAPORE · BEIJING · SHANGHAI · HONG KONG · TAIPEI · CHENNAI · TOKYO

Published by

World Scientific Publishing Co. Pte. Ltd.
5 Toh Tuck Link, Singapore 596224
USA office: 27 Warren Street, Suite 401-402, Hackensack, NJ 07601
UK office: 57 Shelton Street, Covent Garden, London WC2H 9HE

British Library Cataloguing-in-Publication Data
A catalogue record for this book is available from the British Library.

Series on China's Belt and Road Initiative — Vol. 2
CHINA'S BELT AND ROAD
The Initiative and Its Financial Focus

Copyright © 2018 by World Scientific Publishing Co. Pte. Ltd.

ISBN 978-981-3239-53-1

For any available supplementary material, please visit
http://www.worldscientific.com/worldscibooks/10.1142/10971#t=suppl

Desk Editors: Chandrima Maitra/Dong Lixi

Typeset by Stallion Press
Email: enquiries@stallionpress.com

Printed in Singapore

Foreword

OBOR: An Upgraded Silk Road for the 21st Century

This book provides an organized introduction to the One Belt One Road (OBOR) Initiative, which is more popularly known as "The Belt and Road" (B&R). This Initiative, which has already been embodied in China's strategic plan, is not easy to define because it encompasses a wide array of issues. While it can certainly be interpreted as China's new foreign policy manifesto, it is also a collection of interlinked trade deals and infrastructure projects throughout the Eurasia and Pacific regions. When taken together, these trade deals and infrastructure projects aim at better integrating this part of the world and enhancing the trade relationships among all the countries involved in the Initiative.

Furthermore, according to Chinese leaders, this Initiative is also intended to be a project to strengthen the globalization process, of which China has become a champion. Globalization is, in China's eyes, the solution to revive the world economy, and drive it forward. That being said, a clear and unequivocal definition of what exactly qualifies as a B&R project (or, for that matter, which countries are even involved in this Initiative) is often fuzzy. The Initiative is large and still growing, with more facets and implications than can be easily summarized or explained.

The authors assembled in this book have deftly explored the many aspects which compose and surround the B&R Initiative. China has taken the lead to create new institutions, such as the AIIB and the Silk Road Fund, in order to facilitate and sustain this massive plan. The authors have successfully illustrated these institutions and their roles, making a clear distinction between the institutional funding of the B&R on the one hand, and the private sector, which also plays a significant role in financing the different projects connected to the B&R, on the other.

But the funding of the B&R Initiative is only one area that the authors have analyzed and explained. They have also given careful consideration to the impacts and implications of the B&R Initiative at the international level. As it emerges from the pages of this book, there are many collateral effects related to this Initiative, such as the internationalization of the Chinese Yuan, and the growing influence of China in international affairs. Many other aspects are also touched upon, including the inevitable expansion of China in the EU market through new investments. Chinese ODI (Outbound Direct Investments) is likely to surge in the future, especially with the development of the B&R Initiative. Therefore, the authors have given particular attention to the relationship between China and the EU, because it represents a natural result of the new Silk Road.

As the name implies, the "Belt and Road" in fact aims to both restore the ancient Silk Road and to rejuvenate it by adding new meaning. In this book, emphasis is paid to China's connection with Italy, which serves as a stopover for Chinese goods on their way to the rest of the EU. Prof. Fabio E. Ziccardi, an esteemed Italian colleague and distinguished scholar with vast experience in the field of International Law, has contributed another important part related to the transportation of goods. The smooth transportation of goods between China and Europe was a key objective of the ancient Silk Road, and the B&R Initiative shares this goal.

The connection goes beyond trade. Today, Italian and Chinese companies often partner on important infrastructure projects. In doing so, Chinese companies must abide by EU procurement rules and comply with the local regulations. A lucid explanation of those rules is therefore offered, in order to give a complete picture of how Chinese companies can cooperate with their counterparts in the EU. The authors have also elaborated on how China is identifying potential projects in the EU. As a matter of fact, the EU already has its own plan to upgrade the infrastructure in Europe, the so-called Connectivity Platform. This is a priority for the EU, and there is certainly room for further cooperation so as to integrate these initiatives.

Finally, this book is enriched by the contribution of one important bank, namely "UBS" which offer intriguing descriptions of their role in developing the B&R Initiative. An ambitious initiative like the Belt and Road cannot be carried out by the Chinese alone. As the authors make clear, well-coordinated international efforts are imperative in order to achieve this far-sighted goal, which will benefit not only China but all the countries and peoples contributing to it.

Li Guo 郭雳
Professor of Law
Peking University
Beijing

15 November 2017

Preface

This book aims at illustrating the OBOR Initiative, (now also known as "Belt and Road" (B&R) Initiative) and its many facets, including its background, and how the Chinese government intends to develop this ambitious project. Consideration is also given to the different players involved in this huge project. As an incredible amount of money (US$1 trillion, probably more) is involved, the book describes in detail the institutions (lenders especially) which are involved in the B&R Initiative and their role. A brief guidance is also given on how interested parties can participate in the different projects connected to the Initiative.

The views of the different authors, on the main aspects of this Initiative, should also serve as suggestions on how to interpret and take part in this project.

The book provides an exceptional amount of information about how projects are financed, and about how to develop those projects. A Particular focus is given to the relationship between China and the EU because the scope of this Initiative is to boost trade relationships between these two blocks, and not only to create new opportunities for all the countries along the Silk Road.

The eight chapters of this book are intended to illustrate specific topics related to different aspects of the B&R Initiative. Each of the chapters can be seen as individual parts which complement each other — in fact the authors specifically discussed and agreed in this sense. However, the chapters are not simply stitched together. We used a specific logic to connect and link each of the eight chapters. Subsequently, each of the chapters completes each other in a fashion that presents the reader with a complete picture about the B&R Initiative and its many facets and impacts especially on the EU economy.

The information discussed in the eight different chapters is complete and updated as of December 2017. We do hope that the information discussed in the eight chapters of this book will assist the readers in understanding the complicated background and functioning of this project.

The contribution of the UBS helps in better assessing this ambitious project and clearly shows the interest of financial institutions in participating more in financing this Initiative.

Xugang Yu, Cristiano Rizzi, Mario Tettamanti
and Fabio Emilio Ziccardi

About the Authors

Xugang Yu is a Senior Partner at Dentons Law Offices, heading the Capital Market team of Dentons China, with over 20 years of experience in securities transactions domestically and internationally. Yu also serves as Independent Director of Central China Securities, Baoshan and Dafeng ports listed at Shanghai and Hong Kong. Yu has published over 30 academic papers and 10 books. He also advises regulators, courts, arbitration bodies and ministries both domestically and overseas, especially now on the Belt and Road legal issues. Yu is a Visiting Professor at the University of International Business and Economics — School of Law, and Huazhong University of Science and Technology. He holds a Ph.D. (2001), and an LL.M (1998) in International Economic Law from Peking University, and an LL.B from Chinese University of Political Science and Law (1990). Besides having coordinated this work, Yu is the sole author of Chapter 1, and co-author of Chapter 2.

Cristiano Rizzi is a foreign professional who has been working "on the ground" in Mainland China for the past 10 years. Rizzi is a Counsel of Link to Beijing Consulting Partnership Enterprise. He is cooperating also with Xugang Yu, Senior Partner at Dentons, assisting Chinese companies in finding investment opportunities in the EU region. Rizzi is incorporated at the *"Illustre Colegio de Abogados de Salamanca"*, Spain and registered as "Avvocato Stabilito" at the *"Consiglio dell'Ordine degli Avvocati di Milano"*, Italy. Rizzi obtained his LL.M in Chinese Law from Peking University, China, LL.M. in Spanish Law from University of Valladolid, Spain, and LL.M in International Business Law from University of Exeter,

UK. The author contributed to the parts related to the impact on the European economy from the B&R investment. In particular, Rizzi co-authored Chapter 2 with Xugang Yu, and co-authored Chapters 3 and 6 on the financial institutions financing the B&R Initiative with Mario Tettamanti. Rizzi is also the sole author of Chapters 5 and 7.

Mario Tettamanti is a partner and CEO of Link to Beijing Consulting Partnership. Tettamanti holds a Ph.D. in Economics (1981) and has worked in Mainland China for eight consecutive years. Tettamanti was an Editorialist and Chef Redactor of the Economic Section at Corriere del Ticino (Switzerland), Professor at the Centro di Studi Bancari (Lugano). Tettamanti has a vast experience in the financial field. He was the First Vice President and responsible for Italian, French and German clients at UBS New York. He also worked as Deputy Head of the financial department and was Head of the Investment Committee at Banco di Lugano (UBS Group). Tettamanti acts as a point of reference for important private financial groups in China and is assisting several Chinese companies in finding investment opportunities in the EU. Tettamanti is the sole author of Chapter 4 and co-authored Chapters 3 and 6 with Cristiano Rizzi. He also coordinated the UBS's intervention in the book.

Fabio E. Ziccardi is a retired Professor of School of Political Sciences, Milan University. Ziccardi has authored 5 books and about 50 papers and articles on civil, comparative, international private and arbitration laws. He is also an arbitrator in national and international proceedings. Ziccardi contributed to this work with his final notes on the impact of the B&R Initiative on the development of international law, particularly the law of international carriage of goods and international business law in Chapter 8.

Li Guo is a Professor of Law School, Peking University. He obtained his LL.B. and LL.D. from Peking University, LL.M from Southern Methodist University and LL.M from Harvard University. He is also a Visiting Professor at Cornell University, Visiting Scholar at Vanderbilt University and a Humboldt Foundation Researcher at University of Freiburg. Guo supervised the development of this work and helped in structuring the content. He wrote the Foreword highlighting the reasoning behind the topics of this work.

Acknowledgments

This book is the final result of joint efforts by Cristiano Rizzi, Xugang Yu, Mario Tettamanti, Fabio E. Ziccardi, and Guo Li. A team composed by an Italian Lawyer with more than 10 years experience in China, who has authored four books on Chinese issues ranging from M&A in China to the protection of IPRs in China, the functioning of e-commerce in China, and Chinese expansion into the EU; Xugang Yu, a Senior Partner at Dentons, which is considered as one of the most prestigious Chinese law firms at home as well as overseas; a Swiss Economist, Mario Tettamanti who is an ex-top executive at UBS with vast expertise in international finance; Fabio Ziccardi who is an Italian Professor with vast experience in International Law; and a Professor of Law at Peking University, Li Guo who has explained clearly the content of this book in the Foreword.

I would like to express my gratitude in particular to Xugang Yu, who proposed the idea of writing this book together with him. Xugang Yu was the first to realize the importance this work can have for all the participants to the B&R Initiative, because no other books deal with the many facets comprising this Initiative. Naturally, my gratitude also goes to Mario Tettamanti, who encouraged me and believed in my capabilities to connect people, and to Fabio Ziccardi, for having faith in my capabilities and for providing great support all these years with his invaluable advice professionally and personally. Last but not least, I thank Guo Li for his contribution and support.

I express my gratitude to Wang Wei, senior partner at Dentons, for supporting and believing my abilities, and to every other person who encouraged me during the development of this new manuscript.

This work is intended to highlight the new policy China is pursuing in order to contribute to changing global governance, and how China is contributing to that scope; without the help of all the other authors, this piece of work would not have been concluded.

My family and friends also played a fundamental role in the completion of this manuscript by inspiring me as I pursued the final draft of this project.

The organization and the contents of this manuscript have been discussed among the four authors, and the outcome is a complete analysis of the Belt and Road Initiative and its many facets and the impact this Initiative will have on the rest of the global economy.

We do hope our efforts can be of some use for readers from different backgrounds, that is, not only for investors or professionals but also for parties interested in knowing what this huge project also known as the OBOR is all about and how China is developing this Initiative. For this reason, we tried our best to render the contents of this book in the most "readable" possible manner for non-professionals and the vast public.

Cristiano Rizzi

Contents

Abbreviations and Acronyms

ADB	Asian Development Bank
AIC	Administration of Industry and Commerce
AIIB	Asian Infrastructure Investment Bank
APEC	Asia-Pacific Economic Cooperation
ASEAN	Association of Southeast Asian Nations
B&R	Belt and Road
BITs	Bilateral Investment Treaties
BRICS	Brazil, the Russian Federation, India, China, and South Africa
CBRC	China Bank Regulatory Commission
CCPIT	China Council for the Promotion of International Trade
CECIF	China–EU Co-Investment Fund
CIC	China Investment Corporation
CEF	Connecting Europe Facility
CIPA	China Investment Promoting Agency
CNY	Chinese Yuan
CP	Connectivity Platform
CPC	Communist Party of China
CPCC	Communist Party Central Committee
CSRC	China Securities Regulatory Commission
DRC	Development Research Center of the State Council, P. R. China
EC	European Commission

EEC	European Economic Community
EFSI	European Fund for Strategic Investments
EFTA	European Free Trade Association
EIB	European Investment Bank
EIF	European Investment Fund
EU	European Union
FYP (or 5YP)	Five-year Plan
EUR	Euro (unit of currency used in the EU)
FDI	Foreign Direct Investment
FIEs	Foreign Invested Enterprises
FTA	Free Trade Agreement
FTZ	Free Trade Zone
GATT	General Agreement on Tariffs and Trade
GDP	Gross Domestic Product
GEM	Growth Enterprises Market
GNI	Gross National Income
HRS	Household responsibility system
IBRD	International Bank for Reconstruction and Development
ICT	Information and Communication Technology
IDA	International Development Association
IFC	International Finance Corporation
IMF	International Monetary Fund
IPA	Investment Promotion Agency
IP	Intellectual Property
IPO	Initial Public Offering
IPRs	Intellectual Property Rights
IT	Information Technology
M&A	Mergers and Acquisitions
MFN	Most-favored Nation
MIIT	Ministry of Industry and Information Technology
MOF	Ministry of Finance (of the People's Republic of China)
MOFCOM	Ministry of Commerce (of the People's Republic of China)
MNCs	Multinational Corporations
MSR	Maritime Silk Road
NAPA	Northern Adriatic Port Association

NDB	New Development Bank
NBSC	National Bureau of Statistics of China
NDRC	National Development and Reform Commission
NPC	National People's Congress
OBOR	One Belt, One Road
ODI	Outbound Direct Investment
OECD	Organization of Economic Co-operation and Development
OFDI	Outward Foreign Direct Investment
OFIC	Outbound Foreign Investment Catalogue
PBoC	People's Bank of China
PPP	Public–Private Partnership
PSU	Public Service Unit
PRC	People's Republic of China
QDII	Qualified Domestic Institutional Investor
QFII	Qualified Foreign Institutional Investor
R-QFII	RMB-Qualified Foreign Institutional Investor
R&D	Research and Development
RMB	Renminbi
SAIC	State Administration for Industry and Commerce
SAFE	State Administration of Foreign Exchange
SAMC	State Asset-management Company
SASAC	State-owned Assets Supervision and Administration Commission
SAR	Special Administration Region
SC	State Council
SCO	Shanghai Cooperation Organization
SIPO	State Intellectual Property Office
SFI	State Financial Institutions
SME	Small and Medium Enterprise
SOEs	State-owned Enterprises
SPFTZ	Shanghai Pilot Free Trade Zone
SRF	Silk Road Fund
S&T	Science & Technology
SWF	Sovereign Wealth Fund
TEU	Treaty on the European Union

UN	United Nations
US	United States of America
UNEP	United Nations Environment Program
VAT	Value-added Tax
WIPO	World Intellectual Property Organization
WTO	World Trade Organization

Introduction

The first part of this book, namely Chapter 1, illustrates the background and the very necessary conditions which have allowed to seed the terrain for the Reforms and consequently for the Beijing Consensus, allowing the conceivement of the Belt & Road (B&R) Initiative. In fact, it is possible to affirm that the "B&R" is the direct result and consequence of the Beijing Consensus. It is necessary to introduce these concepts because without them China would not have achieved all its great goals and acquired a leading position in world affairs.

The B&R Initiative represents an enormous opportunity for China to regain its splendor and to play a major role not only in trade relationships, but also at the international stage, if the many difficulties to be dealt with in order to realize this ambitious project will be properly and efficiently overcome. The project is extremely challenging because it involves more than 60 nations belonging to three different continents, i.e. Asia, Africa and Europe, representing roughly the 60% of the world population, and 1/3 (probably more) or the aggregate GDP. The whole project is destined to reshape the world economy and also rebalance China's geopolitics, putting emphasis on the relations with the EU, consequently diminishing the role of the US' commercial ties with China.

Before introducing the many aspects surrounding the B&R Initiative, it is extremely important to clarify the concept of this Initiative. In fact, the term itself can be a little confusing, so just to make it clearer the "belt" is a series of overland corridors connecting China with Europe, via

Central Asia and the Middle East; the "road" does not refer to a road in the strict sense but rather to a sea route linking China's southern coast to East Africa and the Mediterranean.

President Xi Jinping in February 2017 in his keynote speech at the World Economic Forum in Davos, Switzerland,[1] announced that the B&R Initiative will be a platform for the countries to look for solutions to global economic problems. The attendance of the Chinese President at the Forum showed China's active stance in participating in global governance, and especially China's interest in expanding cooperation with the other countries. China's major concern, however, is to stimulate the world economy and to keep the pace of the expansion of its own economy implementing the B&R project, which will have enormous economic impact not only for China but also, and in particular, for the countries on the track of the new Silk Road.

Chinese President Xi also spoke about on globalization, trade protectionism and climate change during his Davos speech, giving a Chinese perspective on global issues and clearly marking out a strategy for global recovery and prosperity. Moreover, at Davos Forum President Xi stressed the importance of economic openness, pointing out that many of the problems troubling the world are not caused by economic globalization: "Global economic depression strains the relations between growth and distribution, between capital and labor, and between efficiency and equity. Both developed and developing countries have felt the punch,"[2] he affirmed; to counter such problems, "we should strike a balance between efficiency and equity to ensure that different countries, different social stratus and different groups of people all share in the benefits of economic globalization."[3]

Concerning the second issue, President Xi used an appropriate metaphor to depict trade protectionism in his speech in Davos: "Pursuing protectionism is like locking oneself in a dark room. While wind and rain

---

[1] Chinese President Xi Jinping delivered a keynote speech at the opening session of the World Economic Forum Annual Meeting 2017 in Davos, Switzerland, on January 17. The Davos Forum is not only the world's premier annual elite fest, but is also seen as a weathervane of global economy.

[2] Xi Jinping's speech at Davos Forum, January 17, 2017.

[3] *Ibid.*

may be kept outside, that dark room will also block light and air. No one will emerge as a winner in a trade war."[4] Finally, on climate change President Xi affirmed that "It is important to protect the environment while pursuing economic and social progress — to achieve harmony between man and nature, and harmony between man and society;" and also he added "The Paris agreement is a hard-won achievement ... all signatories should stick to it rather walk away."[5]

All these statements show the interest of China in maintaining the necessary consensus on major issues which impact the economic development of the entire world and are critical for putting in place China's plans for better integrating itself and assuming a reference role for international affairs.

China is perfectly aware that its influence is growing and its role in defining a new world order is undeniable, but the wise Chinese leadership is also aware that in order to achieve internal objectives, and properly play the role China is assuming, it is a priority to assure that its vision is accepted not only by the other major powers but also by the rest of the nations. China's investment policies are of great importance not only for sustaining internal economic growth but also for contributing to enhance trade and economic relations with third-party nations. The plan to build a new Silk Road is also showing the preferences and focus China is now putting on the EU, this also considered the more attractiveness the EU is offering to Chinese investments. Thus, the B&R Initiative will positively influence investment trends toward the EU, though not directly aimed at this. Chinese investments in the infrastructure sector will surge dramatically. However, many obstacles will have to be overcome in order to realize this ambitious project. The Chinese will have to make an effort to understand the rules of each single country touched by the project, just as when foreigners invest in China, for the success of the project itself.

---

[4] *Ibid.*
[5] *Ibid.*

CHAPTER 1

"Belt & Road Initiative" as a Continuation of China's Reforms and Opening up and as a Consequence of the Beijing Consensus

Xugang Yu

Any circumstance hitting a limit will begin to change. Change will in turn lead to an unimpeded state, and then lead to continuity.

Laozi, Chinese Philosopher

Before illustrating the Belt & Road (B&R) Initiative in its many facets, this chapter aims at providing a clear picture of the background and of the opening-up policy China has adopted in the last part of its modern history, which has allowed not only the development of China but also the conceivement of the B&R Initiative which can be considered as a consequence of the opening up and also of the Beijing Consensus.

1.1 The Formation of China's Reform and Opening-up Policy

1.1.1 *Deng Xiaoping's Enlightenment Works and His Rehabilitations: The Turning Point of Socialist China*

Deng Xiaoping will always be remembered as one of the greatest Chinese politicians. Deng's efforts in serving China was disturbed by many historical events, however, his legacy is of paramount importance to China. Without the guidance of Deng Xiaoping, China would have never achieved its goals. Although Deng had a troubled political career (he was rehabilitated more than once), he contributed enormously to the advancements in China.

It is necessary to retrace Deng's experience in order to focus on all the events which have brought China forward to its present position at the international stage.

In May 1966, the Culture Revolution began, while Deng was the General Secretary of the Central Committee of the Communist Party of China (CPC) and also a Member of the Standing Committee of the Political Bureau of the Central Committee of CPC. From September 1966 to October 1967, Deng was "isolated" in his house in Zhongnanhai, then he was sent to Nanchang, Jiangxi Province, and during this period, his role was greatly diminished. In March 1973, Deng was rehabilitated as the Vice Premier of the State Council. On January 5, 1975, he was appointed as the Vice Chairman of the Central Military Commission of the CPC and the Chief of the General Staff of the Chinese People's Liberation Army. On January 10, he was selected as the Vice Chairman of the Central Committee of the CPC and as a Member of the Standing Committee of the Political Bureau of the Central Committee of the CPC by the 2nd Plenary Session of the 10th Central Committee of the CPC; on January 17, he was appointed as the first Vice Premier of the State Council by the 1st Session of the 4th National People's Congress (NPC).

On April 7, 1976, Deng Xiaoping was once again removed from all of his positions, but kept within the Party membership. On July 21, 1977, Deng was again rehabilitated by the 3rd Plenary Session of the 10th Central Committee of the CPC and he reassumed all his positions.

Before his second rehabilitation, Deng continued to study and prepare material, today considered as "enlightenment work," which would have been useful for the reform and opening-up policy in the years to come.

An episode is of particular significance in Deng's experience, which convinced the Chinese leader to follow the path of reforms. In November 1977, Shenzhen came into Deng Xiaoping's view when he inspected Guangdong Province as the first stop after his comeback as the Chinese leader. It is necessary to give a brief background here:

On October 19, 1949, Shenzhen of Guangdong Province was liberated from the Guomindang government, but because of the tensions between the People's Republic of China and the United Kingdom, the border between Hong Kong and Shenzhen was closed from 1951 onward. This situation, however, did not prevent the successive 20 years of four massive waves of stealing and incursions into Hong Kong from Shenzhen (counting around 1 million people) in 1957, 1961, 1972 and 1979. During this time, one of the main missions of the police was to prevent people from crossing the borders, and these actions were becoming increasingly fierce.[1]

At this time, there were two villages on both sides of the Sino-British border, both named Luofang Village, one in Shenzhen, one in Hong Kong, separated by a river. The GDP of the Hong Kong Luofang was HKD 13,000, the other in Shenzhen was RMB 134 only; the income of Luofang villagers in Hong Kong was 100 times that of the villagers in Shenzhen.

Naturally, this situation came to Deng Xioaping's attention, and during his visit to Guangdong Province on November 17, 1977, while the leaders of the Guangdong Committee of the CPC reported to him about the escaping or "transhumance" trend, Deng firmly said, "escaping to Hong Kong is mainly because life is not good and difference is too big"[2] and stressed that "something was wrong with our policy, and the armed forces could not control this kind of situation." These statements shocked the reporters, and they got the sense that Deng Xiaoping was completely indifferent to this delicate and complex issue. These two sentences also puzzled the leaders of Guangdong Province: How should they deal with this situation? If it is not convenient using the armed forces (the police) to

---

[1] See Chen Hong, *Folk Observation on Important Decisions and Events of Shenzhen in 1979–2000*, Yangtze River Literature and Art Publishing House, 2006, p. 3–4.
[2] See CCCPC Party Literature Research Office, *The Chronicle of Deng Xiaoping's Life (1975–1997)*, Central Literature Publishing House, 2004, p. 238.

control this situation, in which manner could it be better managed? The answers to these questions can be found in the reforms China gradually adopted to solve the differences and transit the country toward a more just and harmonious society.

Deng Xiaoping realized that the only way to grant China a steady development was to introduce changes through gradual reforms and also open up to the outside world. China, under Deng's guidance, chose Socialism, but a Socialism with Chinese characteristics, which Deng firmly believed was the most suitable model for his country. In one of his speeches, he affirmed, "Currently, although we are engaging in Socialism, … only until the middle period of next century, when we achieve the moderately developed countries' level, we could say that we are really engaging in Socialism and we could self-confidently say that socialism excels capitalism."[3]

This specific historical moment marked the time China started a period of reforms and gradually implemented the opening-up policy, leading the country to more prosperous shores.

1.1.2 *The Resolution of the 3rd Plenary Session of the 11th CPC Central Committee: Starting Point of China's Reform and Opening-up Policy*

Although Deng Xiaoping was rehabilitated, there was an erroneous notion still puzzling the country, the "Two Whatevers,"[4] which was pursued by then Party Chairman Hua Guofeng after the death of Chairman Mao. Hua became Communist Party Chairman in September 1976, and he pursued the notion that "whatever policy decisions Mao had made must be firmly upheld and whatever instructions he had given must be followed unswervingly." The statement first appeared in an editorial entitled *Study the*

---

[3] See Chen Hong, Folk Observation on Important Decisions and Events of Shenzhen in 1979–2000, Yangtze River Literature and Art Publishing House, 2006, at p. 8.

[4] The Two Whatevers (simplified Chinese: 两个凡是; traditional Chinese: 兩個凡是; pinyin: *Liǎng gè fán shì*) refers to the statement that *"We will resolutely uphold whatever policy decisions Chairman Mao made, and unswervingly follow whatever instructions Chairman Mao gave"* (凡是毛主席作出的决策, 我们都坚决维护; 凡是毛主席的指示, 我们都始终不渝地遵循).

Documents Carefully and Grasp the Key Link, which was published simultaneously in the *People's Daily,* the Liberation Army Daily and later in the monthly journal *Hongqi* or the "Red Flag."[5]

The remarks, however, were replaced by the more pragmatic slogan given by Deng Xiaoping that "it doesn't matter if a cat is black or white, as long as it catches mice."

On April 10, 1977, although Deng Xiaoping was still not rehabilitated, he wrote to the Central Committee of CPC, bringing forward his theories using accurate and complete Mao Zedong Thoughts, to direct the Party's work. Then he talked with comrades from the Party illustrating this issue. On May 24, 1977, he affirmed that the "Two Whatevers" principle was not accorded with Marxism; it was not "workable." What comrade Mao Zedong had spoken was to be interpreted according to the time and situation he expressed himself. Comrade Mao Zedong himself had expressed several times that some of what he had said was wrong.[6] And then there was a nationwide debate against the ideological principles of emancipating the mind and seeking truth from facts and bringing order out of chaos. On May 11, 1978, "Practice is the sole criterion for testing truth," published in *Guangming Daily,* emphasized that the criterion for testing truth was only a social practice, and that the integration of practice and theory was one of the most fundamental principles of Marxism, which in fact criticized the wrong guideline of the "Two Whatevers." The publication of this piece of article initiated a nationwide debate on the "truth criterion," suppressed by Hua Guofeng, but led and supported positively by Deng Xiaoping and majority of the other central leaders. This debate broke through the tie of "Left" wrong thought for a long time and prepared in theory and in ideas for the convening of the 3rd Plenary Session of the 11th Central Committee of CPC, which was a pivotal meeting of the Central Committee of CPC.

From August 12 to August 18, 1977, the 11th National Congress of the CPC was held,[7] which firmly and unequivocally decided to achieve

---

[5] All on February 7, 1977.

[6] See *Selected Works of Deng Xiaoping (1975–1982)*, Foreign Languages Press, 1983, p. 51.

[7] According to Article 19 of the Constitution of the CPC (amended and adopted at the 18th National Congress of the CPC on October 24, 2017), "The National Congress of the Party is held once every five years and convened by the Central Committee. It may be convened

the "four modernizations" of industry, agriculture, national defense, and science and technology in the new period.[8]

From November 10 to December 15, 1978, the "Central Working Conference" was held in Beijing. At the opening ceremony, Hua Guofeng announced a decision of the Central Political Bureau, putting forward the

before the normally scheduled date if the Central Committee deems it necessary or if more than one third of the organizations at the provincial level so request. Except under extraordinary circumstances, the Congress may not be postponed." According to Article 22, "The Central Committee of the Party is elected for a term of five years. However, when the next National Congress is convened before or after its normally scheduled date, the term shall be correspondingly shortened or extended. Members and alternate members of the Central Committee must have a Party standing of five years or more. The number of members and alternate members of the Central Committee shall be determined by the National Congress. Vacancies on the Central Committee shall be filled by its alternate members in the order of the number of votes by which they were elected. The Central Committee of the Party meets in plenary session at least once a year, and such sessions are convened by its Political Bureau. The Political Bureau reports its work to these sessions and accepts their oversight. When the National Congress is not in session, the Central Committee carries out its resolutions, directs the entire work of the Party and represents the Communist Party of China in its external relations."

[8] During the first session of the 1st NPC, four modernizations of industry, agriculture, transportation and national defense were first explicitly brought forward, which was written into the Party Constitution at the 8th National Congress of the CPC in 1956. During the fourth session of the 2nd NPC from November 17 to December 3, 1963, NPC called on the whole nation to make China a modern, powerful socialist country with four modernizations of industry, agriculture, national defense, and science and technology. From December 20, 1964 to January 4, 1965, during the first session of the 3rd NPC, Premier Zhou Enlai brought out as the task of the country, the four modernizations of industry, agriculture, national defense, and science and technology. In January, 1975, in the first session of the 4th NPC, Premier Zhou Enlai, according to Mao Zedong's direction, reaffirmed the four modernizations of industry, agriculture, national defense, and science and technology. And therefore, the four modernizations of industry, agriculture, national defense, and science and technology formed a historical notion, theoretically being brought out by Mao Zedong. See *Selected Works of Mao Zedong*, 2nd Edition, People's Publishing House, 1991, Vol. 3, p. 1081, Vol. 4, p. 1433; *Collected Works of Mao Zedong*, People's Publishing House, 1996, Vol. 6, pp. 329, 357, Vol. 7, p. 268; 1999, Vol. 8, pp. 116, 162. For this issue, Deng Xiaoping is very clear, "the four modernizations we are talking about in fact has been brought out by Chairman Mao, which was told out by Premier Zhou in his Government Work Reporter." See *Selected Works of Deng Xiaoping (1975–1982)*, People's Publishing House, 2nd Edition, 1994, p. 311–312.

fundamental guiding principle of shifting the focus of all Party work to the four modernizations.[9] At the closing session, Deng Xiaoping delivered a speech, i.e. *Emancipate the Mind, Seek Truth from Facts and Unite as One in Looking to the Future.* Deng Xiaoping affirmed, "when it comes to emancipating our minds, using our heads, seeking truth from facts and uniting as one in looking to the future, the primary task is to emancipate our minds. Only then can we, guided as we should be by Marxism–Leninism and Mao Zedong Thought, find correct solutions to the emerging as well as inherited problems, fruitfully reform those aspects of the relations of production and of the superstructure that do not correspond with the rapid development of our productive forces, and chart the specific course and formulate the specific policies, methods and measures needed to achieve the four modernizations under our actual conditions." Emancipating the mind is a vital political task; now that the question of political lines has been settled, the quality of leadership given by the Party committee in an economic unit should be judged mainly by the unit's adoption of advanced methods of management, by the progress of its technical innovation, and by the margins of increase of its productivity of labor, its profits, the personal income of its workers and the collective benefits it provides. The quality of leadership by Party committee in all fields should be judged with similar criteria. This would be of major political importance in the years to come. Without these criteria as its key elements, our politics would be empty and separated from the highest interests of both the Party and the people. Deng also has emphasized that "the whole Party must start to study Marxism–Leninism and Mao Zedong Thought and try to integrate the universal principles of Marxism with the concrete practice of China modernization drive."[10] Deng Xiaoping's Theory is taking shape and can be defined as "a socialism with Chinese characteristics." This Central Working Conference made preparations for the 3rd Plenary Session of the 11th Central Committee of CPC that immediately followed. In essence, this speech served as the keynote address for the 3rd Plenary Session.

---

[9] See Xinhua Monthly Report, *Chronicle of Events of China 30 Years Reform and Openning-up*, People's Publishing House, 2008, Vol. I, p. 26.

[10] Deng Xiaoping, *Selected Works of Deng Xiaoping*, Foreign Languages Press, 1984, pp. 152, 162, 165.

From December 18 to December 22, 1978, the 3rd Plenary Session of the 11th Central Committee of CPC was held in Beijing.

The conference marked the beginning of the "Reform and Opening-up" policy, and is widely seen as the moment when Deng Xiaoping became the most acclaimed leader of China replacing Hua Guofeng, who remained the nominal Chairman of the CPC until 1981. The meeting was a decisive turning point since post-1949 Chinese history, marking the beginning of the wholesale repudiation of Cultural Revolution policies, and set China on the course for nationwide economic reforms.

Before the plenum, demands for a repudiation of the Cultural Revolution increased, especially by those who were persecuted during that period. In October 1976, the radical Gang of Four was arrested, and the "Counterattack the Right-Deviationist Reversal-of-Verdicts Trend" campaign aimed against Deng was openly rejected, and Peng Dehuai, Tao Zhu, Bo Yibo and Yang Shangkun were rehabilitated.

Although Hua Guofeng, who succeeded "the great helmsman" in 1976, tried to carry on the Maoist rhetoric and to gain an authority like that of Mao, he also allowed the rehabilitation of many of Deng's allies calling for economic reform. At the same conference, Deng said it was necessary to go over the ideological barriers.

Trying to distance from the Cultural Revolution practice which put politics before economy, the 3rd Plenary Session argued that extensive criticism campaigns against Lin Biao and the Gang of Four were to be abandoned in favor of a greater attention to economic issues. The "four modernizations" of industry, agriculture, national defense, and science and technology were considered as the Party's key tasks for the new period. Former President Liu Shaoqi's theory, that under socialism, mass class struggle came to an end, and it was necessary to develop relations of production in order to follow the growth of social forces, was openly endorsed, while Mao's theory of continued revolution under socialism was abandoned. Changes in economic management were called for.

The 3rd Plenary Session of the 11th Central Committee decisively discarded the slogan "Take class struggle as the key link," the "Left" political line which had become unsuitable in a socialist society, and made the strategic decision to concentrate instead on socialist modernization. The Party made efforts to set things right and started the all-round reform, which took economic development as the central task.

The new slogan was to "make China a modern, powerful socialist country before the end of this century."

Also, as an important contribution, this plenary session brought out the bud of market economy: should uncompromisingly work according to the canon of economics, lay more stress on the rule of law and pay attention to handle ideological and political education and economic means together.[11]

However, the most important decision taken by the Central Committee was the opening up to the outside world.

1.1.2.1 Establishing Diplomatic Relations with the USA as of January 1, 1979

On December 15, 1978, the Joint Communique[12] of the United States of America and the People's Republic of China was released in Washington and Beijing, announcing the following:

1. The United States of America and the People's Republic of China have agreed to recognize each other and establish diplomatic relations as of January 1, 1979.
2. The United States of America recognizes the Government of the People's Republic of China as the sole legal Government of China. Within this context, the people of the United States will maintain cultural, commercial and other unofficial relations with the people of Taiwan.
3. The United States of America and the People's Republic of China reaffirm the principles agreed on by the two sides in the Shanghai Communique and emphasize once again that:

    i. Both wish to reduce the danger of international military conflicts.
    ii. Neither should seek hegemony in the Asia-Pacific region or in any other regions of the world and each is opposed to efforts by any other country or group of countries to establish such hegemony.

---

[11] See the gazette of the 3rd Plenary Session of the 11th Central Committee of CPC.

[12] Joint Communique on the establishment of Diplomatic relations between the United States of America and the People's Republic of China, January 1, 1976. The communiqué was released on December 15, 1978, in Washington and Peking. The document is available at: https://photos.state.gov/libraries/ait-taiwan/171414/ait-pages/prc_e.pdf.

iii. Neither is prepared to negotiate on behalf of any third party or to enter into agreements or understandings with the other directed at other states.

iv. The Government of the United States of America acknowledges the Chinese position that there is but one China and Taiwan is part of China.

v. Both believe that normalization of Sino-American relations is not only in the interest of the Chinese and American people but also contributes to the cause of peace in Asia and the world.

vi. The United States of America and the People's Republic of China will exchange Ambassadors and establish Embassies on March 1, 1979.

1.1.2.2 Opposing Hegemonism

After the forces of the United States of America left Vietnam, this country began to carry out a disputable policy and tried to exercise hegemonism threatening China's interests. Vietnam tried to conquer Cambodia and invade China, pushing the Chinese to take action.

The Sino-Vietnamese War in February 1979 was an 18-day limited incursion to "teach the Vietnamese a lesson" in response to Vietnam's full-scale invasion of Cambodia. China's action was legitimized by a friend-ship treaty signed between the Maoist Pol Pot and China, and the agreement in The Geneva Accords, 1954, that should have protected Cambodia from Vietnamese aggression.[13]

---

[13] It should be remembered that Pol Pot, the leader of Cambodia's Khmer Rouge regime, had also been backed by US and Britain during his genocidal rule. See John Pilger, How Thatcher Gave Pol Pot a Hand, *NewStatesman*, April 17, 2000. Vietnam's (pop. 40m) heavy-handed military strike on Cambodia (pop. 7m) came about because of Khmer Rouge's military incursions into Vietnam. Those incursions were driven by propaganda of fear of Soviet-backed Marxist (Vietnam). The Sino-Vietnamese War began on February 17, 1979. The Chinese first advanced and captured major high grounds around Lang Son city (pop. 100k, less than 10 miles from China–Vietnam border and 100 miles from capital Hanoi). Vietnam redeployed its main forces from southern Vietnam and occupied Cambodia, transporting them 800 miles North. On satellite intelligence given by Soviets, the Vietnamese held these troops in Hanoi, and were not tempted to move them to Lang Son as they would fall into a strategic trap. The Chinese fought into towns and territories

In July, 1978, the 4th Plenary Session of the 4th Central Committee of the Vietnamese Communist Party passed a resolution, i.e. *New Situation and New Task*, pointing out: "although the basic and long-term enemy is the USA, the direct enemy is China and Cambodia. ...Further depending on the support of the Soviet Union, capture political and military victory in the Southwest (Cambodia), prevent north threat, and prepare to fight against China." And then the Central Committee of the Vietnamese Communist Party issued instructions to its armies and provinces and cities: "China is the most direct and the most dangerous enemy, dangerous enemy, new target to fight against, to carry out offensive strategy, and to counterattack and attack in borders." Just in 1978, Vietnam stirred up 1,108 times of armed clash in China border. On November 3, 1978, the Soviet Union and Vietnam signed a 25-year mutual defense treaty, which made Vietnam the "linchpin" in the Soviet Union's "drive to contain China." On December 25, Vietnam invaded Cambodia.

Although the Vietnamese Communists and the Khmer Rouge had previously cooperated, the relationship deteriorated when Khmer Rouge leader Pol Pot came to power and established Democratic Kampuchea on April 17, 1975. After numerous clashes along the border between Vietnam and Cambodia, and with encouragement from Khmer Rouge defectors fleeing a purge of the Eastern Zone, Vietnam invaded Cambodia on December 25, 1978. By January 7, 1979 Vietnamese forces had entered Phnom Penh and the Khmer Rouge leadership fled to western Cambodia.[14]

From January 28 to February 5 1979, Deng Xiaoping paid a visit to the United States of America. On February 1, the *Joint News Communique of the United States of America and the People Republic of China* was released emphasizing that China and America oppose any country or country group seeking hegemony or dominating other countries.

From February 17 to March 16 1979, China sponsored self-defense fight against Vietnam, guarding the borderland and also forcing Vietnam

---

all along other border regions, but still the Vietnamese held back their main forces. On March 6, the Chinese moved into Lang Son and declared (in their opinion) a successful end of their objective. It was probable that on his visit to US in January 1979, Deng Xiaoping would have informed the US President on the limited scale of any options available to him in response to Vietnam invading Cambodia.

[14] See https://en.wikipedia.org/wiki/Sino-Vietnamese_War (accessed on December 20, 2017).

to withdraw from Cambodia. Border skirmishes continued throughout the 1980s, including a significant skirmish in April 1984 and a naval battle over the Spratly Islands in 1988. Armed conflict only ended in 1989 after the Vietnamese agreed to fully withdraw from Cambodia. Both nations planned the normalization of their relations in a secret summit in Chengdu in September 1990 and officially normalized ties in November 1991.

Chinese society, including Chinese people, is built on harmony and the achievements of the last two decades were possible because of stability and peace, but China does not fear to take actions for peace and for granting the conditions allowing further sustainable development. The self-defense fight against Vietnam can be regarded as a model case. At the end of the conflict with its neighbor, China has gained a long-term peaceful environment which allowed the reform and opening-up period.

1.1.2.3 Upholding the Four Cardinal Principles

During the reforms and opening-up processes, at least at the early stage, some people wondered whether China was still a socialist country; there were people who negated Mao Zedong's Thought, and some others even opposed the Party's leadership. Theoretical work did not look good enough, and therefore from January 18 to April 3, 1979, a Forum on the Principles guiding the Party's theoretical work was held in Beijing in order to clarify those principles.

At the end of the aforementioned Forum, on March 30, Deng Xiaoping delivered a speech clarifying the following aspects: *Uphold the Four Cardinal Principles*: "What is our main task at present and for a fairly long time to come? To put it briefly, it is to carry out the modernization programme. The destiny of our country and people hinges on its success. Given our present conditions, it will be precisely by succeeding in the four modernizations that we will be adhering to Marxism and holding high the great banner of Mao Zedong Thought. And if we fail to proceed from this reality and to concentrate on the four modernizations points, it will mean that we are departing from Marxism while indulging in empty talk about it. At present, socialist modernization is of supreme political importance for us, because it represents the most fundamental interest of our people. Today every member of the Communist Party and the Communist Youth

League and every patriotic citizen must devote all his energies to the modernization drive and do all he can to overcome every difficulty under the unified leadership of the Party and government."

Deng Xiaoping affirmed that in order to achieve the four modernizations points and make China a powerful socialist country would be a gigantic task. Two important features must be taken into account, i.e. a weak base and a large population, but he also underlined that Chinese people can surely find ways of solving these problems. To carry out China's four modernizations points, China must uphold the four cardinal principles ideologically and politically, which is the basic prerequisite for achieving modernization: "we must stay stick to the socialist road, we must uphold the dictatorship of the proletariat, we must uphold the leadership of the Communist Party, and we must uphold Marxism–Leninism and Mao Zedong's Thought." About the Socialist Road, Deng Xiaoping said: "some people are openly saying that socialism is inferior to capitalism. We must demolish this contention. In first place, socialism and socialism alone can save China — this is the unshakable historical conclusion that the Chinese people have drawn from their own experience in the 60 years since the May 4th Movement [1919]. Deviating from socialism, China will inevitably retrogress to semi-feudalism and semi-colonialism … in the second place, although it is a fact that socialist China lags behind the developed capitalist countries in its economy, technology and culture, this is not due to the socialist system but basically to China's historical development before Liberation; it is the result of imperialism and feudalism. The socialist revolution has greatly narrowed the gap in economic development between China and the advanced capitalist countries. …As for the question of what was the principal contradiction in the current period — what was the main issue or central task confronting the Party and the people in the current period — actually this question had been answered by the decision of the 3rd Plenary Session of the 11th Central Committee to shift the focus of our work to socialist modernization. The level of our productive forces was very low and was far from meeting the needs of our people and country. This was the principal contradiction in the current period, and to resolve was our central task."[15]

---

[15] Deng Xiaoping, *Selected Works of Deng Xiaoping*, Foreign Languages Press, 1984, pp. 166, 174, 189, 190.

In his speech, Deng Xiaoping explained in detail why China should uphold the Four Cardinal Principles historically, theoretically, politically and philosophically. This speech was considered as the sister of the speech *Emancipate the Mind, Seek Truth from Facts and Unite as One in Looking to the Future* also by Deng Xiaoping, constituting the core base of the Communist Party's basic line on the initial stage of socialism.

1.1.2.4 Setting up Special Economic Zones

Setting up Special Economic Zones is an integral part of the reform and opening up policy. Attracting foreign capitals also is of basic importance for China to expand its economy. This is why particular emphasis is posed on these projects which should serve as an example and experiment for the rest of Mainland China.

On November 17, 1977, facing the Shenzhen "fleeing" and the awkward situation, Deng Xiaoping said, "something was wrong with our policy, and the armed forces could not control this kind of situation," which puzzled lots of leaders of Guangdong Provincial Committee, but Wu Nansheng, the Secretary of Guangdong Provincial Committee of the Communist Party, recognized the sound beyond the string and consequently he thought that changing the policy should be the right answer to overcome the situation.

On January 16, 1979, Wu Nansheng, went back to his hometown, Shantou, a city in Guangdong Province, to propagandize the meeting's spirit of the 3rd Plenary Session of the 11th Central Committee. At his hometown, what he saw deeply shocked him, the buildings, which were familiar to him, looked dilapidated, shaky and unsteady; on each side of the streets were, scattered, bamboo scaffolds, crowded with tens of thousands of men and women; no clear road, no bright light, even electricity was not always available, no telephones to communicate, and everywhere in the night it was deep dark.

The fact is that 100 years earlier, Shantou was considered by Friedrich Engels as a vibrant city, and a city with a commercial soul in the Far-East region. Not to mention the fact that only 50 years earlier, the same city was named the "Little Shanghai." Thirty years earlier, commerce in this city was flourishing and the city was considered as a prosperous place, similar to Hong Kong. But all this disappeared and everything had changed during the last 30 years period when China experienced internal "turbulence and readjustments." During the same period Hong Kong became one of the Four Small Dragons of Asia, and Shantou, instead, experienced a regression and now it looked ran-down and full of grief everywhere.

"Any circumstance hitting a limit will begin to change. Change will in turn lead to an unimpeded state, and then lead to continuity (Laozi)." How to become wealthy as fast as possible? A friend from Singapore posed the following questions to Wu Nansheng: "Do you dare to establish an export processing zone like in Taiwan? Do you dare to establish something like a free port?" "Singapore and Hong Kong's economies are so developed!" "Yes, we also should establish Shantou as an Export Processing Zone," Wu Nansheng thought, "to open to the outside world, to attract foreign investments." This thought soon become a reality: July 15, 1979, the Central Committee of CPC and the State Council approved the reports of Guangdong and Fujian Provinces, and consented to set up "Export Special Zones" in Shenzhen, Zhuhai, Shantou and Xiamen.[16]

On May 16, 1980, the Central Committee of the CPC and the State Council formally established the Special Economic Zones in Shenzhen, Zhuhai, Shantou, and Xiamen as Experimental Economic Special Zones to attract international investments, advanced technology and to learn "international management experience.[17] On August 26, 1980, the NPC of China passed the "Regulations of Guangdong Special Economic Zone." But most importantly the approval of these Regulations also symbolized the importance of the "Rule of Law" for China.

The establishment of Special Economic Zone for China has represented an "epochal" change, and a new kind of development model which encompasses several elements, such as peace, development, ideology, opening up, socialism, with this last element being the most important.

---

[16] See Chen Hong, *Folk Observation on Important Decisions and Events of Shenzhen in 1979–2000*, Yangtze River Literature and Art Publishing House, 2006, pp. 7–17.
[17] See CCCPC Party Literature Research Office, *The Chronicle of Events of the Forming and Development of the Socialism System with the Chinese Characteristics*, Central Literature Publishing House, 2008, p. 10.

From January 24 to February 17, 1984, Deng Xiaoping left Beijing to inspect Shenzhen, Zhuhai, Xiamen and Shanghai. On February 24, he talked with a few leading members of the Central Committee of the CPC after he returned to Beijing. He said, "In establishing special economic zones and implementing an open policy, we must make it clear that our guideline is just that — to open and not to close." Deng Xiaping also affirmed that, "A special economic zone is a medium for introducing technology, management and knowledge. It is also a window for our foreign policy. Through the special economic zones we can import foreign technology, obtain knowledge and learn management, which is also a kind of knowledge. As the base for our open policy, these zones will not only benefit our economy and train people but enhance our nation's influence in the world."

From the 3rd Plenary Session onward, China stepped on a new journey, a new story about China's fast rising begun, and after only four decades these changes have brought China to become the second largest economy in the world and probably in a few years to come its economy will become even stronger and China's influence will increase thanks to the new policies and plans which include the B&R Initiative launched by the new leadership and advocated by President Xi Jiping.

1.1.3 *Bringing Forward the Theory of Building a Socialism with Chinese Characteristics: The 12th National Congress of CPC*

On May 6, 1982, Deng Xiaoping met with the Liberian Head of State Samuel Kanyon Doe, and the Chinese leader in this occasion stated that, "in this decade, the economy will not develop too fast because there are too many issues left to be dealt with, and all of the (economic) ratios have lost balance; in the next five to ten years, the speed of the economic development could only reach four percent, and five percent would be incredible. We hope in the next decade, is to say, the last ten years of this century, the speed of our economic development will be higher."[18] Such is

---

[18] See *Selected Works of Deng Xiaoping (1975–1982)*, People's Publishing House, 1983, p. 62.

ratio of GDP increase of China

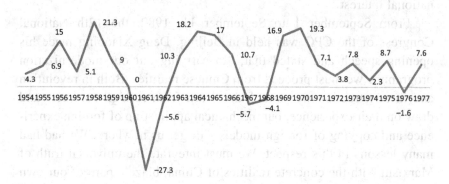

Source: The website of National Bureau of China.

the fact: from 1979 to 1981, the growth rates of GDP are 7.6%, 7.8% and 5.1%, respectively, but compared with the first 27 years of the People's Republic of China, it is still a miracle and a turning point.

In the initial 27 years of the People's Republic of China, the economic trend looks like an emotional roller coaster. We may have a lot of circumstances to take into account which can explain the situation, and surely one of the main reasons is because from the formation of the new People's Republic of China only a few years have passed.

The reason why China's economy was so weak in the initial 27 years of PRC is because the country lost its direction. Some members of the CPC only dared to initiate revolution but not to promote production. Certainly the situation in China was confused and this let the country lose its focus on the right priorities to be pursued for China. What is the main interest for China? Economic development. The Reports on the Work of the Government at the first sessions of the 3rd and 4th NPC both envisaged a two-stage development of the economy: the first stage is to build an independent and relatively comprehensive industrial and economic system by 1980. The second phase will be to turn China into a powerful socialist country fostering modern agriculture, industry, national defense and also science and technology by the end of the 20th century. The entire Party and nation must strive for the attainment of this great objective. This constitutes the overall national interest.[19]

From September 1 to September 11, 1982, the 12th National Congress of the CPC was held in Beijing. Deng Xiaoping made his opening speech and stated that, "In carrying out our modernization programme we must proceed from Chinese realities. Both in revolution and in construction we should also learn from foreign countries and draw on their experience, but mechanical application of foreign experience and copying of foreign models will get us nowhere. We had had many lessons in this respect. We must integrate the universal truth of Marxism with the concrete realities of China, blaze a path of our own and build a socialism with Chinese characteristics — that is the basic conclusion we had reached after reviewing our long history. China's affairs should be run according to China's specific conditions and by the Chinese people themselves. Independence and self-reliance have always been and will always be their basic stand. The 1980s will be an important decade in the history of our Party and state. To accelerate socialist modernization, to strive for China's reunification and particularly for the return of Taiwan to the motherland, and to oppose hegemonism and work to safeguard world peace — these are the three major tasks of our people in this decade. Economic development is at the core of these tasks; it is the basis for the solution of our external and internal problems."[20]

Deng Xiaoping's Theory, "Socialism with Chinese Characteristics," was formally in place and in progress. No doubt Deng's vision and the

---

[19] Deng Xiaoping, *The Whole Party Should Take the Overall Interest into Account and Push the Economy Forward*, a speech at a meeting of secretaries in charge of industrial affairs from the Party committee of provinces, municipalities and autonomous regions dated March 5, 1975, in *Selected Works of Deng Xiaoping*, Foreign Languages Press, 1984, p. 14.

[20] Deng Xiaoping, *Selected Works of Deng Xiaoping*, Vol. 3 (1982–1922), p. 11, available at: https://archive.org/stream/SelectedWorksOfDengXiaopingVol.3/Deng03#page/n9/mode/2up.

subsequent reforms have allowed China to transform this country into the second world economy.

An economic miracle, seemingly impossible, happened anyway:

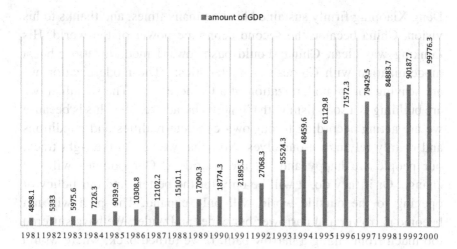

Sources: National Bureau of Statistics of PRC, statistics according to GDP, RMB.

The statistics indicates in the last 20 years of the 20th century, China's economy, in particular its GDP, has increased more than 20 times — from RMB 489.8 billion to RMB 9,977.63 billion — this is beyond any imagination, which proves that the lines, the principles and the policies adopted by China have proved to be absolutely correct, and a "Socialism with the Chinese Characteristics" is possible and it will be further developed by introducing the necessary adjustments to grant a sustainable development for the country and all the people.[21]

---

[21] The target of economic construction was counted in the annual industrial and agricultural output value in the 12th National Congress of the CPC. Internationally and normally, gross domestic product, GDP, is used to measure a country's economic outcome. And so for better reflecting the real level of the Chinese economic development, from 1985 onward, China uses GDP to count the economic goal. See *Selected Works of Deng Xiaoping*, Vol. 3, People's Publishing House, 1993, p. 386.

1.1.4 *Further Development of the Socialism with Chinese Characteristics*

1.1.4.1 Opening up of Costal Harbor Cities

Deng Xiaoping firmly sustained his line many times, and thanks to his vision, China became the second economic power of the world. His thinking was clear. China should push toward modernization, but a modernization with Chinese characteristics: "The modernization we are striving for is modernization of a Chinese type. The socialism we are building is a socialism with Chinese characteristics. This is because we are acting according to our own concrete realities and conditions and mainly relying on ourselves. Now that we are on the right track, our people are happy and we are confident. Our policies will not change. Or if they do, it will be only for the better. And our policy of opening to the outside world will only expand. The path will not become narrower and narrower but wider and wider. We have suffered too much from taking a narrow path. If we turned back, where would we be headed? We would only be returning to backwardness and poverty."[22]

In order to carry out the spirit of Deng Xiaoping's instructions (February 24), from March 26 to April 6, 1984, the Secretariat of the Central Committee of the CPC and the State Council held a Forum attended by some coastal cities. At the Forum, it was decided to enlarge the Xiamen Economic Zone to the whole island, carrying out the so-called "free harbor policies": opening up Dalian, Qinhuangdao, Tianjin, Yantai, Qingdao, Lianyungang, Nantong, Shanghai, Ningbo, Fuzhou, Guangzhou, Zhanjiang, and Beihai.[23]

Opening up the coastal port cities represents a big step since the Central Committee of the CPC and the State Council decided to establish the Special Economic Zones in Shenzhen, Zhuhai, Shantou, and Xiamen in July 1979.

---

[22] See *Selected Works of Deng Xiaoping*, Vol. 3, People's Publishing House, 1993, p. 29.

[23] See CCCPC Party Literature Research Office, *The Chronicle of Deng Xiaoping's Life (1975–1997)*, Central Literature Publishing House, 2004, p. 963.

1.1.4.2 Upholding the Basic Line for Further Development

On June 30, 1984, Deng Xiaoping met with the Japanese delegation at the second session of the Council of Sino-Japanese Non-Governmental Persons, and again reaffirmed that China would follow its own path for further developing "Socialism with Chinese Characteristics." Deng Xiaoping also made clear what is Socialism and Marxism in his view, and he affirmed, "Marxism attaches utmost importance to developing the productive forces. [.....] Therefore, the fundamental task [...] is to develop the productive forces. The superiority of the socialist system is demonstrated, in the final analysis, by faster and greater development of those forces than under the capitalist system." And again he stressed, "Our political line is to focus on the modernization program and on continued development of the productive forces. Nothing short of a world war could tear us away from this line. And even if a world war broke out, we would engage in reconstruction after the war." Underlining the latest advancements he added, "We have opened 14 large and medium-sized coastal cities. We welcome foreign investment and advanced techniques. Management is also a technique. Will they undermine our socialism? Not likely, because the socialist sector is the mainstay of our economy. Our socialist economic base is so huge that it can absorb tens and hundreds of billions of dollars' worth of foreign funds without being shaken. Foreign investment will doubtless serve as a major supplement in the building of socialism in our country. And as things stand now, that supplement is indispensable."[24]

Deng Xiaoping could not be clearer when he explained "Socialism with Chinese Characteristics." It is evident that the Chinese interpretation of Socialism with Chinese Characteristics is mainly focused on Socialism, linked to economic construction, reforms and opening up. This basic line must be upheld for further development.

1.1.4.3 Reform of the Economic Structure

The 3rd Plenary Session of the 11th Party Central Committee shifted the emphasis of the Party's work and the attention of the people of the whole

---

[24] See *Selected Works of Deng Xiaoping*, Vol. 3, People's Publishing House, 1993, at pp. 62–66.

country to socialist modernization. But most of the reform was focused on questions concerning agriculture, and held that the whole Party should concentrate its main energy and efforts on advancing agriculture as fast as possible. Therefore, the reform mainly had an impact on agriculture and countryside, where enormous progress was made, but touched the urban economy marginally.

On April 20, 1984, the 3rd Plenary Session of the 12th Party Central Committee unanimously adopted a Decision on the Reform of Economic Structure, by combining basic Marxist principles with China's current situation. The decision explained the necessity and urgency of speeding up the reforms of the country's entire economic structure, with special attention devoted to the urban economy. The document adopted by the session, defines the nature, sets the orientation and tasks while outlining the policies and principles of the reforms.

The session called on the whole Party, the whole army and the people of all China's nationalities to study conscientiously the "Decision of the Central Committee of the Communist Party of China on Reform of the Economic Structure" and work seriously and effectively, with full confidence and courage, to make the reform successful, while striving for a new and better situation for socialist modernization.[25]

1.1.4.4 Conditions for Further Developments: Disarmament and Peace

Along with the Chinese social and economic development, the world situation has also followed a peaceful direction. China's foreign policy especially during Deng Xiaoping's era, can be summed up with two points as Deng pointed out: (i) to safeguard world peace we oppose hegemony; (ii) China will always belong to the Third World. It belongs to the Third World today, and even when it will become prosperous and powerful China will maintain its position with the Third World, this is because it shares a common destiny with all Third World countries. China will never

---

[25] See Decision of the Central Committee of the Communist Party of China on Reform of the Economic Structure, approved by the Third Plenary Session of the 12th Party Central Committee on April, 1984.

seek hegemony or bully others, but will always side with the Third World. China sincerely hopes that no war will break out and that peace will be long-lasting, so that we can concentrate on driving our country to modernization.[26] When he spoke to a delegation from the Japanese Chamber of Commerce and Industry on March 4, 1985, Deng Xiaoping said: "China seeks to preserve world peace and stability, not to destroy them. The stronger China grows, the better the chances are for preserving world peace...Only the two superpowers have the capacity to launch world war, while the other countries, such as China, Japan and the European countries, are not in a position to do so. It follows that opposing superpower hegemony means preserving world peace. Since the downfall of the Gang of Four, we too have made it a state policy to oppose superpower hegemony and keep world peace. ... We now think that although there is still the danger of war, the forces that can deter it are growing, and we find that encouraging. The Japanese people do not want war, nor do the people of Europe. The Third World countries, including China, hope for national development, and war will bring them nothing good. The growing strength of the Third World — and of the most populous country, China, in particular — is an important factor for world peace. So from the political point of view, a stronger China will help promote peace and stability in the Asia-Pacific region and in the rest of the world as well."[27]

From May 23 to June 6, 1985, an enlarged meeting of the Military Commission of the CPC was held in Beijing, where it was decided to reduce the People's Liberation Army by one million men, which was based on China's new evaluation of the internal (and external) situation. The country had maintained an Army of this size because China used to believe that war was inevitable and imminent. Many of our policy decisions were based on this belief, including the decision to disperse production projects and to locate some of them in the mountains and concealing others in the caves. In recent years, after a careful analysis of the situation, China had come to believe that only the two superpowers, the Soviet

---

[26] See *Selected Works of Deng Xiaoping*, Vol. 3, People's Publishing House, 1993, at pp. 56–57.

[27] See *Selected Works of Deng Xiaoping*, Vol. 3, People's Publishing House, 1993, pp. 104–105.

Union and the United States, were in a position to trigger a world war. But wisely these superpowers were able to maintain an equilibrium though they both possess mass destruction weapons and other conventional weapons, and the military strength to destroy each other. These two countries were striving for global strategic supremacy but had suffered setbacks and met with failures, so they changed their focuses, especially the US, and were able to strengthen their economy. It is possible to affirm that the entire world has benefited from this long period of peace. The world forces for peace were growing faster than the forces for war. China recognized that the new revolution in science and technology all over the world was developing vigorously and that economic strength, and in particular science and technology, played an extremely important role for economic development and competition all around the world. Neither the United States and the Soviet Union, nor the other developed countries, nor the developing countries could ignore this. Thus, we can conclude that it has been possible and there is hope today to maintain peace, especially with the contribution of China considering its increasing influence in the world's affairs (including the delicate question of "Climate Change") if all the parties and countries involved in the managing of world affairs can meet to discuss and compromise for the benefit of the entire humankind. Therefore, after analyzing the general trends all around the world and the global situations which have an impact on our society, China has changed its view, and having understood that it is unlikely to have another world conflict, it has wisely concentrated its efforts on building a more harmonious and equable world, and China is also now striving to contribute in establishing a more just and "globalized" world. No doubt the role China will play in the near future is of basic importance for stimulating the entire world economy, and its influence will grow especially thanks to the massive investments China is realizing everywhere, and in particular, the B&R Initiative is a factual plan already attracting the attention of a great part of the world, which will contribute to creating new wealth for all the parties involved in its realization.

It must be noted that reducing the armed forces does not mean that China underestimates the construction of an efficient and modern army. "The four modernization points include the modernization of defense. Without that modernization there would be only three [agriculture, industry, and science and technology]. But the four modernizations should be achieved in order of priority. Only when we have a good economic foundation will it be possible for us to modernize the army's equipment. So we must wait patiently for a few years. By the end of the century we can surpass the goal of quadrupling the GNP (Gross National Product). At that time, when we are strong economically, we shall be able to spend more money on updating equipment. We can also buy some from abroad, but we should rely on ourselves to conduct research and design superior airplanes for the air force and equipment for the navy and army. If the economy develops, we can accomplish anything. What we have to do now is to put all our efforts into developing the economy. That is the most important thing, and everything else must be subordinated to it."[28]

China's move to reduce the army represents a significant move (toward Peace) for the whole world, indicating China's confidence in its new path, namely, the Reforms to further modernize China, the opening-up policy, and the creation of new (investment) opportunities also for third parties which are to be sought in projects like the B&R Initiative.

1.1.4.5 "Basic Line" Must be Upheld and Reforms Should Be Continued

Reforms and the opening-up policy have broken down the rigid economic structure and revitalized the economy. Indeed, the economy has grown vigorously and with irresistible momentum. The coastal areas from south to north are now forming a vast strip opened to the outside world. The enthusiasm of the masses has also played a fundamental role, and this has further liberated the productive forces.

Reforms and the opening-up policy have also further emancipated the minds of the people, battering down many old concepts that have long stifled their thinking. It is becoming a trend for people to seek change, to blaze new trails and to stress practical results. All this was possible because the CPC upheld the "Basic line" and further introduced new reforms.

---

[28] See *Selected Works of Deng Xiaoping*, Vol. 3, People's Publishing House, 1993, at pp. 126–129.

With the passage of time, the importance of all the reforms introduced in recent history will emerge more clearly, the last lustre has been an extraordinary period of time for China and has attracted worldwide attention. It is because during this period a great number of new ideas have emerged which conform to social progress, and these new ideas represent the foundation of a new model of economic growth (referred to as the *Beijing Consensus*) which also brings a new significance of "advancements" for the entire country, and its development (as a new model of economic grow) will have an impact on the world economy also. In terms of the breadth and depth of the changes it is bringing about in the Chinese society, this new socialist structural reform, and the opening up, can be regarded as another revolution.

As for the present historical stage of Chinese society, the 12th National Congress considered that a correct understanding of the Chinese reality was of paramount importance for building Socialism with Chinese characteristics, and it laid the essential basis on which a correct policy line and correct policies to further develop the country can be formulated and implemented.

China did not jump into this reality. Under the specific historical conditions of contemporary China, transformation occurred gradually. From a preliminary stage of socialism, in which the productive forces were to be developed, reforms have allowed a gradual transformation and have brought China to become the second world economy.

China's new Development Model (*Beijing Consensus*) has been introduced. In the following section, it is now necessary to explain how it was nourished in order to understand how China successfully developed itself and how the new policies have shaped China, also allowing to conceive the "B&R" Initiative which represents an expression of the so-called Beijing Consensus.

1.2 Washington Consensus vs. Beijing Consensus

Taking some specific political decisions determines the direction in which a country is developing and heading, and consequently the fate it will face. Both the US and China have chosen their own path. The formation and functioning of their decision-making process is completely different and has its own characteristics. The two systems have proved to work "fine" according to the circumstances and situations in which the two countries found themselves in determined historical moments.

It is possible, though not intentionally, that when a country is developing and advancing toward a more modern society, based on its past experiences, its decisions can influence the direction in which other countries are evolving. How developed the society of a certain country is and how good its economy and welfare are in general depend on the characteristics of that country reflected in the events in the history of the country in question.

In a very broad sense, it is possible to affirm that the so-called "Washington Consensus" and "Beijing Consensus" represent not only a model of development but also two distinct ways to gain support and get the approval for determined decisions and actions which lead to the determination of some policies having an impact on economic matters (but not only in this field) for the concerned country. It is worthwhile to briefly analyze how these two models have evolved in order to better understand the differences and similarities. However, Beijing Consensus it seems has proved to be more efficient having contributed to the fast development of China and having also triggered the implementation of decisive reforms which have lead to the formulation of the B&R Initiative.

1.2.1 What Is Washington Consensus and Where Does It Come From?

In the 1980s, while China was carrying out the reform and opening-up policy, the outside world was also experiencing changeful movement both theoretically and practically. Future historians may well look upon the years 1978–1980 as a revolutionary turning point in the world's social and economic history.[29]

The most important movements were Neoliberalism in theory and Washington Consensus in practice in the international political economic

---

[29] See David Harvey, *A Brief History of Neoliberalism*, Oxford University Press, 2005, p. 1.

fields, the former of which was the compass of the latter, profoundly changing the whole world, especially in Latin America, Africa, East Europe and Soviet Union, until today.

1.2.2 Neoliberalism: Theoretical Base of Washington Consensus

Neoliberalism or neo-liberalism refers primarily to the 20th-century resurgence of 19th-century ideas associated with *laissez-faire* economic liberalism, normally reinventing liberalism.[30] Such ideas include economic liberalization policies such as privatization, austerity, deregulation, free trade, and reductions in government spending in order to increase the role of the private sector in the economy and society. The concept goes to the heart of the public–private divide and, consequently, of (neo)liberalism itself, by conceptually delineating a sphere of private ownership and autonomy that no state institution may legitimately invade. As the Austrian economist Ludwig von Mises has commented: "The programme of (neo) liberalism, if condensed into a single word, would have to read: property, that is, private ownership of the means of production. All the other demands of liberalism result from this fundamental demand."[31]

However, neoliberalism is still a rather broad and general concept referring to an economic model or "paradigm" that rose to prominence in the 1980s. Built upon the classical liberal ideal of the self-regulating market, neoliberalism comes in several strands and variations. Perhaps the best way to conceptualize neoliberalism is to think of it as three intertwined manifestations: (1) an ideology; (2) a mode of governance; (3) a policy package,[32] which are interwoven together philosophically, politically and economically. The ideology of neoliberalism directs the establishment of a neoliberal governance, which lays down a policy package of neoliberalism.

---

[30] See Rachel S. Turner, *Neo-Liberal Ideology: History, Concepts and Policies*, Edinburgh University Press, 2008, Chapter 3.

[31] See Ludwig von Mises, *Liberalism: In the Classical Tradition*, Cobden Press, 1800, and The Foundation for Economic Education, Inc., 1985, p. 15.

[32] See Manfred B. Steger and Ravi K. Roy, *Neoliberalism — A Very Short Introduction*, Oxford University Press, 2010, p. 11.

It is noteworthy that in the 1960s, the usage of the term "neoliberal" heavily declined. When the term reappeared in the 1980s in connection with Augusto Pinochet's economic reforms in Chile, the usage of the term had shifted. It had not only become a term with negative connotations employed principally by critics of market reform, but it also had shifted in meaning from a moderate form of liberalism to a more radical and *laissez-faire* capitalist set of ideas. These market-based ideas and the policies they inspired constitute a paradigm shift away from the post-war Keynesian consensus which lasted from 1945 to 1980.[33]

Neoliberalism is certainly linked to the Washington Consensus, and in the recent past, scholars have tended to associate it with the theories of economists such as Friedrich Hayek and Milton Friedman, not to mention the adherence with the vision of some great politicians and policymakers, again of the recent past, such as Margaret Thatcher, Ronald Reagan and Alan Greenspan.[34] The importance of "neoliberalism" cannot be underestimated

---

[33] See https://en.wikipedia.org/wiki/Neoliberalism (December 27, 2017). Also see Rachel S. Turner, *Neo-Liberal Ideology: History, Concepts and Policies*, Edinburgh University Press, 2008, pp. 1–2.

[34] See https://en.wikipedia.org/wiki/Neoliberalism (December 27, 2017). Also see Stefan Halper, *The Beijing Consensus: How China's Authoritarian Model Will Dominate the Twenty First Century*, CNHK Publications Limited, 2011, at pp. 81–83. Halper in this book considered neoliberalism as neoconservatism. Contemporary neoconservatives are not "conservative" in the classical sense, as defined by 18th-century thinkers like Edmund Burke, who expressed a fondness for aristocratic virtues, bemoaned radical social change, disliked republican principles, and distrusted progress and reason. Rather, the neoconservativism of Reagan and Thatcher resembles a muscular liberalism that is often associated with political figures like Theodore Roosevelt, Harry Truman or Winston Churchill. In general, neoconservatives agree with neoliberals on the importance of free markets, free trade, corporate power, and elite governance. But neoconservatives are much more inclined to combine their hands-off attitude toward big business with intrusive government action for the regulation of the ordinary citizenry in the name of public security and traditional morality. Their appeals to "law and order" sometimes drown out their concern for individual rights — albeit not for the individual as the building block of society. In foreign affairs, neoconservatives advocate an assertive and expansive use of both economic and military power, ostensibly for the purpose of promoting freedom, free markets, and democracy around the world. Both Reagan and Thatcher sought to merge their economic neoliberalism with more traditional conservative agendas. Some commentators have even gone so far as to suggest that "neoliberalism" and "neoconservatism" should be used as

in the development of the Washington Consensus, and the theories of the aforementioned economists and politicians have played a fundamental role in refining the concept, which formally was created in 1989 by the English economist John Williamson.[35]

In fact, the first written usage of the term "Washington Consensus" is found in John WIliamson's paper titled "What Washington Means by Policy Reform," which he prepared for the conference that the Institute for International Economics convened in order to examine how Latin America had been governed, since the 1950s, from the economic point of view, considering the concepts and ideas that had long been accepted as appropriate within the Organisation for Economic Co-operation and Development (OECD). Williamson prepared a list of 10 policies[36] that he

---

interchangeable terms. However, such assertions appear somewhat exaggerated, for these ideologies are not identical. At the same time, however, there were significant areas of overlap between neoliberalism and neoconservatism — especially as applied to Reaganomics and Thatcherism. And consequently although Reagan and Thatcher are neo-conservative, they carried out lots of neoliberalism policies, and so we continue considering Reagan and Thatcher as neoliberalists, even though they never acknowledged the same. See Manfred B. Steger and Ravi K. Roy, *Neoliberalism — A Very Short Introduction*, Oxford University Press, 2010, pp. 22–23.

[35] Williamson has been a Senior Fellow at the Peterson Institute for International Economics since 1981. He was the Project Director for the United Nations High-Level Panel on Financing for Development (the Zedillo Report) in 2001. He was also on leave as Chief Economist for South Asia at the World Bank during 1996–1999. He was an adviser to the International Monetary Fund from 1972 to 1974 and economic consultant to the UK Treasury from 1968 to 1970. Williamson used the term to summarize commonly shared themes among policy advice by Washington-based institutions at the time, such as the International Monetary Fund, World Bank, and US Treasury Department, which were believed to be necessary for the recovery of countries in Latin America from the economic and financial crises of the 1980s.

[36] These 10 policies can be summarized as follows: (1) Fiscal policy discipline, with avoidance of large fiscal deficits relative to GDP; (2) Redirection of public spending from subsidies ("especially indiscriminate subsidies") toward broad-based provision of key pro-growth, pro-poor services like primary education, primary healthcare and infrastructure investment; (3) Tax reform, broadening the tax base and adopting moderate marginal tax rates; (4) Interest rates that are market determined and positive (but moderate) in real terms; (5) Competitive exchange rates; (6) Trade liberalization: liberalization of imports, with particular emphasis on elimination of quantitative restrictions (licensing, etc.); any trade protection to be provided by low and relatively uniform tariffs; (7) Liberalization of

thought policymakers in Washington would agree were needed in almost all Latin America and labeled this as the "Washington Consensus." Since then, the "Washington Consensus" has assumed new and variegated significances close to the interests of powers sustaining institutions such as the IMF and the World Bank which in any case have begun to rethink their time-worn strategies.

1.2.3 *Neoliberalism Did Not Respond to the Emergencies of a Changing (Global) Economy*

Neoliberalism and *laissez-faire* have not solved problems afflicting countries where distressed economies have caused further dysfunctions, and the intervention of sovranational institutions have worsened the financial situation rather than ameliorate the position of those countries which recurred to external aids.

"Laissez-faire is finished," French President Nicolas Sarkozy affirmed in January 2009. "The global financial crisis is a crisis which is simultaneously individual, national, and global. It is a crisis of both the developed and developing world. It is a crisis which is at once institutional, intellectual, and ideological. It has called into question the prevailing neoliberal economic orthodoxy of the past 30 years – the orthodoxy that has underpinned the national and global regulatory frameworks that have so spectacularly failed to prevent the economic mayhem which has been visited upon us." Australian Prime Minister Kevin Rudd affirmed in February 2009. To make it more clear: "The old world of the Washington Consensus is over," was British Prime Minister Gordon Brown's judgment in April 2009.

By the mid-1990s, it became increasingly clear that neither of the extremes — the Washington Consensus or state-dominated planning — provided much help. The success of the East Asian countries, even after taking into account the setback of the financial crisis of 1997–1998, stood

---

inward foreign direct investment; (8) Privatization of state enterprises; (9) Deregulation: abolition of regulations that impede market entry or restrict competition, except for those justified on safety, environmental and consumer protection grounds, and prudential oversight of financial institutions; (10) Legal security for property rights.

in marked contrast to the experiences of those that had tried one or the other of these recipes for success. The East Asian countries had been more successful not only in producing growth but also in reducing poverty. Markets were seen to be at the center of development, but government had a vital role in catalyzing change and in helping to make the markets work better, to transform the economy and society through education and technology, and to regulate the economy so that it could function better. Greater attention was focused on how to make not only markets but also governments work better.[37]

It is now necessary to introduce the so-called "Beijing Consensus" as it can be considered as the base for the B&R Initiative and new policies China has adopted in order to project the Middle Kingdom toward a new era characterized by a more market-oriented economy, which remains a socialist economy with Chinese characteristics.

1.3 Beijing Consensus: The Opposite Pole to the Washington Consensus

In this section, it is exposed how China was able to develop itself by adhering to the principles of the CPC which contributed to the formation of the so-called *Beijing Consensus*, which can now be seen as an example for developing countries as a new economic growth model.

1.3.1 *What is the So-called Beijing Consensus?*

The *Beijing Consensus*,[38] which is also known as the "China Model" (or "Chinese Economic Model"), refers to the political and economic policies

---

[37] See Joseph E. Stiglitz and Carl E. Walsh, *Economics*, 4th Edition, W. W. Norton & Company, Inc., 2005, p. 804.

[38] The term "Beijing Consensus" was coined by Joshua Cooper Ramo to frame China's economic development model as an alternative — especially for developing countries — to the Washington Consensus of market-friendly policies promoted by the IMF, World Bank, Based in Beijing and New York, Ramo serves as an advisor to some of the largest companies and investors in the world. He is a member of the boards of directors of Starbucks and Fedex. Ramo is a Mandarin speaker, who is also known as "one of China's leading

of the People's Republic of China instituted after Mao Zedong's death in 1976 by Deng Xiaoping, and further elaborated by the Chinese leadership and never abandoned, though disturbances have occurred.[39]

Deng Xiaoping repeatedly sustained and explained the Chinese socialist system and the line of the CPC to many foreign politicians and journalist,[40] and he stressed the importance for China to follow its own path in developing its economy, refusing to embrace other ideologies like, for example, neoliberalism and capitalism as interpreted and applied in the Western countries. In many of his speeches, he underlined the necessity for China to stay stick to the socialist road and also the importance of modernization, which would have brought foreign capitals into China, and lured China toward western ideals and

---

foreign-born scholars" by the World Economic Forum. He was the Senior Editor of *Time Magazine* from 1995 to 2003, and Managing Partner of JL Thornton & Co., LLC.

[39] Disturbances were caused by external factors which had an influence in China's internal affairs, but also because according to Deng Xiaoping the leadership has failed to take a firm position, a clear-cut stand and it did not do enough to educate the people to stay stick to the fundamental principles of the Socialist China.

On January 20, 1987, while Deng Xiaoping interacted with Prime Minister Robert Mugabe of Zimbabwe, about the students' disturbances occurred on December 30, 1986, he said, "basically, it was because of weak leadership. Since we called for upholding the Four Cardinal Principles, we must conduct constant education in these principles among the people. In the last few years we have witnessed the emergence of an ideological trend in favour of bourgeois liberalization that has not been effectively countered. Although I have warned against this trend on many occasions, our Party has failed to provide adequate leadership in combating it. This was a major mistake made by Comrade Hu Yaobang. So the Central Committee accepted his resignation from the post of General Secretary." See *Selected Works of Deng Xiaoping*, Vol. 3, People's Publishing House, 1993, p. 201.

[40] Talking with the Italian journalist Oriana Fallaci and asking if modernization and foreign capitals would inevitably give rise to private investment, "would that not lead to a miniaturized capitalism"? in an interview back in August 1980, Deng Xiaoping reaffirmed that "China though absorbing foreign capitals and technology and even allowing foreigners to construct plants in China, this can only play a complementary role to our effort to develop the socialist productive forces. Of course, this would bring some decadent capitalist influences into China. We were aware of this possibility; it was nothing to be afraid of." See *Selected Works of Deng Xiaoping*, Vol. 2, People's Publishing House, 1983, p. 310.

"bourgeois liberalization,"[41] but clearly pointed out the necessity for China to remain on its path.[42]

1.3.1.1   1989 Student Movement: A Provocative Demand for Reforms

The advancement toward a Socialist market-oriented economy and the formation of the Beijing Consensus encountered some obstacles and "disturbances," but the CPC's line prevailed and the gradual reforms introduced have led China to where it is now. Disturbances come not only from outside China but also from Student Movements like, for example, the 1989 movement which led to the Tiananmen Square incident. The

---

[41] On September 28, 1986, the 6th Plenary Session of the 12th Party Central Committee was held in Beijing, and made *a resolution on guide line of socialist spiritual construction*, definitely opposing bourgeois liberalization. At the meeting, Deng Xiaoping remarked, "with regard to the question of opposing bourgeois liberalization, I am the one who has talked about it most often and most insistently. Why? First, because there is now a trend of thought among the masses, especially among the young people, in favour of liberalization. Second, because this trend has found support from the sidelines. For example, there have been some comments from people in Hong Kong and Taiwan who are opposed to our Four Cardinal Principles and who think we should introduce the capitalist system lock, stock and barrel, as if that were the only genuine modernization. What is this liberalization? It is an attempt to turn China's present policies in the direction of capitalism. The exponents of this trend are trying to lead us towards capitalism. That is why I have explained time and again that our modernization programme is a socialist one. Our decision to introduce the open policy and assimilate useful things from capitalist societies was made only to supplement the development of our socialist productive forces."

[42] Deng Xiaoping expressed his thoughts, which also are the Party's line, in many occasions, and his repulsion for capitalism is clearly reported in numerous of his speeches: "The mainland will maintain the socialist system and not turn off onto the wrong road, the road to capitalism. One of the features distinguishing socialism from capitalism is that socialism means common prosperity, not polarization of income. The wealth created belongs first to the state and second to the people; it is therefore impossible for a new bourgeoisie to emerge." And again "Since the downfall of the Gang of Four an ideological trend has appeared that we call bourgeois liberalization. Its exponents worship the "democracy" and "freedom" of the Western capitalist countries and reject socialism. This cannot be allowed. China must modernize; it must absolutely not liberalize or take the capitalist road, as countries of the West have done." See *Selected Works of Deng Xiaoping*, Vol. 3, People's Publishing House, 1993, pp. 123–124.

incident, which was ended by the Central authorities in a disputable manner, forced the leadership to take into consideration some of the questions raised by the protesters like, for example, the problem of the corruption and the necessity to introduce some reforms to ameliorate the rigid scheme China has adopted to advance toward a more advanced society. The demand for radical changes and more "democracy" was too provocative, but the leadership has proved to have taken those concerns into consideration too, if we look at the changes and reforms which gradually took place.

Deng Xiaoping fearlessly expressed his personal vision about this episode.[43] However, the event has stimulated the necessity for the

---

[43] "In upholding the line, principles and policies formulated since the 3rd Plenary Session of the Eleventh Central Committee of the CPC, it is essential to adhere to the principle of 'one central task and two basic points.' If we did not adhere to socialism, implement the policies of reform and opening to the outside world, develop the economy and raise living standards, we would find ourselves in a blind alley. We should adhere to the basic line for a hundred years, with no vacillation. That is the only way to win the trust and support of the people. Anyone who attempted to change the line, principles and policies adopted since the 3rd Plenary Session of the Eleventh Central Committee would not be countenanced by the people; he would be toppled. I have said this several times. Had it not been for the achievements of the reform and the open policy, we could not have weathered June 4th. And if we had failed that test, there would have been chaos and civil war. The 'cultural revolution' was a civil war. Why was it that our country could remain stable after the June 4th Incident? It was precisely because we had carried out the reform and the open policy, which have promoted economic growth and raised living standards. The army and the government should therefore safeguard the socialist system and these policies." Deng Xiaoping, Excerpts from talks given in Wuchang, Shenzhen, Zhuhai and Shanghai, January 18–February 21, 1992.

On October 31, 1989, while Deng Xiaoping met former President of the United States Richard Nixon, he said, "Frankly, the recent disturbances and the counter-revolutionary rebellion that took place in Beijing were fanned by international anti-communism and anti-socialism. It's a pity that the United States was so deeply involved in this matter and that it keeps denouncing China; actually China is the victim. China has done nothing to harm the United States. Each country can have its own views of this event, but you cannot ask us to accept incorrect criticism from others. The American public got its information from the Voice of America and from American newspapers and periodicals, which reported that blood was flowing like a river in Tian'anmen Square and that tens of thousands of people had died. They even gave the exact number of casualties. The Voice of America has gone too far. The people working for it tell lies; they are completely

introduction of some changes. The gradual reforms China introduced since then have also contributed in shaping the Beijing Consensus and establishing a new model of Socialist market-oriented economy, which substantially offers an alternative to the Washington Consensus and (the former) demands for a more "equitable" international order and global governance reform.

1.3.2 Contribution of the Beijing Consensus to the Establishment of the Socialist Market-oriented Economy and the "Courage to Experiment"

The advancements experienced by China in the recent past, especially in the economic area, are the result of the reforms and opening-up policy, which embody the Beijing Consensus. The key to China's success is the perseverance and conviction of the leadership to strictly adhere to the CPC's line and principles which have produced the policies and allowed China to conquer the position it holds now. In the following section, China's path toward its success is clearly explained. Using Deng Xiaoping's words, it reflects more clearly why China had no choice but to stick to its principles, though it was not always easy. Now, this model, the "Beijing Consensus," is also a reference for other developing countries.

It is noteworthy to regard the new direction toward which China was heading. The 14th National Congress of CPC (October of 1992) is a great landmark in the history of the PRC. This Congress summarized the Party's theory of building socialism with Chinese characteristics and the socialist essence. It was decided to establish a socialist market economy, and most importantly this Congress amended the Party's Constitution, written with the aim of building socialism with Chinese characteristics, reflecting the

---

dishonest. If the American leaders determine their state policies on the basis of information provided by the Voice of America, they will be in trouble... the United States should take the initiative in putting the past behind us, ... China is the victim." See *Selected Works of Deng Xiaoping*, Vol. 3, People's Publishing House, 1993, pp. 330–331.

On December 10, 1989, Deng Xiaoping met with Brent Scowcroft, special envoy of President George Bush and Assistant to the President for National Security Affairs. Deng in this occasion affirmed, that Sino-US relationships must be improved. See *Selected Works of Deng Xiaoping*, Vol. 3, People's Publishing House, 1993, p. 350.

basic line of CPC. One year later, on November 1993, the 3rd Plenary Session of the 14th Central Committee of CPC was held in Beijing, which adopted a decision concerning the establishment of a socialist market economic system. Basically, the Central Committee specified and upheld the goals and basic principles set by the 14th National Party Congress held in October the previous year. This can be seen as a decisive turning point for establishing a socialist market economic system with Chinese characteristics. It would have had a major impact on the country's reforms and opening up, and also it can be seen as a socialist modernization drive.

1.3.2.1 Continuing Exploration of Socialist Market Economy

After the Tiananmen incident, along with the western countries' economic sanctions, the relationship between China and the west became cold, as a consequence, the Chinese economy grew at a snail's pace: 4.2% in 1989 and only 3.9% in 1990 according to GDP data available. Consequently, the leaders of China decided to pay more attention to this theme, and they were determined to boost and enhance China's economic development. Although Deng Xiaoping had retired, he was concerned with China's development situation, and he was always ready to offer his vision and suggestions.[44]

---

[44] On March 3, 1990, while talking with the leading members of the Central Committee of CPC, Deng Xiaoping said, "We should pay particular attention to the question of the drop in the economic growth rate. I am worried about this. If our economy grows at the rate of only four or five per cent a year, it will be all right for a couple of years. But if that rate continues for a long time, it will represent a decline compared with the growth in the rest of the world, especially in the East Asian and Southeast Asian countries and regions. Some countries have problems basically because they have failed to push their economy forward. In those countries people don't have enough food and clothing, their wage increases are wiped out by inflation, their living standards keep dropping and for a long time they have had to tighten their belts. If our economy continues to grow at a slow rate, it will be hard to raise living standards. ...In short, it is still a big question whether we can prevent the economy from going downhill and quadruple the GNP by the end of this century. I am afraid that for at least the next ten years this question will keep us awake at night. If China wants to withstand the pressure of hegemonism and power politics and to uphold the socialist system, it is crucial for us to achieve rapid economic growth and to carry out our development strategy." See *Selected Works of Deng Xiaoping*, Vol. 3, People's Publishing House, 1993, p. 327.

The opening-up and reform policies have promoted economic growth and raised the living standards, and in Deng Xiaoping's words, "We should be bolder than before in conducting reform and opening to the outside, and have the courage to experiment. We must not act like women with bound feet. Once we are sure that something should be done, we should dare to experiment and break a new path." (Deng Xiaoping, 1992) [Excerpts from talks given in Wuchang, Shenzhen, Zhuhai and Shanghai January 18–February 21, 1992.]

It is worth noting Deng Xiaoping's words because they represent not only the new policy but also contribute in bringing into reality the Beijing Consensus, the Chinese leadership having then embraced these elements implementing the new reforms: "Since we introduced the reform and open policy, we have drawn up many rules and regulations covering all fields of endeavor. Clear-cut guidelines and policies concerning economic and political affairs, science and technology, education, culture and military and foreign affairs have been worked out and expressed in precise terms." This is the basis of Beijing Consensus. "The reason some people hesitate to carry out the reform and the open-up policy and dare not break new ground is, in essence, that they're afraid it would mean introducing too many elements of capitalism and, indeed, taking the capitalist road. The crux of the matter is whether the road is capitalist or socialist. The chief criterion for making that judgment should be whether it promotes the growth of the productive forces in a socialist society, increases the overall strength of the socialist state and raises living standards. As for building special economic zones, some people disagreed with the idea right from the start, wondering whether it would not mean introducing capitalism. The achievements in the construction of Shenzhen have given these people a definite answer: special economic zones are socialist, not capitalist. In the case of Shenzhen, the publicly owned sector is the mainstay of the economy, while the foreign invested sector accounts for only a quarter. And even in that sector, we benefit from taxes and employment opportunities. We should have more of the three kinds of foreign-invested ventures." [Here, Deng Xiaoping is referring to: equity joint-venture, cooperative joint venture and wholly foreign-owned enterprise.] "There is no reason to be afraid of them. So long as we keep level-headed, there is no cause for alarm. We have our advantages: we have the large and medium-sized state-owned enterprises and the rural enterprises. More important, political power is in our hands. Some people argue that the more foreign investment flows in and the more ventures of the three kinds are established, the more elements of capitalism will be introduced and the more capitalism will expand in China. These people lack basic knowledge." And he also stressed: "The proportion of planning to market forces is not the essential difference between socialism and capitalism. A planned economy is not equivalent to socialism, because there is planning under capitalism too; a market economy is not capitalism, because there are markets under socialism too. Planning and market forces are both means of controlling economic activity. The essence of socialism is liberation and development of the productive forces, elimination of exploitation and polarization, and the ultimate achievement of prosperity for all. This concept must be made clear to the people."[45]

These were the thoughts of Deng Xiaoping which he had expressed during his visit in Wuchang, Shenzhen, Zhuhai and Shanghai, from January 18 to February 21, 1992. During his tour, he met with different leaders in different cities and he expressed his thoughts in these terms.

This tour was Deng Xiaoping's last public activities, and his speeches are also the last piece compiled in his *Selected Works of Deng Xiaoping*. That year, he was 88 years old, retired for 3 years, but still concerned with China's development.

This tour also restarted China's reform and opening-up processes. From this tour on, China has begun to experience an incredible historic momentum on the road to civilization and prosperity. Naturally, all this was possible thanks to the new elements introduced into China's ecosystem which have contributed in forming the so-called *Beijing Consensus*, now regarded as a concrete alternative of development for all the other developing countries, and an example for all the countries involved in the development of the B&R Initiative.

China has continued to explore the path of its development toward a socialist market-oriented economy and in doing so, the highest political organs of the CPC have introduced many "adjustments" which to be described would take us to write an entire tome, and it is not the aim of

---

[45] See *Selected Works of Deng Xiaoping*, Vol. 3, People's Publishing House, 1993, pp. 370–373.

this book to describe in detail all these elements, however it is worthwhile to remember China's objectives which can be found in *The Two Centenary Goals* briefly described in the following section.

1.3.2.2 Two Centenary Goals: Further Planned Improvements for Chinese Economy

The 18th National Congress of the CPC set forth a master blueprint for building a comprehensively moderate prosperous society and accelerating socialist modernization and it issued a call for achieving the *Two Centenary Goals*.

Before this Congress, back in 1997 at the 15th National Congress of the CPC, Jiang Zeming in his report titled *Hold High The Great Banner of Deng Xiaoping Theory for an All-Round Advancement of the Cause of Building Socialism with Chinese Characteristics into the 21st Century*, introduced these goals.[46]

The first Centenary Goal, marking the 100th anniversary of the CPC's founding in 1921, is to double the 2010 GDP and double the

---

[46] At the congress, Jiang Zemin, on behalf of the 14th CPC Central Committee, delivered a report titled *Hold High the Great Banner of Deng Xiaoping Theory for an All-Round Advancement of the Cause of Building Socialism with Chinese Characteristics into the 21st Century*. The report, which made a scientific summary of the history, prepared for the future, and drew up a cross-century blueprint for China's reform, opening and socialist modernization drive, served as the CPC's political declaration and program of action for the next century. The congress endorsed a resolution on Jiang's report and approved the reforming and development programs in economic, political and cultural fields expounded in the report. The resolution pointed out that the coming period until the first decade of the next century will be crucial for China's modernization drive, and efforts must be made relating to the following aspects: to promote the fundamental shift of the economic system and of the mode of economic growth; to establish a sound socialist market economy and to maintain sustained, rapid and sound development of the national economy so as to lay a solid foundation for achieving basic modernization by the middle of the next century; under the precondition of adhering to the Four Cardinal Principles, to continue to press ahead with the reform of the political structure, further extend the scope of socialist democracy and improve the socialist legal system, governing the country according to the law and making it a socialist country ruled by the law; to strengthen ideological and ethic building, see to it that science and technology as well as education are made a priority, and positively develop various cultural undertakings.

2010 income of both urban and rural residents by 2020, completing the building of a moderately prosperous society.

The second Centenary Goal, commemorating the 100th anniversary of founding of the People's Republic of China in 1949, is to build a modern socialist country that is prosperous, strong, democratic, culturally advanced and harmonious by the time the People's Republic of China celebrates its centenary in 2049 — the great renewal of the Chinese nation.

These goals were put down in writing by the 18th Party Congress in 2012 — the same Party Congress that saw Xi Jinping assume the position of China's top leader. Xi himself linked these goals to a catchier slogan: the "Chinese dream." In Xi's speeches, the "two centenary goals" are often paired with the "Chinese dream" or the "great rejuvenation of the Chinese nation as twin aspirations." "At present, the Chinese people are striving to realize the Two Centenary Goals and the Chinese Dream of the rejuvenation of the Chinese nation," Xi said in July 2014.

1.3.3 *Beijing Consensus as a Key Model to China's Success and the Necessity to Remain on Track*

No doubt the reforms and opening-up policy, and thus the Beijing Consensus, have guided China and favored its success, but this process has not ended, on the contrary, China has to insist on this path, and the B&R Initiative, which is a consequence of the Beijing Consensus, was conceived not only to further stimulate its economy but also for granting further development and enhancing trade relationship with all the countries involved in offering at the same time a model of growth, however some basic elements must be upheld to achieve its new goals.

These elements have already been discussed and they should always be kept in mind when discussing further developments China is putting into place, which will also favor the Third World countries.

1.3.3.1 Upholding the Basic Line

The first of these elements is the adherence to the Basic Line of the CPC. Socialism with Chinese characteristics must always be the central theme of China's development in every field and direction. China must not deviate from its principles, which have not only proved to fit a country with more than 1.42 billion people,[47] granting a sustainable development and a better standard of living, but also has created prosperity for a great portion of China's population which must be better distributed following the path of further reforms and adjustments.

The Basic Line is the fountainhead of anything in China, from China Development to China economic model, and anyone who dare to change it would fall.[48]

1.3.3.2 Maintaining Stability as Top Priority

Managing such a big country with 1.42 billion population certainly is a huge challenge for any party. After the Tiananmen incident, Chinese leaders came to understand that stability must be of top priority, also for further social and economic development. Development is the purpose and a priority for China, reforms are the means, stability is the prerequisite and an essential condition and all these elements are inter-related and interdependent: reforms and stability serve development, development improves reforms and stability, and reforms must lead to development, which benefits the people.

---

[47] See http://www.worldometers.info/world-population/china-population/.

[48] While talking with the Chinese-American physicist and Nobel Prize winner Professor Tsung-Dao Lee of Columbia University on September 16, 1989, Deng Xiaoping said, "Please believe me when I say that the principles and policies formulated during the reform and opening to the outside world over the past ten years will not change. The line set at the Party's Thirteenth National Congress will not change. Anyone who changed it would fall.

In the recent past we have had two General Secretaries who did not retain the post for long. That was not because they were not qualified when they were elected. It was right to elect them, but later on they made mistakes with regard to the fundamental issue, the issue of adhering to the Four Cardinal Principles, so they stumbled and fell. Of the four principles, the two most important are that we should uphold leadership by the Party and that we should uphold socialism. The opposite of the four principles is bourgeois liberalization. In the last few years I have stressed on many occasions the need to uphold the Four Cardinal Principles and oppose bourgeois liberalization. But they didn't do that." See *Selected Works of Deng Xiaoping*, Vol. 3, People's Publishing House, 1993, p. 24.

China's main objective is to develop a modern, harmonious and creative high-income society. This has made the government aware that to develop in a sustainable way, to manage, regulate and maintain both progress and stability, a just and harmonious society is needed. "Heaven and people in harmony" is a perennial theme in Chinese philosophy and culture. In recent years, this desire for harmony has intensified as China's rapid economic growth has continued to drive enormous social change.

In 2006, the Chinese government enshrined the building of a harmonious society as a central theme in the country's economic, social and political mission.

The economic and social changes of the past three decades have brought the Chinese people benefits and opportunities through the introduction of gradual reforms, but also major challenges; one of the most serious issues is the unequal distribution of the new created wealth. The country's leaders believe that creating a harmonious society is strategically important in dealing with the problem of uneven urban, rural and regional economic development, increasing pressures from human resource conditions, employment, social security, wealth distribution, education, healthcare, housing, industrial safety, crime prevention and public security that affect people's daily lives. All these delicate questions can be managed by adopting a pragmatic attitude and following the precise line of the CPC and persevering in building a socialist market-oriented economy with Chinese characteristics, and acknowledging the leadership of the CPC which grants the stability China needs.[49]

---

[49] As Deng Xiaoping stressed, "China's overriding interest is in stability." Stability is not only of leaders' concern but also the center of policy. For example, the report of the 16th National Congress of CPC, *Build a Well-off Society in an All-round Way and Create a New Situation in Building Socialism with Chinese Characteristics, said*, "ensure stability as a principle of overriding importance and balance reform, development and stability. Stability is a prerequisite for reform and development. We should take into full consideration the momentum of reform, the speed of development and the sustainability of the general public. Continued improvement of people's lives must be regarded as an important link in balancing reform, development and stability. We should press ahead with reform and development amidst social stability and promote social stability through reform and development." See *Selected Works of Deng Xiaoping*, Vol. 3, People's Publishing House, 1993, p. 313.

1.3.3.3 Evolution of the Socialist Market Economy: Importance of the Five Years Plans

The 18th National Congress of CPC, held in November 8–14, 2012 and the 3rd Plenary Session of 18th Central Committee of CPC, decided to deepen the reforms comprehensively. As Hu Jintao stressed in his report titled, "Firmly March on the Path of Socialism with Chinese Characteristics and Strive To Complete the Building of a Moderately Prosperous Society In All Respect," he affirmed that "Taking economic development as the central task is vital to national renewal, and development still holds the key to addressing all the problems we have in China. Only by promoting sustained and sound economic development can we lay a solid material foundation for enhancing the country's prosperity and strength, improving the people's well being and ensuring social harmony and stability. We must unwaveringly adhere to the strategic thinking that only development counts."[50]

China now has to further elaborate the Party's line: "The overall goal of deepening the reform comprehensively is to improve and develop socialism with Chinese characteristics, and to promote the modernization of the national governance system and capacity. We must pay more attention to implementing systematic, integrated and coordinated reforms, promoting the development of socialist market economy, democratic politics, advanced culture, a harmonious society and ecological progress."

Xi Jiping delivered a work report at the 3rd Plenary Session of the Party's 18th Central Committee (held from November 9 to 12, 2013, in Beijing)[51] substantially upholding the guidelines of the CPC. Xi Jinping said the Party has worked to speed up the development of a socialist market economy, democracy, cultural development, social harmony and

---

[50] Hu Jintao, Report to the Eighteenth National Congress of the CPC on November 8, 2012. This is the start of Section IV, *Accelerating the Improvement of the Socialist Market Economy and the Change of the Growth Model*, the full text of the report is available at: http://www.chinadaily.com.cn/china/19thcpcnationalcongress/2012-11/18/content_29578562.htm.

[51] The 3rd Plenary Session of the 18th CPC Central Committee was held from November 9 to 12 in Beijing, during the session the Political Bureau reports its work to the CPC Central Committee and the session discusses major issues concerning comprehensive and deepened reforms. The meeting comes as China faces major economic and social challenges. It will, to some extent, determine the direction of reform of the new leadership.

environmental protection. The reform guidelines affirm the work accomplished by the Party's political bureau since the 18th CPC National Congress held in 2012.

China cannot deviate from its path now, and all the efforts put in place, which are a manifestation of the Beijing Consensus, have allowed to elaborate new plans also incarnated in the so-called "Five Years Plans"[52] (also FYP) which express the strategies China has conceived to transit the country toward a more integrated and globalized world, and the B&R Initiative serves exactly to reach this goal.

The FYP is an instrument serving to guide China's (economic) development, and the 13th FYP (2016–2020)[53] encompasses and reaffirms Xi Jinping's policy vision for China.

In the 13th FYP period (2016–2020), the Chinese government aims to bring all rural residents out of poverty, while also promising higher quality education, healthcare and public services for all citizens. The proposal hints at further reform of China's household registration (*hukou*) system, and states that the urban welfare services will be extended to all residents. Urbanization will be an integral part of spurring consumption and lessening the disparity between urban and rural residents. The proposal says that the government will target an urbanization rate of 60% by 2020, up from the current 55%. Notably, the government recently loosened the one-child

---

[52] China's five-year plans are blueprints containing the country's social, economic and political goals. They encompass and intertwine with existing policies, regional plans and strategic initiatives. A five-year plan signals the Chinese government's vision for future reforms and communicates this to other parts of the bureaucracy, industry players and Chinese citizens. It is a living document that will go through constant review and revision over the next five years.

[53] The 13th FYP Proposal contains five main principles underpinning the policies for China's future development. None of these ideas are new, but have been put into one place for the first time. They are to work in tandem to achieve the overall goal of creating "a moderately prosperous society." The first principle is innovation, primarily as a driver of economic development and to shift China's economic structure into a higher-quality growth pattern. The document pledges openness, stating that China should utilize both domestic and global markets and be more active in global governance. Green development means protecting the environment and pursuing environmentally friendly economic growth. Coordination to ensure balanced development among rural and urban areas, and across different industries is also emphasized.

policy allowing citizens to have a second child, a move to alleviate China's growing demographics imbalance. At the same time, the government also announced that social security will be extended to the entire elderly population.

Emphasis was also put in the area of environmental protection, with oversight mechanisms such as a water management system, an emission permit system and an outright ban on commercial deforestation. From the FYP clearly emerges the need to modernize China's agriculture in an environmentally friendly way. There is also continued emphasis on green development and creating an ecological civilization which includes promoting a low-carbon economic system and performance indicators to wean government officials off of the growth-at-all-costs mindset.

1.4 The Linkage Between the "Beijing Consensus" and the "B&R" Initiative

Having developed such a good system to achieve its goals, not only in the economic area but also to build a more harmonious society through the introduction of gradual reforms, instead of embracing western ideals or models, the so-called Beijing Consensus has demonstrated its validity and in particular has proved the Chinese model to function and respond perfectly to the needs of this particular ecosystem which is China. The Chinese leadership and its organs, *in primis* the CPC, and the Central Committee of the CPC, have elaborated policies which have been implemented through gradual reforms, which now are accompanying China toward a new modernization. This new modernization, however, needs to be fostered by new investments in different areas, included investments in the infrastructure sectors. As China sees this as a priority to help internal regions to develop faster, and because China needs to reinforce trade relations with its neighboring nations and to find new commercial outlets, from its new plans, and thus from what now we can call the Beijing Consensus, it has spurred on this new initiative, it is to say the B&R Initiative, which will have a huge impact not only on Chinese economy but also on the economies of all the countries which are contributing in bringing it into reality.

1.4.1 *B&R: Not Only Investments in Infrastructures and Enhanced Trade Relationships but Also an Opportunity to Connect Cultures*

In particular the "B&R" Initiative will serve to ameliorate the transportation and communication systems (not only in China), and certainly will enhance trade relationships, but it can also be seen as a tool to bring different cultures closer to one another, and working together for a common destiny. Moreover, according to the Chinese leadership, the "B&R" also serves at bringing about a more just globalization.

President Xi Jinping delivered a speech about "civilization" at the UNESCO headquarters in Paris on March 27, 2014, and he affirmed that, "Today, we live in a world with different cultures, ethnic groups, skin colors, religions and social systems, and the people of various countries have become members of an intimate community of shared destiny. The Chinese have long come to appreciate the wisdom of 'harmony without uniformity.' Zuo Qiuming, a Chinese historian who lived 2,500 years ago, recorded in the *Chronicle of Zuo* the following comments by Yan Ying, Prime Minister of the State of Qi during the Spring and Autumn Period: 'Achieving harmony is like preparing the thick soup. Only with the right amount of water, fire, vinegar, meat sauce, salt and plum can fish and meat be cooked with the right taste.' 'It is the same when it comes to music. Only by combining the sounds of different instruments with the right rhythm and pitch as well as tone and style can you produce an excellent melody.' 'Who can eat the soup with nothing but water in it? What ear can tolerate the same tone played repeatedly on one instrument?'"

There are 200-odd countries and regions, over 2,500 ethnic groups and a multitude of religions in the world today. We can hardly imagine if this world has only one lifestyle, one language, one kind of music and one style of costume.

Victor Hugo once said, "'There is a prospect greater than the sea, and it is the sky; there is a prospect greater than the sky, and it is the human soul.' Indeed, we need a mind that is broader than the sky as we approach different civilizations. Civilizations are like water, moistening everything silently. We need to encourage different civilizations to respect each other and live together in harmony while promoting their exchanges and mutual learning as a bridge of friendship among peoples, a driving force behind human society, and a strong bond for world peace. We should seek wisdom and nourishment from various civilizations to provide support and consolation for people's mind, and work together to tackle the challenges facing mankind."[54]

1.4.2 Interpretation of the "B&R" by the National Development and Reform Commission, Ministry of Foreign Affairs, and Ministry of Commerce of the People's Republic of China

It is also worth reporting a passage of the "Vision and Actions on Jointly Building Silk Road Economic Belt and 21st-Century Maritime Silk Road" issued by the National Development and Reform Commission, Ministry of Foreign Affairs, and Ministry of Commerce of the People's Republic of China, with State Council authorization, to have a clear interpretation of what represents this project: *The Belt and Road Initiative is in line with the purposes and principles of the UN Charter. It upholds the Five Principles of Peaceful Coexistence: mutual respect for each other's sovereignty and territorial integrity, mutual non-aggression, mutual non-interference in each other's internal affairs, equality and mutual benefit, and peaceful coexistence.*

The Initiative is open for cooperation. It covers, but is not limited to, the area of the ancient Silk Road. It is open to all countries, and international and regional organizations for engagement, so that the results of the concerted efforts will benefit wider areas.

The Initiative is harmonious and inclusive. It advocates tolerance among civilizations, respects the paths and modes of development chosen by different countries, and supports dialogues among different civilizations on the principles of seeking common ground while shelving differences and drawing on each other's strengths, so that all countries can coexist in peace for common prosperity.

---

[54] Speech by H.E. Xi Jinping President of the People's Republic of China At UNESCO Headquarters, March 28, 2014. See: http://www.fmprc.gov.cn/mfa_eng/wjdt_665385/zyjh_665391/t1142560.shtml.

The Initiative follows market operation. It will abide by market rules and international norms, give play to the decisive role of the market in resource allocation and the primary role of enterprises, and let the governments perform their due functions.

The Initiative seeks mutual benefit. It accommodates the interests and concerns of all parties involved, and seeks a conjunction of interests and the "biggest common denominator" for cooperation so as to give full play to the wisdom and creativity, strengths and potentials of all parties.[55]

1.4.3 The B&R Initiative as a Conglomerate of New Policies and an Economic Engine for China

The Belt and Road Initiative is not a single policy, but a conglomerate of initiatives which are aimed at letting China play a bigger role at the international stage and gaining the position China deserves considering its growing importance. Being a Chinese initiative, the B&R is designed to serve Chinese interests first, but at the same time, all the countries touched by the Initiative will also benefit from this project, especially those actively involved in its development. It is possible to affirm that the B&R represents one of China's economic engines; other initiatives will concentrate more on internal affairs and further reforms aimed at building a moderate prosperous society, and at reaching the centenary goals.

After having described the background, and the historical circumstances in which China found itself, and thus how China was able to overcome all the obstacles it has encountered introducing a series of gradual reforms which have led to the formation of the Beijing Consensus, we have to turn now to the main theme describing how it is possible for China to bring into reality this Initiative. The realization of

---

[55] See *Vision and Actions on Jointly Building Silk Road Economic Belt and 21st-Century Maritime Silk Road*, issued by the National Development and Reform Commission, Ministry of Foreign Affairs, and Ministry of Commerce of the People's Republic of China, with State Council authorization on March 28, 2015 (http://en.ndrc.gov.cn/news-release/201503/t20150330_669367.html) (accessed on January 24, 2018).

the B&R will absorb a great part of the China's resources, financially speaking, and not only that many aspects are to be treated and fully analyzed. All the aspects related to the realization of the B&R, together with the many other facets of this Initiative, will be discussed in the following chapters. Particular attention shall be given to the financial aspects which are of paramount importance for the factual implementation of this ambitious plan.

CHAPTER 2

China and the "Belt and Road" Initiative: What Is It All About?

Xugang Yu and Cristiano Rizzi

Essentially, the "One Belt, One Road" Initiative (also referred to as "The Belt & Road") is an immensely ambitious development campaign aimed at modernizing infrastructure and better connecting China with the EU, but it is not limited to this, as explained in this chapter. Many other facets in fact compose this ambitious project. China is preparing to play a bigger role at the international stage and to gain a leading position in introducing new policies not only aimed at granting China a linear development, but also directed at stimulating global economic growth if its leadership will be able to properly implement the so-called "Silk Road Economic Belt" and "21st Century Maritime Silk Road" which are initiatives first introduced by President Xi Jinping in 2013 during his visit to Kazakhstan and Indonesia, respectively, and which are now referred to jointly as the "Belt, and Road" Initiative, or the "B&R." This Initiative has continued to expand in its scope and now includes promotion of enhanced policy coordination across the Asian continent, financial integration, trade liberalization and people-to-people connectivity.

China's efforts to implement the B&R Initiative not only will likely have important effects in the economic architecture of the entire Asia region but also will have strategic implications for China and for the other major powers. President Xi is actively promoting this Initiative because it is an integral part of China's plan to enhance its economy and features prominently in China's 13th Five-Year Plan (2016–2020), which guides the national investment strategy throughout that period.

2.1 "The Belt and Road" Initiative: Essential Background

The "Belt, and Road" Initiative has significant implications for China and it will have a tremendous impact on the countries involved in the development of this Initiative. In order to begin this analysis on the [B&R] Initiative, which is also transiting China into a new and more connected world, where its role will assume an unprecedented importance (at least concerning the economic development of a great part of the world), we provide in the following section an introduction to President Xi's vision that helps understand the more precise significance of this Initiative.

2.1.1 *President Xi Jinping's Vision of the Belt and Road Initiative*

President Xi Jinping launched the B&R Initiative in 2013 when he made a speech titled "Promote People-to-People Friendship and Create a Better Future"[1] at Kazakhstan's Nazarbayev University during his State visit.[2]

---

[1] Ministry of Foreign Affairs of the People's Republic of China, *President Xi Jinping Delivers Important Speech and Proposes to Build a Silk Economic Belt with Central Asian Countries,* http://www.fmprc.gov.cn/mfa_eng/topics_665678/xjpfwzysiesgjtfhshzzfh_665686/t1076334.shtml (accessed on September 7, 2013).

[2] *President Xi Jinping Delivers Important Speech and Proposes to Build a Silk Road Economic Belt with Central Asian Countries,* Xi Jinping expressed that more than 2,100 years ago, during China's Western Han Dynasty (206 BC–AD 24), imperial envoy Zhang Qian was sent to Central Asia twice to open the door to friendly contacts between China and Central Asian countries as well as the transcontinental Silk Road linking East and West, Asia and Europe. Kazakhstan, as a major stop along the ancient Silk Road, has made important contributions to the exchanges and cooperation between different nationalities and cultures. People in regional countries created the history of friendship along the ancient Silk Road through the ages. See President Xi's speech at Ministry of Foreign Affairs of the People's Republic

Substantially, President Xi Jinping proposed to revisit the ancient Silk Road[3] and to join hands and build a new economic belt with innovative cooperation mode. President Xi put in evidence that over the 20-plus years, the ancient Silk Road is becoming full of new vitality with the rapid development of China's relations with Asian and European countries. It is a foreign-policy priority for China to develop a friendly and cooperative relation with the Central Asian countries. China hopes to work with Central Asian countries and engage them into this project because they are part of it. Thus, unceasingly enhancing mutual trust, consolidating friendship, and strengthening cooperation with these countries are also priorities for China, so as to push forward the common development and prosperity, and work for the happiness and well-being of the people in these countries. This is also a condition to further develop this Initiative and reach Europe in a smooth manner. President Xi also assured the audience that China "respects the development path as well as the domestic and foreign policies Central Asian people have independently chosen for themselves. China will never intervene in internal affairs of Central Asian countries, seek leadership in regional affairs, or operate sphere of influence."[4] However, it seems reasonable to affirm that a certain influence is inevitable especially because of the Chinese investments (in the infrastructure sector in particular). Thus, China will play a delicate role and should keep its promises limiting its intervention to only the necessary issues in order to allow the realization of the project and all the infrastructure together with the cooperation of all these nations.

---

of China: http://www.fmprc.gov.cn/mfa_eng/topics_665678/xjpfwzysiesgjtfhshzzfh_665686/t1076334.shtml (accessed on June 6, 2017).

[3]The Silk Road was a network of trade routes, formally established during the Han Dynasty. The road originated from Chang'an (now Xian) in the east and ended in the Mediterranean in the west, linking China with the Roman Empire. Soon after the Roman conquest of Egypt in 30 BCE regular communications and trade between China, Southeast Asia, India, the Middle East, Africa, and Europe blossomed on an unprecedented scale. More info available at: https://en.wikipedia.org/wiki/Silk_Road.

[4]President Xi Jinping Delivers Important Speech and Proposes to Build a Silk Road Economic Belt with Central Asian Countries. Ministry of Foreign Affairs of the People's Republic of China. http://www.fmprc.gov.cn/mfa_eng/topics_665678/xjpfwzysiesgjtfhshzzfh_665686/t1076334.shtml (accessed on June 6, 2017).

2.1.2 *Reinforced Cooperation with Eurasian Countries*

Through the implementation of this Initiative, naturally the relations between China and Eurasian Countries are destined to assume a new importance. President Xi Jinping proposed that in order to make these economic ties stronger, it is necessary to develop deeper cooperation and broader relationships among Eurasian countries. Substantially, China and these countries have to innovate their mode of cooperation, and what is most important for China is to jointly build the "Silk Road Economic Belt" step by step to gradually form an overall regional cooperation. Clearly, this is one of the main goals of the Initiative.

President Xi Jinping has stressed five points which, though are referred to those Eurasian countries, have the same importance and significance in the relations with third countries: "**First**, to strengthen policy communication. Countries in the region can communicate with each other on economic development strategies, and make plans and measures for regional cooperation through consultations. **Second**, to improve road connectivity. To open up the transportation channel from the Pacific to the Baltic Sea and to gradually form a transportation network that connects East Asia, West Asia, and South Asia. **Third**, to promote trade facilitation. All the parties should discuss the issues concerning trade and investment facilitation and make appropriate arrangements. **Fourth**, to enhance monetary circulation. All the parties should promote the realization of exchange and settlement of local currency, increase the ability to fend off financial risks and make the region more economically competitive in the world. **Fifth**, to strengthen people-to-people exchanges. All the parties should strengthen the friendly exchanges between their peoples to promote understanding and friendship with each other."[5]

As it can be inferred from President Xi's speech, his vision for this Initiative is broad in scope. In fact, in order to underline the importance of the B&R Initiative and further stimulate (and push) its implementation, on March 28, 2015, China's top economic planning agency, i.e. the National Development and Reform Commission (NDRC), released a new action plan[6] outlining the key details of Beijing's "One Belt, One Road"

---

[5]*Ibid.*

[6]National Development and Reform Commission (NDRC) — new action plan for the B&R Initiative.

Initiative. It is now clear that the B&R is a centerpiece of China's foreign policy and an important part for its domestic economic strategy. China aims at promoting and enhancing policy coordination across the Asian continent, and more importantly China is seeking more financial integration and trade liberalization.

2.1.3 *What China is Trying to Achieve with This Initiative? B&R and Its Strategic Significance*

Economic and geopolitical reasons are the most important drivers of the Initiative and trade cooperation also plays a decisive role.

Basically, on the one hand, the economic belt of the Silk Road, i.e. "the Belt," designates the land network of the Silk Roads linking China to Europe, thereby reviving the ancient Silk Road and improving the trade relationships between China and Europe. This is of course one of the main goals that will be achieved only through increasing cooperation between China and Europe. On the other hand, the new maritime Silk Road, i.e. "the Road," aims to intensify maritime trade between Chinese ports and Europe. This immense project involves cooperation agreements and investments in Southeast Asia, the Indian Ocean, the Arabic peninsula, the Mediterranean Sea and the East African coastline. The new maritime Silk Road also aims at modernizing infrastructure and simplifying trade formalities to intensify and accelerate exchanges along this route.

However, it is also necessary to underline that China is seeking a more sustainable economic growth and also needs stimulus to help cushion the effects of the currently deepening slowdown and this initiative certainly can represent the solution.

It is evident that by building convenient trade routes, implementing trade and investment facilitation measures, strengthening infrastructure construction, it is possible to promote economic and trade cooperation especially between China and the countries along the B&R, thus, it is also possible to share development opportunities. All the infrastructure projects and constructions are intended to help make use of China's enormous industrial overcapacity and ease the entry of Chinese goods into regional markets. Beijing is also hoping that improving connectivity between its underdeveloped southern and western provinces with its richer coast will improve China's internal economic integration and competitiveness and spur more regional balance growth.

Another explicit intent by the Chinese government is to push forward the construction of international trunk passageways, "build a new Eurasian Land Bridge and develop China–Mongolia–Russia, China–Central Asia–West Asia and China–Indochina Peninsula economic corridors. Especially the China-Pakistan Economic corridor, starting from Kashgar, Xinjiang of China, reaching the Indian Ocean via Gwadar Port of Pakistan, is an important strategic route, which can bypass the Malacca Strait. The three big oil and gas pipelines of China–Russia, China–Myanmar and China–Central Asia greatly reduced China's oil import dependence on the Malacca Strait."[7]

It is also necessary to stress that the B&R Initiative embodies many of China's priorities on the "foreign policy front." In fact, China's efforts focus on improving diplomacy with neighboring states and more strategic use of the economies as part of China's overall diplomatic toolkit. "Against the backdrop of a regional 'infrastructure gap' estimated in the trillions of dollars, the initiative highlights China's enormous and growing resources and will provide a major financial carrot to incentivize governments in Asia to pursue greater cooperation with Beijing."[8]

The B&R project comes at a time when many large state-owned enterprises are struggling to stay afloat and banks are stuck in a cycle of rolling over ever-growing and progressively less viable loan portfolios. This Initiative is for certain a well-reasoned project by Chinese leaders to put China at the centre of the International attention. At the same time, "the projects that make up the Belt and Road could provide vital life support and serve as a useful patronage tool for compensating vested interests threatened by efforts to implement market-oriented reforms."[9]

---

[7] In this sense, Zhu Ruixue, Liu Xiuling and Cai Li, Background and Strategic Significance of the Belt and Road Initiative of China, *Journal of Behavioural Economics, Finance, Entrepreneurship, Accounting and Transport*, Vol. 4, No. 3, 2016.

[8] In this sense, Scott Kennedy and David A. Parker, "Building China-s One Belt, One Road," CSIS / Center for Strategies and International Studies, April 3, 2015. https://www.csis.org/analysis/building-china%E2%80%99s-%E2%80%9Cone-belt-one-road%E2%80%9D.

[9] *Ibid.*

Apart from all these reasons, which are of fundamental importance and significance, this Initiative is the clear materialization of China's growing capacity and her economic clout. To conclude this section, it is worthwhile to stress that according to the Asian Development Bank, there is an annual "gap" between the supply and demand for infrastructure spending in Asia on the order of US$800 billion. Thus, given that infrastructure is at the heart of the B&R, there is room for the initiative to play a constructive role in regional economic architecture.

2.1.4 *Infrastructure is Not the Only Focus*

The B&R is a centerpiece of China's foreign policy and an important part of its domestic economic strategy. It is evident that China aims at promoting and enhancing policy coordination across the Asian continent and China is also seeking more financial integration and trade liberalization, therefore the scope of the initiative extends well beyond infrastructure construction.

It seems appropriate to affirm that this ambitious program also includes efforts to promote greater financial integration and the use of the Renminbi by foreign countries.

2.1.4.1 Financial Integration

The B&R proposes that financial cooperation between Eurasian countries should be deepened, but China also seeks other countries' cooperation, and efforts should be made in building a currency stability system, investment and financing system, and credit information in Asia. Therefore, financial integration is an important underpinning for implementing the B&R Initiative.

As a priority for the next stage, financial cooperation and connectivity are seen as key to success and smooth development of the B&R.

At the Belt and Road Forum for International Cooperation held in Beijing in May 2017,[10] a joint communiqué was issued vowing to work

---

[10]Belt and Road Forum for International Cooperation, *Strengthening International Cooperation and Co-building the "Belt and Road" for Win–win Development*, Beijing

on a long-term, stable and sustainable financing system, as well as to enhance financial infrastructure connectivity by exploring new finance models, platforms and services.

2.1.4.2 RMB Internationalization: Brief Introduction

The B&R Initiative is helpful not only in removing financial barriers between China and the countries along the B&R but also in accelerating the process of "RMB internationalization."

As for the RMB internationalization, it is worth remembering that in 2014 China's trade volume accounted for 12% of the world, but the share of RMB in the global payment currency market was only 2%. With the implementation of the B&R Initiative, RMB exchange and settlement businesses will be carried out in more countries, and countries holding Chinese yuan as their reserve will be more and more. Consequently, the size of the financial assets denominated in Chinese yuan will surge. Another consequence is that capital markets will pay more attention to the Chinese currency.

The B&R Initiative seems to already promote RMB internationalization. The gradual full convertibility of the Chinese yuan is of fundamental importance to introduce China into the club of the real economic powers allowing the "Middle Kingdom" to play the role it deserves considering the growing importance of China's economy (for more details on this topic, see Secs. 4.4.1-4.4.3).

2.1.5 *Energy Security*

The source of China's energy import mainly focuses on the Middle East and Africa, but due to the political unrest, religious disputes and ethnic conflicts, oil and gas production in these regions are not stable, and this

---

May 14–15, 2017. The conference mainly discussed and exchanged ideas on eight aspects, including infrastructure, industry investment, economic and trade cooperation, energy and resources, financial cooperation, people-to-people and cultural exchanges, ecological civilization and maritime cooperation, discuss the direction of cooperation, come up with implementation path, pool cooperation consensus and push forward practical results. http://english.mofcom.gov.cn/article/zt_ydyl_english/.

situation threatens China's energy import security. The oil imported from the Middle East and Africa has to be transported by sea via the Indian Ocean–Malacca Strait–South China Sea, and the amount of oil transported by this route accounts approximately for 75% of China's total oil import. The problem is that "this route is subject to 'the Malacca Dilemma,' and China is troubled by the singles of the energy transportation route due to the intensified dispute in the South China Sea."[11] Consequently, "energy cooperation" between China and the countries along the B&R has great significance to the diversification of energy import channels and the insurance of energy supply security for China. The three big oil and gas pipelines of China–Russia, China–Myanmar and China–Central Asia will greatly improve China's oil supply security. It is a matter of fact that the Central Asian countries have abundant resources of oil, gas and uranium (for the new electric power stations China is planning to build). Central Asian countries are promoting the process of diversification of energy export and have great potential for cooperation with China, and no doubt the B&R Initiative will facilitate this cooperation.

2.1.6 *Potential Risks*

Naturally, implementing the B&R Initiative will entail significant risks and challenges for China. The central question is whether the infrastructure projects can bring China sufficient return on investment, especially since the political and economic environment in the countries involved in the Initiative is uncertain at its best. Investing in these countries might risk increasing China's debt burden for the sake of limited returns.

China's past difficulties investing in infrastructure abroad, especially through bilateral arrangements, suggest that many of the proposed projects could well end up as little more than a series of expensive boondoggles. This is something to keep in mind, and this is also why cooperation among the countries involved in the Initiative is of paramount importance. "Given Chinese construction companies' poor track record operating in

---

[11] In this sense, Zhu Ruixue, Liu Xiuling and Cai Li, Background and Strategic Significance of the Belt and Road Initiative of China, *Journal of Behavioural Economics, Finance, Entrepreneurship, Accounting and Transport*, Vol. 4, No. 3, 2016.

foreign countries (including frequent mistreatment of local workers), a major increase in the scale of their external activities increases the risk of damaging political blowback that could harm Beijing's image or lead to instability in host countries particularly if the efforts do not generate lasting benefits for local economies. Enhanced regional connectivity might also increase the likelihood of the consequences of poor conduct abroad finding their way back to China."[12]

It is worth stressing that infrastructure investment already represents a quarter of China's total investment and returns on infrastructure investments are currently very low in China, often not even covering financial outlay. This has created the potential for a debt crisis in the country. Even so, in the Silk Road projects, China plans to continue investing in infrastructure, both in China and in countries where returns are even less stable and certain. "Therefore, developing the OBOR Initiative carries significant micro-hazard for China. From a macro perspective, infrastructure projects could, on the other hand, have an indirect benefit for China. Only part of the investment would go into China itself, but the infrastructure build would help link China to its neighboring countries, thus easing the pressure on natural and energy resources and goods transport."[13]

Another risk is that many countries in Asia, and abroad (including the United States), are concerned about the geopolitical impact of the B&R Initiative. Although Beijing is stressing the "win–win" potential of the Initiative, its efforts will have important foreign policy implications for a number of key regional players, including Japan, India and Russia. Moscow is particularly concerned about the initiative translating into increased Chinese influence in Central Asia, an area it has long viewed as

---

[12] In this sense, Scott Kennedy and David A. Parker, "Building China-s One Belt, One Road," CSIS / Center for Strategies and International Studies, April 3, 2015. https://www.csis.org/analysis/building-china%E2%80%99s-%E2%80%9Cone-belt-one-road%E2%80%9D.

[13] See the document prepared by the European Council on Foreign Relations (*ECFR) titled "One Belt, One Road": China's Great Leap outward, European Council on Foreign Relations," June 2015. This article is available at: http://china-trade-research.hktdc.com/business-news/article/The-Belt-and-Road-Initiative/One-Belt-One-Road-China-s-Great-Leap-Outward/obor/en/1/1X000000/1X0A8B12.htm.

within its sphere of influence and where Sino-Russia competition has been noticeably intensifying of late. Meanwhile, India has been especially alarmed by Chinese investments in Sri Lanka, which New Delhi likewise views as part of its backyard. All this is an inevitable consequence of the implementation of the B&R Initiative. Diplomatic relations with all the countries involved should be intensified in order to facilitate the development of all the planned projects. The potential of the Initiative and its impact on the economies of all the countries involved are huge, but only with joint efforts, it will be possible to grasp the benefits of the Initiative.

Finally, it is important to stress that there are also direct security implications of the project. The Maritime Silk Road in particular will likely expand China's capacity to project its growing naval power abroad, while increased Chinese involvement in building regional information technology infrastructure could create new channels for Beijing to exert its influence in the region.

2.1.7 *Information Silk Road: The Concept Explained*

Another important theme which is embodied in the B&R Initiative is the attempt to create an "Information Silk Road"[14] linking regional information and communication technology networks. The idea of incorporating digital sectors like telecommunications, Internet of things infrastructure and e-commerce into the B&R is not new. The March 2015 White Paper[15] articulating the vision for B&R called for growth in digital trade and expansion of communication networks to develop "an information silk road." The concept even received a "shout-out" in the joint communiqué from the recent Belt and Road Forum (Beijing, May 14, 2017) with a

---

[14]*"Information Silk Road"* represents a third prong of the B&R Initiative. Many aspects of the concept are a natural extension of the "going out" policies pursued by Chinese telecommunications companies and could fill unmet needs for digital connectivity. Greater connectivity could in turn open new markets for China firms in e-commerce and other areas.

[15]The document issued by the National Development and Reform Commission (NDRC) is available at: http://en.ndrc.gov.cn/newsrelease/201503/t20150330_669367.htm (accessed, June 15, 2017).

pledge to support innovation action plans for e-commerce, digital economy, smart cities and science and technology parks. In particular:

> "g) Expanding trade by nurturing new areas of trade growth, promoting trade balance and promoting e-commerce and digital economy, welcoming the development of free trade areas and signing of free trade agreements by interested countries."[16]

But apart from the bland formulation of policy documents, what will the digital new Silk Road actually look like?

Many aspects of the concept are a natural extension of the "going-out" policies pursued by Chinese telecommunications companies and could fill unmet needs for digital connectivity; greater connectivity could in turn open new markets for Chinese firms in e-commerce and other areas. But overall, the digital new Silk Road looks less like a cohesive concept and more like a catchall phrase applied to everything which can be considered "digital." It seems appropriate to affirm that there are, at least, three sectors that fit into the so-called "Information Silk Road" concept, as identified in the following section.

2.1.7.1 Telecommunications and Satellite Network

In addition to new railways, ports, and power plants, another infrastructure priority[17] under the B&R Initiative is improving "international communications connectivity" through "the construction of cross-border optical cables and other communications trunk line networks." State-owned enterprises including China Telecom, China Unicom and China Mobile have already embarked on B&R-related projects[18] and are building out the

---

[16] See the "Joint communiqué of leaders roundtable of the Belt and Road forum," Beijing, May 15, 2017. http://news.xinhuanet.com/english/2017-05/15/c_136286378.htm.

[17] See the content of the document: "Vision and Actions on Jointly Building Silk Road Economic Belt and 21st Century Maritime Silk Road" available at: http://en.ndrc.gov.cn/newsrelease/201503/t20150330_669367.html.

[18] See, "Key connectivity improvements along the Belt and Road in telecommunications & aviation sectors," September 2016, available at: http://www.ey.com/Publication/vwLUAssets/ey-china-go-abroad-4th-issue-2016-en/%24FILE/ey-china-go-abroad-4th-issue-2016-en.pdf.

infrastructure to underlie the digital new Silk Road. Among the ambitious programs are the construction by China and Russia of overland cable links between Asia and Europe.

In addition to cable networks, B&R also offers the Chinese government a chance to encourage the adoption of its Beidou satellite network,[19] a competitor to GPS, through a "space-based Silk Road."[20] The government aims to roll out basic services along the B&R route by 2018 and the State Council Information Office is promoting Beidou's use in everything from power transmission to transportation.

These new projects, it is understood, will not only enhance digital connectivity in underserved Central and Southeast Asian countries but also facilitate faster and easier to maintain data connections. While the expansion of the Beidou system could improve the accuracy of consumer satellite navigation, it could also squeeze foreign companies out of satellite navigation markets in China and certain B&R nations. Furthermore, Beidou's development could also have implication in the national security realm as the People's Liberation Army improves its weapons and tracking capabilities.

It is too early and there are scarce elements to determine whether these additional project(s) can have a significant impact on the economies

---

[19] BeiDou Navigation Satellite System is China's global navigation satellite system which has been developed independently. The system's target: maintain independence and keep the initiative in Chinese hands, keep open, compatible, stable and reliable on technology, offer global service, thereby accelerating the foundation of navigation satellite industrial chain, consummating the sustaining extending and guaranteeing system, expanding the range of application in the country's economic and social sector.

BeiDou Navigation Satellite System is composed of three parts: the space section, the ground section and the user section. The space section contains five geostationary orbit satellites and 30 non-geostationary orbit satellites. The ground section consists of a certain number of stations: including the main control stations, the injection stations and the monitoring stations. And the user section includes terminators of BeiDou system, and some compatible with other navigation satellite system. http://en.beidou.gov.cn/.

[20] The space-based Silk Road initiative was proposed in 2014 by the International Alliance of Satellite Application Service (ASAS), a China-based organization of aerospace companies, institutions and scholars that promotes Chinese satellite services around the world. Jiang Jie, Nation Considers Space-based 'Silk Road of Satellites' to Provide Data Services," *Global Times*, May 31, 2015. *China can build a "Space-based Silk Road" by strengthening cooperation in satellite services with other countries, with the aim of supporting the country's "One Belt, One Road" initiative.* See article at: http://www.globaltimes.cn/content/924600.shtml.

of the involved countries, however their relevance cannot be ignored or underestimated.

2.1.7.2 Smart Cities

Another digital infrastructure frontier for Chinese firms is the construction of "smart cities." Smart cities are broadly defined as urban areas that integrate information and communications technology to improve city operations in everything from traffic flows to water conservation to crime prevention. In recent years, ZTE[21] and Huawei have expanded their efforts to supply smart city projects in B&R nations such as Malaysia, Kenya, and Germany. Even China's model smart city, Yinchuan,[22] lies along the path of the original Silk Road in a region now poised to benefit from new trade routes. Yinchuan offers citizens an array of innovative services including access to city information via QR codes and the ability to pay bus fares upon boarding through facial recognition software. Last December, ZTE's chief information and strategy officer, Chen Jie, stressed the company's commitment to sharing its smart cities know-how across the B&R route. One of the company's subsidiaries, ZTEsoft, has even co-opted the B&R name for its new initiative, the "Data Belt, Information Road."[23] Such collaborations could help modernize cities, increase their efficiency, and promote greater standardization of technologies. However, the increasing reliance of cities on technology also raises cyber-security risks. Moreover, for countries with often tense relationships with China,

---

[21] ZTEsoft, a leading provider of telecom software, solutions and services.

[22] *Leading the Global Transition to Smart Cities in China TM Forum's* "Smart City InFocus 2016: Yinchuan," a summary of the three days Forum held on September 9, 2016, Shenzhen, China is available at: http://www.zte.com.cn/global/about/press-center/news/201609ma/0909ma.

[23] "Data Belt, Information Road" strategy is based on China national strategy "One belt, One Road," which focuses on strengthening the collaboration among Asia countries, Europe countries and Africa countries (regional cooperation). ZTEsoft will take the role of regional collaboration enabler to combine smart city experience, ecosystem resources, investment capabilities, technology advantages among China, Singapore and other countries based on ZTEsoft international capabilities and smart city operation capabilities. ZSmart "Data Belt, Information Road" Strategy — To Innovate a Regional Cooperation Platform to Connect the Smart Nation and Smart Cities. http://www.ztesoft.com/en/content/details_36_1954.html.

there could be broader worries about depending on digital infrastructure supplied by Chinese firms.

2.1.7.3 E-commerce

E-commerce represents one of the pillars of Chinese economy, and its further development is of paramount importance for China. In fact, an increased Internet connectivity could also pave the way for more Chinese e-commerce sales along the B&R route. It is significant that two of China's e-commerce giants, i.e. Alibaba and JD.com, have already sought to link their global expansion to B&R. It is interesting to note that JD.com plans to set up "more than 20 overseas warehouses to store and transfer goods from over 100 countries and regions including those along the Belt and Road Initiative."[24] Also, Alibaba[25] founder, Jack Ma, has cited countries along the B&R route[26] as among the most important regions for his company and plans further expansion in Russia, Central Asia and Southeast Asia. Jack Ma's vision is to implement an "e-road" and this can be achieved by integrating standards and reducing trade barriers in e-commerce via an "Electronic World Trade Platform." It is evident that Ma's dream of promoting greater global online trade is consistent with B&R mission of expanding commerce along new routes. However, many obstacles have to be overcome, especially regulatory obstacles because of the different legal framework in certain B&R nations. It seems that Ma is willing to play a significant role with his company in order to contribute in developing his international e-commerce ambitions, much like Chinese leaders themselves with the entire B&R project.

This short section is only aimed at highlighting the close relation between the B&R Initiative and the silk e-road, however it is necessary to

---

[24] See: Chen Yongrong and Liu Xin, Xinhua Insight: Belt and Road Initiative Boosts China's E-commerce, *XinhuaNet*, April 29, 2017, available at: http://news.xinhuanet.com/english/2017-04/29/c_136245718.htm.

[25] Alibaba this year (2017) went even further and partnered with the Malaysian government to establish the first "digital free-trade-zone," the project will offer logistic and fulfillment capabilities as well as online services platform. https://www.mdec.my/news/malaysia-launches-worlds-first-digital-free-trade-zone.

[26] Vikas Shukla, Alibaba follows Beijing's One Belt and One Road, *Valuewalk*, June 17, 2017, available at: http://www.valuewalk.com/2016/06/alibaba-follows-one-road-one-belt/.

stress that e-commerce, in particular, is at the center of Chinese strategy to further reinforce its economy. "China not only is emerging as one of the new economic powers of this century, and regaining its importance and brightness lost in the last part of our modern history, but the Middle Kingdom is also imposing itself as a new model to be imitated in order to shape the future characteristics of the world economy. This is particularly evident when it comes to the development of the 'new digital economy' which will play a role of paramount importance for China. In order to sustain its growth a robust development of the internal consumptions is needed, and one of the channel the leadership has chosen to grant China its destiny is to implement a new 'Digital Economy' based on the further development of e-commerce and its facets."[27]

E-commerce has been indicated by the Chinese government as one of the pillars of its economic development and it is not surprising that new projects are attempted to further integrate into China's vision of a more connected world and make it a part of this new Initiative.

2.1.8 Connecting the World: Chinese Enterprises Dedicated to Building the Information Silk Road

This theme, i.e. information interconnectivity, as it has already emerged above, is one of the basic elements, if not even a priority, of the B&R Initiative. As clearly expressed in the document titled, "Vision and Actions on Jointly Building Silk Road Economic Belt and 21st Century Maritime Silk Road" among other priorities, the necessity of advancing the construction of cross-border optical cables and other trunk line networks and creating what has been defined as an "Information Silk Road" is pointed out.[28] It is worth noting that the "Guidelines on Boosting International Cooperation in Production Capacity and Equipment Manufacturing"[29] also encourage

---

[27] Cristiano Rizzi, *E-Commerce Law in China — The Functioning of e-commerce in China and the Influence of the EU Model*, Wolters Kluwer, Law & Business, September, 2013.

[28] *Vision and Actions Outlined on Jointly Building Silk Road Economic Belt and 21st-Century Maritime Silk Road*, jointly published by MOFCOM, NDRC and MOFA, March 2015. Document available at: http://en.ndrc.gov.cn/newsrelease/201503/t20150330_669367.html.

[29] *Guideline on Boosting International Cooperation in Production Capacity and Equipment Manufacturing*, published by the State Council, May 2015. The Guidelines are available

telecommunications enterprises to speed up their global market expansion, increase their outbound investment and establish overseas research and development institutions, and the B&R Initiative could prepare the terrain to be inseminated with new dedicated investment projects.

Not only Chinese e-commerce companies but also Chinese telecommunication enterprises are planning to expand their business abroad to improve communication connectivity and to create new opportunities through the B&R Initiative, which not only enhances regional economic integration but also helps the industry to find new spaces for growing abroad in the ambit of the "going-out policy" encouraged by the Chinese government. It is worth stressing that the "Chinese government has embarked on a 'go global' strategy recently, to allocate the enormous resources Chinese enterprises (State Owned or not) have accumulated in recent years when they were focused on manufacturing and export (this, in fact, has resulted in a significant foreign exchange reserve for China). This particular situation has permitted China to push their 'going out policy' to funnel their foreign exchange resources to international investments not only in Asia Pacific, but also in the Americas, Europe and Africa."[30]

2.1.8.1 State-owned Operators: Actions to Accelerate Overseas Expansion in Line with the B&R Initiative

It is of significance and worth noting that the top three Chinese state-owned telecommunications carriers have already set up international companies in Hong Kong in the recent years, positioning Hong Kong as a key platform for their internationalization. Hong Kong has sound information infrastructure and a large number of international talents in the telecommunications, legal, finance and other business service areas.[31]

---

at the following website: http://english.gov.cn/policies/infographics/2015/07/07/content_281475142209946.htm.

[30] Cristiano Rizzi, Paolo Rizzi, Lex Smith and Li Guo, *Chinese Expansion in the EU – Strategies and Policies of the Two Blocks and the Role of the U.S.*, American Bar Association, August 2016.

[31] Key connectivity Improvements along the Belt and Road in telecommunications & aviation sectors, September 2016, Part 2. Document available at: http://www.ey.com/Publication/vwLUAssets/ey-china-go-abroad-4th-issue-2016-en/%24FILE/ey-china-go-abroad-4th-issue-2016-en.pdf.

The strategies of these three operators are highlighted in the following table:

China Mobile International Limited (established in December 2010)	China Telecom Global Limited (established in August 2012)	China Unicom Global Limited (established in July 2015)
China Mobile established China Mobile International Limited (CMI) by integrating some of the functions of its overseas investment office, global business division (affiliated with the marketing department) and China Mobile Hong Kong Company. CMI, headquartered in Hong Kong, is in charge of China Mobile's overseas businesses including those in the UK. In July, 2015, CMCC initiated the "Join Hands Program." The program is designed to cooperate with international operators in areas such as data, international voice call and transmission networks, to provide more reliable and faster telecommunications services for the "One Belt, One Road" initiative. Its partners have included VimpelCom, A1, Telenor and other international giants.	In 2012, China Telecom integrated its international business resources and human resources to found China Telecom Global Limited (CTG), which is headquartered in Hong Kong. Leveraging its abundant resources in mainland China, CTG connects the Asia-Pacific region and the world. CTG has become a world-class integrated provider of communications services including network deployment, service support and product supply. In response to the "One Belt, One Road" initiative, China Telecom has focused on three regions: Eurasia, Greater Mekong and Africa. China Comservice, a subsidiary of China Telecom, planned the "Joint Construction of Africa's Information Superhighway Between China and Africa," with investment amounting to USD15 billion. The planned length of optical cable is 150,000 kilometers covering 48 African countries.	By integrating its overseas businesses in Hong Kong, the Americas, Europe, Singapore, Japan, Australia, South Africa and Burma, China Unicom established its wholly owned subsidiary — China Unicom Global Limited, headquartered in Hong Kong. China Unicom is expanding the network layout in countries along the Belt and Road, laying optical cables to connect Central Asia, Southeast Asia, Africa and South America. In June 2016, led by China Unicom, ChinaASEAN Information Harbor Co., Ltd. was founded to integrate information resources across the regions and establish the Internet plus industrial ecosystem.

Source: EY: Building a better working world, *Key Connectivity Improvements Along the Belt and Road in Telecommunications & Aviation Sectors*, September 2016.

It is evident that the B&R serves as a stimulus, however these Chinese telecommunications enterprises are already engaged in this "internationalization" process to improve their international communications connectivity through the "Belt and Road" Initiative, which not only enhances regional economic integration but also helps the industry find new growth momentum.

2.1.8.2 Internationalization Process: Adapting Strategies to Grasp This Opportunity

It is a matter of fact that with the acceleration of internationalization, the markets along the Belt and Road offer huge development potential. Certainly, for many Chinese enterprises, the M&A methods represents the preferred form to expand their presence abroad, however some obstacles can be encountered, especially regulatory hurdles, and of course this is true not only for telecommunications companies but also for other types of businesses seeking to gain more space abroad. However, regardless of the ways used in "going out," all enterprises need to consolidate their strengths in order to better grasp the "Belt and Road" investment opportunities. Thus, developing an internationalization strategy that embodies the vision of President Xi of the B&R Initiative is an obliged path. In doing so, Chinese companies should be aware that cooperation with third countries is a must. For instance, policy restrictions are stricter in the telecommunications sector, thus enterprises need to understand the market and legal framework of the host country and strengthen cooperation with local governments and authorities to ensure that an investment project can be developed in the smoothest way.

Generally, construction and operation of overseas projects require more standardized and refined management, thus in the ambit of the B&R Initiative, all Chinese enterprises wishing to expand their businesses abroad will also have to adapt themselves to the new environment and rules, and work together with their counterpart to make sure projects can be jointly implemented.

Naturally, in implementing all these projects, linked somehow to the B&R Initiative, it is of basic importance for the subjects involved to make the best use of diversified capital sources, and explore investment model, though the Chinese companies have their own resources, it would be wise to take advantage of multiple platforms, such as AIIB, Silk Road Fund, local government funds and private capitals, to innovate the investment, construction, and operating models, and brake through the bottleneck of investment and financing. These issues will be treated in the book when developing the relative parts concerning financial institutions and the way of financing the projects (see Chapters 3 and 4).

2.1.9 *Efficiency in Transportation of Goods: Brief Introduction*

Connectivity is one of the priorities for implementing the B&R Initiative. However, because one of the major objectives is also to enhance the transportation of goods, China's focus on land routes may seem counterintuitive. In fact, from port to port, sea freight will always be cheaper than overland transportation. Industry trends point toward ever-lower prices as container shipping rates break historic lows. The largest carriers continue to add new megaships to their fleets, with orders placed years ago to be delivered whether companies now want them or not. This is another reason why China is interested in ports, building new ones, or enhancing the efficiency of ports along the Maritime Silk road. China's interest in these infrastructure is evident and more details are to be discussed in Section 5.2, where China's strategy emerges more clear when investing in such infrastructure. In this context, the construction of new railroads is of course welcome and they will enhance connectivity between countries, but when it comes to transportation of goods, it is evident that the Maritime Silk Road plays a major role.

2.2 Some Considerations on the Expansion of Chinese Companies' Presence Abroad

When Chinese companies expand their presence abroad or simply enter third countries to do business or cooperate with local companies, as this Initiative aims, it is easy to forget that companies will face unique risks and liabilities in every market they enter to develop specific projects (i.e. any project connected to the B&R Initiative). Thus, as soon as

Chinese companies enter in contact with entities of third countries (local authorities, and businesses), they should make every effort not only to assure local rules are respected but also to comply with all the regulations. Some of these aspects have been examined in a previous book, i.e. *Chinese Expansion in the EU — Strategies and Policies of the Two Blocks and the Role of the U.S.*[32] However, because the focus was on Chinese investment in the EU, only certain aspects were covered. However, because the aim of this book is limited to highlighting how the B&R Initiative was born and how it is possible to put in place such an ambitious program, the scope of this work is limited to illustrating some facets, otherwise it would be necessary to write entire tomes considering the legal framework of 68 different nations regulating not only the infrastructure sector but also the almost countless rules and laws related to inbound investments.

The Chinese leadership is pushing to accelerate the implementation of the "B&R" strategy, and in doing so, it is inevitable that China has to also continue its policy reforms; these two elements combined will bring a new wave of outbound investments.

A certain background is common and it is necessary to have it exposed to better understand how the B&R Initiative is developing. And also it will be necessary to explain who the players are and their roles, especially at the financial level, helping China in making this Initiative real. Therefore, the following information is of extreme importance to put every single piece of the puzzle together in order to have a clear image of the Belt and Road Initiative.

Companies building an overseas presence should carefully consider the governance requirements for each market in which they will operate, even in a joint modality like, for example, operating a Joint Venture for the realization of a specific infrastructure project.

As many Chinese companies will have the opportunity, thanks to the B&R Initiative, to become more international, they should consider employing local expertise and local operational capabilities in order to

---

[32]Cristiano Rizzi, Paolo Rizzi, Lex Smith and Li Guo, *Chinese Expansion in the EU — Strategies and Policies of the Two Blocks and the Role of the U.S.*, American Bar Association, August 2016.

adapt themselves more easily to the new legal environment, this should also be a key consideration for Chinese corporations, of any size, as they move ahead with global expansion plans, both organically and through acquisitions.

2.2.1 *New Guidelines for Chinese Companies Operating Abroad*

Considering what we have just exposed above, it seems now appropriate to briefly introduce some rules, which usually are considered "marginal" when discussing and planning Outbound Chinese investments or "Chinese ODI" (Outbound Direct Investment), but which are of basic importance and should be considered an integral part of those rules, that Chinese companies must abide to in order not to create frictions with the host recipients of Chinese investments. More precisely in 2013, the Chinese Ministries of Commerce and Environmental Protection jointly released the guidelines for Chinese companies doing business abroad[33] on how to operate sustainably and responsibly, and comply with host country regulations and international standards. The guidelines directly respond to concerns from the international community and help Chinese companies more effectively target the international market. The guidelines consist of 22 comprehensive provisions for corporate responsibility that Chinese companies should take into account when they operate overseas.[34] The following are the most significant points:

- **Environmental conservation:** Analyze potential local environmental impacts, including a baseline survey of the ecosystem, and develop an environmental risk management plan and monitoring, assessment and reporting mechanisms.

---

[33] The "Guidelines for Environmental Protection in Foreign Investment and Cooperation," issued by the Ministry of Commerce of the People's Republic of China, and Ministry of Environmental Protection of the People's Republic of China. Date of Issuance: February 18, 2013, available at: http://english.mofcom.gov.cn/article/policyrelease/bbb/201303/20130300043226.shtml.

[34] https://www.bsr.org/en/ou.r-insights/blog-view/new-guidelines-for-chinese-companies-operating-abroad.

- **Community development:** Create a long-term local community development plan based on potential areas of impact and build monitoring, assessment, and reporting mechanisms —including implementation of a social impact assessment.
- **Stakeholder engagement:** Communicate with local stakeholders and involve them in business strategy as much as possible and secure the social license to operate from local civil society.

The Guidelines will strengthen environmental guidance of overseas Chinese companies, step up environmental protection under the legal framework of host countries, and help host countries achieve sustainable development based on mutual benefit and win–win results. Strengthening guidance on environmental protection of overseas Chinese companies is conducive to improving their capacity of international operation, accelerating business integration, achieving long-term development and promoting the sustainable growth of outbound investment and economic cooperation.[35]

With the Guidelines, the government for the first time offers environmental guidance to companies engaged in outward investment and economic cooperation. It reflects the government's commitment to governance through service and is a concrete step to build a service system for companies investing and operating abroad.

2.2.2 *China's Recent Restriction on Outbound Investment*

The Chinese government on one hand is fostering and encouraging Chinese companies to invest abroad, and now with the B&R Initiative, it is expected to create a new wave of Chinese ODI, however the government is also revising the legal framework for companies to go abroad. Thus, Chinese firms engaged in overseas investments need to be aware of these new trends and prepare to adjust their strategic plans and overseas activities according to the directive of the central government. Recently,

---

[35]Ministry of Commerce, Press Conference, March 1, 2013. In this sense, Yao Jian, MOFCOM spokesperson at: http://english.mofcom.gov.cn/article/newsrelease/press/201303/20130300051296.shtml.

several published rules and public comments by government officials have sent a signal that the Chinese government will take certain measures to tighten its control and supervision over outbound investment by Chinese companies, especially in certain industries.

The most relevant recent rules and policies are provided in the following section, however this is not exhaustive. The framework is extremely vast and complicated, and other references should be used to understand the dynamics of Chinese ODI, nonetheless the following information is useful to clarify the ambit and borders the Chinese regulators are offering to Chinese companies investing abroad.

2.2.2.1 Recent Rules and Policies: Overview

Notably, currency issues are of extreme importance when coming to foreign investments, and in order to further regulate it, the People's Bank of China, on November 29, 2016, promulgated the *Notification on Further Clarifications on Overseas RMB Loans by Domestic Enterprises*, also known as "Circular 306."[36] Circular 306 aims at restricting the arbitrage activities of companies that convert offshore RMB into hard currencies and engage in short-selling of offshore RMB, while stabilizing the RMB exchange rate. Circular 306 also sets forth some new requirements, including the requirement to obtain pre-approval of overseas RMB loans, requirement of equity ownership between debtors and creditors, restrictions on the net outflow amount of RMB, and requirements to tighten the control over intentional breach of loan agreements. Some requirements under Circular 306 are also consistent with the proposed measures that would tighten control over outbound investment by Chinese companies in certain industries, as discussed hereinafter.

The State Administration of Foreign Exchange (SAFE)[37] has simultaneously with the publication of Circular 306 also adopted certain internal

---

[36](YinFa [2016] No. 306) (Circular 306).

[37]One of the State Administration for Foreign Exchange's (SAFE) main functions is to study and propose policy suggestions on the reform of the foreign exchange administration system, prevention of the balance of payments risks, and promotion of the balance of payments equilibrium; to study and implement policy measures for the gradual advancement of the convertibility of the RMB under the capital account and the cultivation and

rules, such as cutting the maximum amount of overseas repatriation by companies established in China (including both domestic companies and foreign-invested enterprises) down from US$50 million to US$5 million, requiring a pre-approval with the SAFE for all overseas transfers by companies established in China of US$5 million or more under capital accounts. These internal rules not only set forth new restrictions over off-shore investment by Chinese companies but also apply to funds trans-ferred between Chinese subsidiaries and their offshore parents and affiliated companies.

On December 6, 2016, officials from the National Development and Reform Commission (NDRC),[38] the Ministry of Commerce, the People's Bank of China and the SAFE, in a press conference (Press Release), stated that the government "will support domestic companies that have the abil-ity and opportunity to make real and legal outbound investment and to participate in projects relating to China's 'One Belt and One Road' strat-egy," but that it "has also noticed some irrational investment activities in real estate, hotels, film studios, the entertainment industry and sports clubs" and "has been alerted to potential risks in association with over-seas investment projects involving (a) large investment in business that is not related to the core business of the Chinese investor, (b) outbound

---

development of the foreign exchange market; to provide suggestions and a foundation for the People's Bank of China to formulate policy on RMB exchange rate. For further infor-mation visit: http://www.safe.gov.cn/wps/portal/english/. The SAFE play an important role in influencing the direction of Chinese investments abroad and it also has several other major functions; more details at: http://www.safe.gov.cn/wps/portal/english/AboutSAFE/Major.

[38] National Development and Reform Commission People's Republic of China (NDRC), 国家发展与改革委员会 is the authority in charge of formulating and implementing strat-egies of national economic and social development, annual plans, medium and long-term development plans; of coordinating economic and social development; to carry out research and analysis on domestic and international economic situation; of putting forward targets and policies concerning the development of the national economy, the regulation of the overall price level and the optimization of major economic structures, and of making recommendations on the employment of various economic instruments and policies; of submitting the plan for national economic and social development to the National People's Congress on behalf of the State Council. Further information is available at: http://en.ndrc.gov.cn//mfndrc/default.htm.

investment made by limited partnerships, (c) investment in offshore targets that have assets value larger than the Chinese acquirers, and (d) projects that have very short investment period." The Press Release "suggests the companies to be cautious when making outbound investment." Is it safe to affirm that though the Chinese government is now pushing on the B&R Initiative, the regulators also want to rationalize ODI, and it is predicted that Chinese investments in the infrastructure sector will be favored because they meet the significance of this policy.

2.2.2.2 (Possible) New Pieces of Legislation to Further Regulate Chinese ODI

It is not surprising if the Chinese government will soon publish a set of rules and regulations with concrete measures to tighten the inspection and supervision of outbound investment activities of Chinese companies, and that those rules and regulations will be broadly applied to outbound investment in all industries. This is not only because of the reasons mentioned in the previous section but also because it is predicted that Chinese investments will surge in connection to the B&R Initiative. It is also expected that domestic examination and approving authorities of outbound investment projects, not only necessary in the infrastructure sector, will scrutinize the approval process from the perspectives of the source of the investment funds, the qualification of the domestic investment entities and the quality of the overseas target companies and/or assets in case the investment is aimed at expanding a presence abroad, and that they will require the Chinese investors (or acquirers) to provide more documents supporting their investment objectives, the estimated investment returns and the rationale of the investment. This in order to better assess every single investment opportunity and to assure that Chinese money going abroad is used according to Chinese priorities.

2.2.2.3 New Rules Also for Foreign Investment in China: Overview

At this point, it is also worth mentioning that along with tightening the control over outbound investment by Chinese companies, the Chinese government is also taking measures to lift restrictions over foreign investment into China and simplifying the examination and approving process for foreign direct investment. For instance, in September 2016, the Standing Committee of the People's Congress made decisions to make revisions to the relevant provisions in the *Wholly Foreign Owned Enterprises Law, Sino-Foreign Equity Joint Ventures Law, Sino-Foreign Cooperative Joint Venture Law* and *The Law on Protection of Investment from Taiwan Enterprises and Individuals*, and some related administrative rules. These regulations represent the core of the legislative framework regulating foreign investment in China.[39] Under those revisions, foreign-invested enterprises (including companies invested by Taiwan enterprises or individuals) in non-restricted industries no longer have to be examined and approved by government authorities, and all such companies only need to file with the government for the record upon formation and changes. The filing for record system for foreign invested enterprises was later formalized by the Ministry of Commerce and the State Administration of Industry and Commerce under the *Tentative Rules on Filing System for the Establishment and Information Change of Foreign Invested Enterprises*,[40] published on October 8, 2016. NDRC and the Ministry of Commerce also published a circular[41] to clarify the industries

---

[39] A more precise description of the instruments at the disposal of the foreign investors to enter the China market is exposed in a detailed manner in the following publication: Cristiano Rizzi, Li Guo and Joseph Christian, *Mergers and Acquisitions and Takeovers in China — A Legal and Cultural Guide to New Forms of Investment*, Wolters Kluwer Law & Business, 2012. This work contains a reasoned explanation of all the form of investments starting from the Representative Office, including the setting up an operational of Equity Joint Ventures, Contractual Joint Ventures and Wholly Owned Foreign Enterprise. At the same time the book also offers a detailed analysis of the M&A legal framework in China for those companies choosing this method to enter the China market.

[40] A clear explanation, and policy interpretation of these rules is available at: http://english. mofcom.gov.cn/article/policyrelease/Cocoon/201610/20161001408728.shtml.

[41] *NDRC & MOFCOM Circular 2016 No.22* (中华人民共和国国家发展和改革委员会 中华人民共和国商务部公告 2016 年第 22 号) ("Circular 22"). China's regulatory regime on inbound foreign investment was modified and entered a new era on October 1, 2016. According to a decision issued by the National People's Congress of China in September 2016, the foreign investment approval requirement has to a large extent been replaced by a filing system across the nation and this "Circular No. 22" has to be read in

in which foreign investments are still subject to special administration (the so-called "Negative List"[42]).

This novelty has to be read in consideration of the revision of the "Catalogue for foreign investment." On December 7, 2016, the NDRC and the Ministry of Commerce issued the draft Seventh Edition of the Catalogue of *Industries for Foreign Investment* for public comments, which further cuts down the restricted industries for foreign investment from 93 categories in 2015 to approximately 60 categories.

However, back to the "Negative-list," although MOFCOM record-filing is not a prerequisite anymore to AIC registration, it is advisable to check the local practice. In some cases, it may be preferable to complete MOFCOM filing first because the filing receipt serves as a confirmation from MOFCOM that the subject matter does not fall within the "negative list," which may facilitate subsequent AIC registration. Under the new system, thus, foreign investment no longer requires the approval from the Ministry of Commerce (MOFCOM) or its local branches, as long as the business undertaken is not on a "negative list." It is also worth noting that a great number of regulations issued by the State Council, MOFCOM, AIC and various industrial regulators are yet to be amended to conform to the new regime. The legislation process may take a considerable amount of time. Therefore, local practice of various government authorities may

---

conjunction with the *Interim Administrative Measures on Record-filing of Establishment and Change of Foreign Invested Enterprises* (外商投资企业设立及变更备案管理暂行办法) ("MOFCOM Measures"), and the *SAIC Notice on Registration of Foreign Invested Enterprises under the Filing System* (工商总局关于做好外商投资企业实行备案管理后有关登记注册工作的通知) ("SAIC Notice").

[42]Negative list: The Chinese regulators did not issue a nationwide "negative list" in the form similar to that of the free trade zones (FTZs). Instead, the "negative list" is made by reference to the current *Foreign Investment Industrial Catalogue* (Catalogue) — the new record-filing regime does not apply to the following types of foreign investment (which will continue to be subject to MOFCOM approval): (i) any investment in the restricted category or prohibited category under the Catalogue; (ii) any investment in the encouraged category under the Catalogue where there are restrictive requirements on foreign equity ratio or foreign nationals being senior management; and (iii) any acquisition of non-foreign-invested companies in China by foreign investors (regardless of industrial sectors). Foreign investment other than the above will only need to go through an online record-filing procedure with local MOFCOM (Filing Procedure).

also vary during the initial phase of implementation of the new system. Foreign investors should closely monitor the developments in this regard.

2.2.3 *Other Focuses of the Chinese Legislator Relating to Outbound Investment Under Recent Trends*

As the focus is Chinese investment abroad, it is necessary to underline here that the overseas investment administrative authorities have emphasized their focus on four types of offshore investment projects: (i) large investment in business that is not related to the core business of the Chinese investor, (ii) outbound investment made by limited partnerships, (iii) investment in offshore targets that have asset value higher than the Chinese acquirers, and (iv) projects that have very short investment period. They have also specifically mentioned the five industries: real estate, hotels, movie theaters, the entertainment industry and sports clubs (collectively, the Targeted Industries), to be more closely scrutinized.

Although these categories of investment are not directly related to the B&R Initiative, it is necessary to briefly treat them because they are included in the more ample "going out policy" that the Chinese government is trying to rationalize while putting into existence the more ambitious and geo-political-oriented project.

It is worth noting that it is not sure yet how the authorities will define "large" and "core business" when deciding what is a "large investment in business that is not related to the core business of the Chinese investor," see point (i) above. To structure around this legal obstacle, is it possible for the Chinese investor to set up an acquiring subsidiary in China with the same business scope as the target company? Is it not possible to formulate a reply to this question. Time will say how Chinese authorities intend to deal with this issue, however, it seems appropriate to hypothesize that the Chinese government will set forth requirements on operating history for the legal entity (for example, two or three years of operation, but this is only a hypothesis) of such an acquiring subsidiary before it can make outbound investment. It is also worth noting that since the Chinese government has long required Chinese companies to "get bigger and get stronger," many Chinese firms have already expanded their "core" business to cover many different industrial areas, or have already been organized as multinational or cross-industry company groups, therefore it will be very difficult to clearly define the "core" business of a company.

Another critical point is how will the authorities define "investment in offshore targets that have asset value larger than the Chinese acquirers"? See point (iii) above. Does it cover acquisition projects that allow acquisition by the Chinese acquirer of target company's assets in two or more different phases? This is also a question that requires new inputs from the Chinese legislator.

This excursus on the new requirements for Chinese ODI only aims at highlighting new trends in the complicated framework. The following sections and chapters will try to stay focused on the many facets of the B&R Initiative, however it should not be forgotten that all Chinese investments taking shape abroad should also be regulated by these new rules if they fall into their ambit.

2.3 Growing Influence of China on the International Stage

China's presence is growing in almost all the parts of the globe, and this is a consequence of the massive amount of money Chinese companies are investing in third countries. And the B&R Initiative will only accelerate investments and consequently enhance China's soft power to influence the policies of the recipients of those Chinese investments.

China's policy to "go abroad" and the B&R Initiative are *de facto* playing an important role in the so-called "globalization" process. At the Davos Forum in January 2017, Chinese President Xi Jinping defended economic globalization and called on all the people of the world to share in its benefits; also, President Xi warned against calls for greater protectionism in Europe and in the USA.[43]

It is evident that China aspires to provide international economic leadership, and also, President Xi reiterated China's desire to pursue and build soft power by promoting herself as a major contributor to the global

---

[43] Xi Jinping's speech at Davos Forum, January 17, 2017. One of the primary themes at the World Economic Forum was strengthening the governance of economic globalization and enhancing international collaboration.

economic governance. President Xi's speech laid out the groundwork for Chinese leadership on global economic integration.

2.3.1 *Granting Internal Stable Growth: A Necessary Condition to Promote Reforms*

In order for China to play the role it deserves, reforms at home must assure a smooth development of the internal market and reaching a sustainable growth because ensuring its own success in achieving this stable economic growth will permit China to be an example for other nations, thus contributing to a new model of global governance. "China responsibilities in economic governance should first be reflected in upholding the principle of free trade. The United States used to be the standard bearer of free trade, in line with the serious resurgence of trade protectionism in recent years, the bellicose trade team appointed by President Donald Trump may further aggravate global trade frictions."[44] China finds herself in this unique position, i.e. to defend globalization, which exactly means global free trade, "not only because it has become the world's second largest economy and a top trading nation, but also because, at the present time of rising uncertainty, China's political system is more conducive to the nation playing the role of free trade advocate."[45]

China is definitely leading the way and making every effort to promoting free trade, development, and economic globalization for mutually beneficial results validating the need for both greater global regulation and this also shows China's determination to continue its own development path while offering policy recommendations to improve the world's economic problems.

2.3.2 *Promoting Reforms*

As China is now involved in the promotion of globalization, Chinese leadership also believes that in order to promote global economic growth, it is

---

[44] In this sense, Mei Xinyu, Growing Influence — China Takes on Greater Global Responsibilities, *Beijing Review*, Vol. 60, No. 5–6, February 2017.
[45] *Ibid.*

necessary to put in place more coordinated efforts sharing the same vision, which in turn implies a move toward a global governance reform. In fact, it is undeniable that the international community is still a complicated and multi-connected machine, wherein great powers are creators and shapers of international rules and norms. However, the complicated mechanism needs to be updated to adequately respond to the different needs of every participant. If we look at the "Brexit issue," this has weakened EU integration, and generally the regional tensions and the economic decline have exposed the necessity to review the existing multilateral trade mechanism. China can play a fundamental role in helping to reshape the current framework, but it is necessary to have a more concrete international cooperation, and the role China is already playing should be recognized and accepted. The EU decision of denying the status of market economy to China can be in part understood for the reasons mentioned in Section 5.3.2, however, if responsibilities are to be shared, China's major role should be recognized.

For instance, China's participation in the global governance reform has provided the world with an alternative approach and also created tangible initiatives and plans, such as the Asian Infrastructure Investment Bank (AIIB), which partially will also serve to help the B&R Initiative. In the next chapter, we will examine more in detail the function and role of this and other new financial institutions, playing a fundamental role in the development of the B&R Initiative. China will shoulder the responsibility of promoting global governance reform through both financial support (AIIB) and trade zone building.

2.3.3 *China's Evolving Role*

China's sound and sustainable growth equates to ensuring the world economy's sound and sustainable growth. It is in the interest of China contributing to establishing a better governance system to create the conditions favoring investment in third countries. Thus, China will involve herself more and more at the international level in order to achieve these goals. In fact, for China to sustainably assume the foregoing global governance responsibilities means also to seek larger global cooperation to improve trade mechanisms. However, naturally, China will assume greater international responsibilities within its capabilities, China is unable to assume excessive responsibilities, and its rights should also be in line with those responsibilities.

2.3.4 *The B&R Initiative Might Encounter Obstacles and Can Be "Downsized," but Not Stopped*

The B&R Initiative, since it was launched by President Xi, has became an important part of China's foreign policy, and it is also intended to have an impact on Chinese economy, boosting its exports to third countries along both the Silk Road Economic Belt and the 21st Century Maritime Silk Road. This Initiative is a multi-faced economic program, which is not easy to realize. The land Silk Road refers to the development of new infrastructure, in particular, railroads and highways, to connect China's interior provinces with Europe by way of Russia, Central Asia, and the Middle East. However, this region, known as Eurasia, is in a state of crisis and Central Asia is one of the world's most unstable places. This alone could impede the development of this ambitious Initiative, as some experts pointed out.[46] However, because the Initiative can be developed in different ways, as we have exposed, and because one of the main objectives is to enhance trade relationships with the EU, the second component of the B&R, i.e. the Maritime Silk Road, plays a fundament role and can only respond to China's interests. It is noteworthy that this part of the plan is meant to create more Chinese ports in countries along the Maritime Silk Road. This makes sense because about 80% of global trade by volume and over 70% of global trade by value are conducted by sea, according to the United Nations Conference and Development.[47]

All these considerations bring to the conclusion that if China encounters difficulties in developing the land Silk Road for geopolitical reasons, a "plan B" already exists and it is to develop the second route(s), and it seems that China has already posed the basis to reach its goals: one example is the acquisition of the Piraeus port by COSCO (see Section 6.2). China has already expressed its interest for other European ports and facilities, and other spots along the Maritime Silk routes. Therefore, from

---

[46] See for example the opinion of George Friedman, *Mauldin Economics*, July 19, 2017, available at: https://amp.businessinsider.com/one-belt-one-road-doomed-to-failure-2017-7.

[47] *Ibid.*

an economic prospective at least, this Initiative, certainly is destined to succeed, though the ambitious plan can be "retouched" and downsized if the land route(s) should not function or operate properly. In any case, the B&R Initiative should also be read in conjunction with the new bilateral investment agreement currently under negotiation between the EU and China. No doubt that the EU and China will strengthen their cooperation to reach their respective goals. However, the EU has its rules and China needs to adapt to those rules in order to grasp all the opportunities this new cooperation can offer.

Now, it is clearer that the project China is pursuing covers different aspects and political implications are not to be undervalued, and that the B&R Initiative is not just aimed at boosting trade relations and stimulating economic growth across Asia and beyond (the particular focus on the EU is evident). It is now necessary to examine and explain in the next chapter about the players and financiers of this Initiative. In fact, the huge amount of money necessary to implement the B&R Initiative will be provided by different financial institutions which have their own scopes in participating in this project.

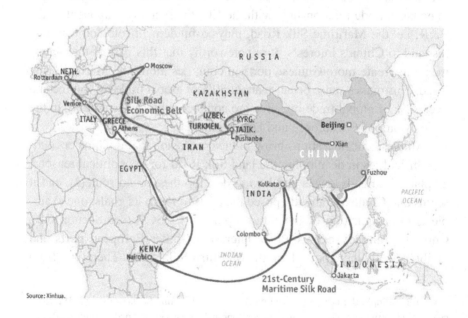

CHAPTER 3

The First Pillar of the B&R Initiative Funding: The Institutional Funding

Cristiano Rizzi and Mario Tettamanti

The B&R Initiative could turn out to be the largest ever infrastructure project with close to a trillion dollars being invested by different players around the globe. China's financial commitments to the Initiative seem huge and naturally China plays a major role: some multilateral and bilateral pledges may overlap, but the project involves up to US$300 billion in infrastructure financing from China in the coming years[1] (and this figure does not include the US$890 billion of public investment recently announced by China Development Bank, one of China's policy banks),[2] this without counting the leveraging effect on private investors and lenders. China's B&R Initiative is arguably the largest overseas investment drive ever launched by a single country. As mentioned, the value of the Initiative is far above the US$900 billion and the planned investments range from ports in Pakistan and Sri Lanka, and Greece, to high-speed

---

[1] Implementation of the B&R Initiative may span a very long time period — as much as 35 years reaching completion in time for the 100th anniversary of the People's Republic of China in 2049.

[2] See: He Yini, China to invest $900 billion in Belt and Road Initiative, *China Daily*, May 28, 2015. Article available at: http://www.chinadaily.com.cn/business/2015-05/28/content_20845654.htm.

railways in East Africa to gas pipelines crossing Central Asia, to finally reach the EU to enhance trade relationships (and not only) with this block.

The huge amount of money needed to finance the B&R Initiative is provided by different financial institutions naturally led by China. In the previous chapters, we have examined the background and how this Initiative was conceived, now we are offering an overview on the Institutions which are making a factual reality of this project. We will also expose how Chinese Institutions and EU Institutions can cooperate together in order to develop this Initiative. The most important reason for China to finance the B&R Initiative is because it will open new opportunities and reinforce trade relations among nations, and also because this Initiative matches with China's needs. However, it must also be underlined that the B&R Initiative is motivated by concerns about slowing domestic growth and a desire to boost China's global influence, but at what cost? It has been argued that "the scheme could simply add to China's fast-growing debt burden, now standing at more than 250 per cent of GDP." "The lack of commercial imperatives behind B&R projects means that it is highly uncertain whether future project returns will be sufficient to fully cover repayments to Chinese creditors," rating agency Fitch said in January.[3]

This chapter intends to illustrate only some facets of the complicated panorama concerning the financing of the B&R Initiative and also the cooperation between China and the EU in developing this Initiative. It seems appropriate to initiate this part analyzing the functioning of these financial institutions and then trying to explain how every single project will be financed and how investors (hopefully) repaid.

3.1 The B&R Initiative and the Institutional Funding

The financing requirements for the B&R Initiative are complex, this is also due to the large sums of money involved. It is not surprising that international players are willing to come together to grant China the realization of its Initiative. Naturally, China will play, *rectius* is already playing a major role, however joint efforts are needed and China is

---

[3] https://www.ft.com/content/0714074a-0334-11e7-aa5b-6bb07f5c8e12.

determined in orchestrating the chorus of International Financial Institutions to better direct the funds. China is also determined to bring in private institutional capital alongside financing from the state-owned Chinese banks and the Asian Infrastructure Investment Bank (AIIB).[4] New regional institutions, such as the New Silk Road Fund (NSFR),[5] is also designed in part to complement and support the Belt and Road's (B&R) development.

3.1.1 *The Asian Infrastructure Investment Bank (AIIB)*

The AIIB has been set up with a view to complementing and cooperating with the multilateral development banks in order to address infrastructure needs in the entire Asian region. However, this is not the only scope of the AIIB, in fact the bank will also focus in other productive sectors and projects in Asia, including energy and power, transportation and telecommunications, rural infrastructures and agriculture development, water supply

---

[4] The AIIB is an international financial institution which is focused on supporting infrastructure construction. The bank was initiated by the government of China and supported by 56 other countries from Europe, Oceania, Africa and South America as members. AIIB is regarded by some as a rival to the IMF, the World Bank and the ADB, which are regarded as dominated by developed countries like the United States. The United Nations has addressed the launch of AIIB as "scaling up financing for sustainable development" for the concern of Global Economic Governance. More information is available at: https://www.aiib.org/en/index.html.

[5] The NSRF, New Silk Road Fund, was established to explicitly support the B&R project. The Fund was established in Beijing on December 29, 2014, with investment from the State Administration of Foreign Exchange, China Investment Corporation, Export-Import Bank of China and China Development Bank. The fund's initial US$10 billion financing is from China's foreign exchange reserves — which contributed the majority of the initial funds — the China Development Bank, China Investment Corporation, and the Export–Import Bank of China. The Chinese government will tap its foreign currency reserves for about 65% of the Silk Road Fund. China Investment Corp. and the Export–Import Bank of China will chip in 15% each, and China Development Bank Capital Co. will invest 5%. The upcoming second and third phases will involve domestic and foreign investors. While based in Beijing and currently supported by a majority of Chinese investors, the Silk Road Fund is not state-owned and will eventually hopefully be dominated by currencies other than the Chinese yuan. More information is available at the following website: http://www.silkroadfund.com.cn/enweb/23775/23767/index.html.

and sanitation, environmental protection, urban development and logistics. So far, AIIB has 80 members (approved membership: 56 members, 24 prospective members).[6]

It is noteworthy that neither the US nor Japan are involved, and both are huge providers of development capital. One of the reasons cited by the USA and Japan against the AIIB is a concern over its governance and whether it will meet satisfactory environmental and social standards. Whether AIIB can meet global environmental and social standards in its lending operations remains to be seen.

Beijing, it seems, either remains wary of the US potential for political interference, or wants to show to the rest of the world it can do it alone. However, the absence of these two nations seems not to have any influence, the only fact is that they will be unable to participate in the benefits derived from the realization of the projects planned by the bank. It is also worth noting that the AIIB is regarded by some as a rival to the IMF, the World Bank and the Asian Development Bank (ADB), which are regarded as dominated by developed countries like the United States. The United Nations has addressed the launch of AIIB as "scaling up financing for sustainable development" for the concern of Global Economic Governance.

3.1.1.1 Government and Management Structure of the AIIB

The bank's governance structure is composed of the Board of Governors[7] as the top-level and highest decision-making body, the Board of Directors[8] as the middle-level, and the Management Team (Senior

---

[6] The AIIB is composed of regional members, and non-regional members, the two complete lists, and the projects approved are available at: https://www.aiib.org/en/about-aiib/governance/members-of-bank/index.html. This information was updated on July 5, 2017.

[7] The Board of governors consists of one governor and one alternate governor appointed by each member country. See: https://www.aiib.org/en/about-aiib/governance/board-governors/index.html.

[8] Board of Directors: *The Board of Directors is responsible for the direction of the Bank's general operations, exercising all powers delegated to it by the Board of Governors. This includes approving the Bank's strategy, annual plan and budget; establishing policies; taking decisions concerning Bank operations; and supervising management and operation of the Bank and establishing an oversight mechanism.* See: https://www.aiib.org/en/about-aiib/governance/board-directors/index.html.

Management Members)[9] which is at the bottom of decision-making pyramidal structure, and an International Advisory Panel[10] to help advise the President and Senior Management on the Bank's strategies and policies, as well as on general operational issue.

In principle, the AIIB could be viewed as the Asian equivalent of the European Investment Bank (EIB).[11] If Europe can have a European Bank for Reconstruction and Development (EBRD) headquartered in London, it seems Asia has an ADB and the AIIB. Despite the fact that over 20 non-Asian countries, including key European countries, became its members, with China's dominant share and its headquarters in Beijing, with a Chinese President, the AIIB is really China's vehicle to challenge the dominance of the Western financial establishment. Moreover, the AIIB seems to perfectly respond to the needs of China with particular reference to the B&R Initiative.

3.1.1.2 A Chinese National as President of the AIIB

As China is the major contributor, it is not surprising a Chinese national was appointed as the President of the AIIB. The President of the AIIB,

---

[9]The senior management team includes the President, the five Vice Presidents, and the General Counsel. The Bank is headed by a President, elected by its shareholders, who is supported by a senior management team which includes: The General Counsel and five Vice Presidents responsible for Policy and Strategy, Investments, Finance, Administration and the Corporate Secretariat. An International Advisory Panel (IAP) comprising global experts provides management with impartial advice and perspectives. The management team comprises individuals from a diverse group of bank member countries, contributing years of experience and a wide range of professional expertise in both the international and private sectors. See: https://www.aiib.org/en/about-aiib/governance/senior-management/index.html.

[10]International Advisory Panel: The Bank has established an International Advisory Panel (IAP) to support the President and Senior Management on the Bank's strategies and policies as well as on general operational issues. The Panel meets in tandem with the Bank's Annual Meeting, or as requested by the President. The President selects and appoints Members of the IAP on two-year terms. Panelists receive a small honorarium and do not receive a salary, and the Bank pays the costs associated with Panel meetings. See: https://www.aiib.org/en/about-aiib/governance/international-advisory-panel/index.html.

[11]EIB is the European Union's non-profit lending institution established in 1958 under the Treaty of Rome. Visit: http://www.eib.org/.

Jin Liqun, is a Chinese politician, banker and professor. Liqun was formerly the Chairman of China International Capital Corporation, the Vice President of the ADB, and the Vice Minister of Finance of the People's Republic of China. According to the words of Lin Liqun, "The Chinese experience illustrates that infrastructure investment paves the way for broad-based economic social development, and poverty alleviation comes as a natural consequence of that."

3.1.1.3 Project Already Approved by the AIIB

The AIIB at the end of 2016 has already approved 16 projects. Of these projects, nine pertain to the B&R Initiative, and the AIIB has allocated for those projects US$1.7 billion. Some of the first loans approved by AIIB included a US$165 million loan for a Power Distribution System Upgrade and Expansion Project in Bangladesh, a US$216.5 million loan for a National Slum Upgrading Project in Indonesia, a US$27.5 million loan for the Dushanbe–Uzbekistan Border Road Improvement Project in Tajikistan, and a US$100 million loan for the Shorkot–Khanewal Section of National Motorway M-4 in Pakistan. All of these, with the exception of the Bangladesh power project, are co-financed by other multilateral institutions. Additional loans were approved in September 2016, including a US$300 million loan for a hydropower project in Pakistan and a US$20 million loan to a power plant in Myanmar. Before the end of 2016, AIIB also approved a US$600 million loan for the construction of the Trans-Anatolian gas pipeline (TANAP), which will connect Azerbaijan to Europe. In this deal, the AIIB has partnered with the World Bank, which has committed to a US$800 million loan. The project will be further financed by other multilateral institutions as well as private finance for a total expected cost of US$11.7 billion.[12]

What is mentioned above serves just to illustrate that the AIIB is already operating and financing projects, some of them directly connected to the B&R Initiative. Naturally, the AIIB alone cannot fulfill the necessities of China concerning the Initiative, so a concerted action

---

[12] A complete list of all the projects approved by the AIIB is available at the following website: https://www.aiib.org/en/projects/approved/.

with all the other Institutions should be the path to follow in order to fully realize this immense project.

3.1.1.4 AIIB Pushes For More Public–Private Partnership in the Realization of the Initiative

The AIIB is particularly interested to finance this Initiative, and Danny Alexander, Vice-President of the AIIB, said that the public–private partnership (PPP) is another path to financing the B&R Initiative. The bank would help the related parties to spread PPPs in Asia, Southeast Asia and the Middle East.

3.1.2 *The New Development Bank (NDB)*

China has also helped create the New Development Bank (NDB) also known as the "BRICS Bank." Basically, the NDB is a multilateral development bank operated by the BRICS states (i.e. Brazil, Russia, India, China and South Africa) as an alternative to the existing US-dominated World Bank and the International Monetary Fund.

The NDB is set up to foster greater financial and development cooperation among the five emerging markets: Brazil, Russia, India, China and South Africa. Together, the four original BRIC countries comprised in 2014 more than 3 billion people or 41.4% of the world's population, covered more than a quarter of the world's land area over three continents, and accounted for more than 25% of global GDP. The New Development Bank was agreed by the BRICS leaders at the BRICS summit held in Durban, South Africa on March 27, 2013. On July 15, 2014, at the sixth BRICS summit held in Fortaleza, Brazil, the group of emerging economies signed the long anticipated document to create the US$100 billion BRICS Development Bank and a reserve currency pool worth over another US$100 billion. Shanghai was selected as the headquarters and an African regional center was set up in Johannesburg. The Bank was formally launched in Shanghai on July 20, 2015. At the launch ceremony, Chinese Finance Minister said, "This bank will place greater emphasis on the needs of developing countries, have greater respect for developing countries' national situation, and more fully embody the values of developing countries."

It is important to underline that the NDB is not directly linked to the B&R strategy, but will fund infrastructure-related projects across the world and work closely with the AIIB.

It has been stressed that "the New Development Bank by itself is not large enough to meet the unmet financing needs for the developing world — so it must leverage its capital. How much capital it will be able to leverage will depend on how it partners with other sources of funding — private capital, local financing and other international financial institutions. If the Bank is able to leverage in other lenders into its projects it could be a catalytic agent in increasing infrastructure investment — which in turn could help crowd in private investment."[13]

It is also worth noting that "the projected steady state lending by the NDB is expected to be $34 billion annually. This is based on a capital base of $100 billion of which $20 billion is paid in capital, based on which the total stock of loans could reach $ 350 billion in twenty years. If the NDB is able to co-finance its projects up to 50% then the size of combined lending could reach $68 billion annually which is about the size of lending of the European Investment Bank and much larger than that of the World Bank."[14]

3.1.3 *The Asian Development Bank (ADB)*

The ADB[15] is a regional development bank established more than 50 years ago in order to promote social and economic development in Asia. The ADB defines itself as a social development organization that is dedicated to reducing poverty in Asia and the Pacific through inclusive economic growth, environment sustainable growth and regional integration. Infrastructure projects represent one of the operational areas,[16] and the

---

[13] See: Ajay Chhibber, *China's One Belt One Road Strategy: The New Financial Institutions and India's Options*, March 2017. This scholar paper-research is available at: https://www2.gwu.edu/~iiep/assets/docs/papers/2017WP/ChhibberIIEPWP2017-7.pdf.
[14] *Ibid.*
[15] More content available at: www.adb.org.
[16] The ADB provides loans, grants and technical assistance to its developing member countries, to the private sector and through PPPs to support the building and maintenance of infrastructure. The majority is in water, energy, transport, urban development, and information and communications technology. https://www.adb.org/about/infrastructure.

ADB supports China's B&R Initiative in Central Asia and South Asia, though ADB is also focused on other areas.[17]

It is worthwhile to note that at the ADB's annual conference in early May 2017, Jin Liqun, President of the AIIB, recalled his interest in the B&R Initiative.[18] Jin said that "AIIB would invest in Belt and Road projects as long as they meet three basic requirements of being financially sustainable, environmentally friendly and welcomed by local people."[19] ADB President Takehido Nakao, too, signaled the organization was open to cooperation on the B&R Initiative, "We can cooperate, but at the same time we should pay attention to the economic feasibility."

Dedicated Institutions like the Silk Road Fund (examined in the following paragraphs) were specifically established to finance the B&R Initiative. The ADB in any case serves as a backbone and of course will complement the B&R Initiative.

3.1.4 *The China Development Bank (CDB)*

China Development Bank is China's largest development bank. CDB was founded in 1994 as a policy financial institution under the direct leadership of the State Council. It was incorporated as China Development Bank Corporation in December 2008 and officially defined by the State Council as a development finance institution in March 2015.[20]

In May 2017, the CDB set up a special lending plan worth 250 billion yuan (approximately US$36.7 billion) to support the B&R cooperation on infrastructure, industrial capacity and financing.

The CDB's assets worth total over 14 trillion yuan and it has more than 500 projects in B&R regions worth over US$350 billion, according to Liang Huijiang, a senior official with CDB.[21]

---

[17] Core operational areas are as follows: (i) Infrastructure, (ii) Education, (iii) Environment, (iv) Regional Cooperation and Integration Strategy, (v) Financial sector. Visit: https://www.adb.org/about/policies-and-strategies.

[18] See: http://asia.nikkei.com/Politics-Economy/International-Relations/AIIB-chief-urges-cooperation-on-Belt-and-Road.

[19] *Ibid.*

[20] More detailed information is available at: http://www.cdb.com.cn/English/.

[21] In this sense, see CDB News, available at the following website: http://www.cdb.com.cn/English/xwzx_715/khdt/201706/t20170602_4345.html.

The CDB will enhance cooperation with other financial institutions at home and abroad, and hopes to attract more private financing to participate in B&R projects.

The CDB in June 2017 signed a memorandum with Deutsche Bank[22] to seek cooperation under the B&R Initiative, including an initial project cooperation plan worth about US$3 billion over five years. The CDB and Deutsche Bank agreed to work together over the next five years to support the projects. The move will make Deutsche Bank one of the first global lenders to participate in the initiative. The two parties also agreed to establish a joint team to cooperate on projects promoting the initiative, including joint lending and project finance that are beneficial to the clients of both the lenders.[23]

3.1.5 *The Silk Road Fund (SRF)*

China has also established in December 2014 the so-called "Silk Road Fund" (SRF) to explicitly finance the B&R Initiative. The fund's initial US$10 billion financing is from China' foreign exchange reserves, however, the total amount of the resources available probably will exceed the US$40 billion contributed so far in total. Contributors include the China's State Administration of Foreign Exchange, the China Development Bank, the China Investment Corporation, and the Export–Import Bank of China. The fund will invest mainly in infrastructure and resources, as well as in industrial and financial cooperation.

The fund operates much as a private equity venture, but with a smaller group of investors committed for longer terms. It is comparable to institutions such as the World Bank's International Finance Corporation in mission and scale, but it is financed by a small number of investors rather than by public funds. The private equity venture-type structure of the fund should help avoid riskier politically-driven deals that are not always in the

---

[22] Deutsche Bank AG, Germany's largest lender. With this Memorandum, the Bank plans to finance US$3 billion worth of projects in partnership with the China Development Bank in the countries and regions taking part in the Belt and Road Initiative. See CDB News, available at: http://www.cdb.com.cn/English/xwzx_715/khdt/201706/t20170602_4344.html.

[23] *Ibid.*

best economic interests. The structure will hopefully depoliticize the fund, allowing its managers to seek lower-risk investments (see SRF's website).

China's Silk Road Fund announced its first project for investment in the B&R Initiative during Chinese President Xi Jinping's state visit to Pakistan, marking a milestone of the all-weather strategic partnership of cooperation between the two countries. The investment into the US$1.65 billion Karot hydropower project in Pakistan, along with other hydropower projects in the region, will help the South Asian country upgrade its power supply and improve its economic performance.

The project is a priority within the broader China–Pakistan Economic Corridor (CPEC) initiative,[24] a flagship program of China's B&R Initiative. The CPEC is a planned network of roads, railways and energy projects linking southwest Pakistan's deep-water Gwadar Port with northwest China's Xinjiang Uygur Autonomous Region. With the CPEC at the center, China and Pakistan could achieve a win–win result and common development, and bring benefit to their people. For China, it would shorten the route for its energy imports.

It is worth noting that the AIIB and the Silk Road Fund represent new mechanisms to channel funds for development outside the existing IFI framework. While the IMF and the World Bank have indicated that they intend to cooperate with the new institutions, the new institutions are not set up to be part of the existing IFI framework.

3.1.6 *The European Investment Bank (EIB) and the EIB Fund: Brief Introduction*

The EIB is the European Union's non-profit lending institution established in 1958 under the Treaty of Rome.[25] The EIB is a part of the

---

[24]Owing to the corridor's geographical position where the B&R meet, the CPEC is expected to combine South Asia, Central Asia, Middle East and China together, and benefit directly about 3 billion people in the region. Based on this, it could function as a bridge in advancing the B&R Initiative after being well developed and successfully operated. The CPEC project has risks as the infrastructure passes through areas with huge disputes.

[25]Treaty of Rome, officially the Treaty establishing the European Economic Community, is an International agreement that brought about the creation of the EEC. This has evolved into the Lisbon Treaty, of 2009, also known as the "EU Treaty" which has shaped the EU into

Institutions constituting the European Union. The EU has a number of other Institutions and inter-institutions bodies that play a specialized role.[26] We are not going to offer an overview of all these bodies here, but what it is important to note is that the EIB is an important piece of the puzzle which makes the EU functioning.[27]

The Bank maintains close working ties with the other members of the EU in pursuit of the Union's objectives and in particular (i) fostering European integration and the balanced development of the Union; (ii) supporting the Union's development aid and cooperation policies toward more than 140 countries throughout the world. It is noteworthy that such cooperation enables the EIB to coordinate its operations with those of the other institutions, while preserving its independence and its own decision-making procedures as provided for in the EU treaties. This maintains the effectiveness of the different EU instruments furnishing loans or grants in support of substantial capital investment, both within and outside the European Union.[28]

EIB has also set up the European Investment Fund and its main scope is to support European small and medium-sized enterprises (SMEs) by improving their access to finance through a wide range of selected financial intermediaries. To this extent, the EIB Fund designs, promotes and implements equity and debt financial instruments.[29]

3.1.6.1 EIB Group Cooperation with China End the New €500 Million Silk Road Fund Equity Investment Initiative

In early June 2017, the European investment Fund and the Silk Road Fund signed a Memorandum of Understanding that outlines new strategic

---

what it is today. The Treaty of Rome was signed on March 25, 1957 by Belgium, France, Italy, Luxembourg, the Netherlands and West Germany and came into force on January 1, 1958. It remains one of the two most important treaties in the modern-day European Union.
[26] An overview of all these Institution is available at the following website: http://europa.eu/about-eu/institutions-bodies/index_en.htm.
[27] A brief introduction about the Institutions composing the EU was also given in the other book prepared by two of the authors, namely *"Chinese Expansion into the EU,"* American Bar Association, August 2016, at §2.01 of the mentioned publication: "Understanding Europe: a brief introduction of the European."
[28] In this sense, the EIB. See: http://www.eib.org/about/eu-family/index.htm.
[29] More information about the EIB Fund available at: http://www.eif.org/who_we_are/index.htm.

cooperation to support equity investment across Europe. It is worth mentioning that the European Commission and China's NDRC have played an important role in supporting discussions which finally led to the signature of the Memorandum of Understanding. Naturally, this initiative can only enhance the dialogue between China and the EU, especially in prospect of the closing of the new bilateral investment agreement.

The agreement to establish the China–EU Co-Investment Fund was signed at the 19th European Union China Summit in Brussels in the presence of the Premier of the People's Republic of China, Li Keqiang, President of the European Commission, Jean-Claude Juncker and the President of the European Council, Donald Tusk. Once operational, the China–EU Co-Investment Fund is expected to provide €500 million, jointly backed by the European Investment Fund and the Silk Road Fund, to support equity investment.[30] The Fund is not aimed at financing infrastructure projects, however it will influence the B&R Initiative, and in any case, the Fund will bring together unique financial and technical expertise from the European Investment Fund and the Silk Road Fund.

Finally, it is possible to affirm that the creation of this China-EU Co-Investment Fund will help to further develop synergies between China's B&R Initiative and the Investment Plan for Europe, also known as "Junker Plan,"[31] which is the EU's strategy to mobilize €315 billion of new public and private investments across Europe.

3.1.7 *Additional Funds Announced by President Xi Jinping*

Considering the dimension of the B&R Initiative, it is not surprising that President Xi Jinping during his speech at the opening of the "Belt and Road" forum held in Beijing in May 2017, pledged at least US$113 billion in extra funding for the Initiative. President Xi also urged countries across

---

[30] See press release of the EIB available at: http://www.eib.org/infocentre/press/releases/all/2017/2017-138-eib-group-cooperation-with-china-to-be-strengthened-with-new-eur-500-million-silk-road-fund-equity-investment-initiative.htm?f=search&media=search.

[31] The European Commission's Investment Plan for Europe (EC IPE) known as the "Juncker Plan" or the "EU Infrastructure Investment Plan" is an ambitious infrastructure investment program first announced by European Commission President Jean-Claude Juncker in November 2014: it aims at unlocking public and private investments in the "real economy" of at least €315 billion over a three years fiscal period (Jan. 2015–Dec. 2017).

the globe to join hands with China in pursuit of globalization. The extra funding will be disbursed through three different sources, namely, the Silk Road Fund, and two Chinese policy banks, i.e. the China Development Bank and the Export–Import Bank of China.

3.1.7.1 Proportion between Chinese ODI and Funds Dedicated to the B&R Initiative

China money is also directed toward ODI. It must be remembered that China is also expanding its presence abroad and in particular Chinese ODI are focused on the EU and with the implementation of the new bilateral investment agreement those investment will surge. The B&R Initiative is new and this is one of the reasons why it is attracting only a small part of Chinese ODI. However, the flow of money for projects related to this Initiative is surely destined to surge. So far investments which went to the B&R Initiative have not been of significance to the total ODI. Apparently, so far, all the countries involved to the B&R Initiative have received 12% only of Chinese ODI (at the end of 2015). A natural factor is that the Initiative is only at its early stage and it is likely that the proportion between Chinese ODI and B&R investment will soon change trend and the latter will increase rapidly.

3.1.7.2 China Becoming a Major Capital Exporter with B&R Initiative

It is expected that more Chinese companies and private funds will join China's B&R Initiative, and this will allow China to become a major capital exporter. China's money in fact will be used for the realization of infrastructure projects in all the countries involved in the Initiative. Moreover, the B&R "Initiative has already boosted trade and investments considerably in these countries. Trade between China and countries along the land and sea routes exceeded US$1 trillion in 2015, which corresponds to a quarter of China's total trade volume. Noteworthy, China's export to B&R countries now exceed those to the US and the EU (China's top two export destinations) and the gap is widening." The B&R Initiative is *de facto* accelerating China's shift from being the world's biggest goods exporter to becoming a major capital exporter. It is also predicted that China's ODI to countries along the B&R will increase dramatically, it is expected that China's cumulative non-financial ODI will reach an impressive US$2 trillion by 2020, more than a doubling of end 2015 levels.[32]

3.1.8 *The Interest of the IMF: Brief Introduction*

The International Monetary Fund (IMF) is an organization of 189 countries, working to foster global monetary cooperation, secure financial stability, facilitate international trade, and also it aims at promoting high employment and sustainable economic growth, and reducing poverty around the world.[33] The IMF's primary purpose is to ensure the stability of the International monetary system — the system of exchange rates and international payments that enable countries, and their citizens, to transact with each other. It is worth noting that the Fund's mandate was updated in 2012 to include all macroeconomic and financial sector issues that bear global stability.

The interest of the IFM in the B&R Initiative was showed by the participation of Christine Lagarde, Managing Director of the International Monetary Fund, at the B&R Forum which was held in Beijing in May 2017. Lagarde at the Forum delivered a meaningful speech, and in particular, she stated that: "The Belt and Road Initiative aims to connect economies, communities, and people. It holds great potential to bring benefits in terms of high-quality infrastructure, inclusiveness, and economic cooperation. The IMF can help in this effort by providing policy advice, financial support as appropriate, and hands-on training and capacity building — so that economies can maximize the benefits of more investment, trade, and financial connectivity, while maintaining economic and financial stability."[34]

---

[32] See also in this sense, La Shen, China's One Belt, One Road Gains Traction, December 2, 2016. Article available at: https://www.sc.com/BeyondBorders/one-belt-one-road-raction/.

[33] See: http://www.imf.org/en/About.

[34] In this sense, Christine Lagarde, Managing Director of the International Monetary Fund, during her speech at the Beijing Forum on the One Belt One Road, May 16, 2017.

It is evident that this illustrates the strong interest of the IMF and its willingness to help in developing this Initiative.

3.1.8.1 The IFM Shows Further Interest in the B&R Initiative

In the context of the Belt and Road Forum in May 2017, the People's Bank of China and the IMF agreed to establish a new "China–IMF Capacity Development Center" to support effective institution-building and policymaking in countries along the B&R and beyond.

Another manifestation of interest was shown at the summer Davos 2017 held in China's northeastern coastal city of Dalian, where leading officials from international financial institutions, including the IMF, urged governments and companies to speed up their financial connectivity and forge closer links with the private sectors to participate in the B&R infrastructure projects.[35] In particular, it was reported that Zhang Tao, Deputy Managing Director of International Monetary Fund, said at the World Economic Forum in Dalian that "measures including cross-border payments and mobile banking products, as well as relaxing financing supply restrictions, would encourage financial institutions to provide more support to the real economy in markets connected with the initiative."[36] Zhang said the IMF will establish a new ability training center in Singapore and other economies involved in the initiative soon after setting one up in Dalian last month, partnered with the People's Bank of China.

3.1.9 *First Concrete Examples of Cooperation between EU Financial Institutions and Chinese Financial Institutions*

There exist a number of international banks specializing in infrastructure projects. Collaboration between these Institutions and Chinese

---

[35] In this sense, Zhong Nan, Top Officials: Boost B&R Finance Links, *China Daily*, June 29, 2017, article available at: http://www.chinadaily.com.cn/business/2017-06/29/content_29926835.htm.

[36] *Ibid.*

Institutions and companies willing to develop infrastructure projects is a must in order to develop the B&R Initiative.

3.1.9.1 Deutsche Bank (DB) Invests in the B&R Initiative

Deutsche Bank,[37] a major financial Institution in the EU and the largest German bank, has already invested in the B&R Initiative.[38] On May 30, 2017, on the eve of the arrival of Chinese Premier Li Keqiang in Europe for an official visit, Deutsche Bank announced that it had reached an agreement with the Chinese bank, i.e. "China Development Bank." Under this deal,[39] Deutsche Bank would invest up to US$3 billion in "Belt and Road" projects over the next five years. This is an example of cooperation between an EU financial institution and a Chinese financial institution which share the same vision on a project which will have important implication for the future also.

3.1.10 *Final Considerations on the Necessity of Pooling Together Resources*

The B&R Initiative requires enormous resources, and China has already put in place a number of initiatives to assure those resources can be available, and China is also orchestrating with other Financial Institutions how to organize the operations of lending money in order to realize projects connected to this Initiative. The AIIB was created to fill a real need in terms of infrastructure financing, as the ADB and the World Bank alone seem cannot supply all the financial support Asia needs in the near future. Thus, the AIIB represents a useful platform to help fill the gap.

---

[37] Deutsche Bank provides commercial and investment banking, retail banking, transaction banking and asset and wealth management products and services to corporations, governments, institutional investors, small and medium-sized businesses, and private individuals. Deutsche Bank is Germany's leading bank, with a strong position in Europe and a significant presence in the Americas and Asia Pacific.

[38] http://www.oboreurope.com/en/deutsche-bank-invests-in-obor/.

[39] China Development Bank (CDB) and Deutsche Bank signed a Memorandum of Understanding at a ceremony in Berlin. The two parties expressed their interest in promoting the renminbi's (RMB) internationalization and in financing economic cooperation between China, Germany and other B&R countries.

CASE STUDY: DEUTSCHE BANK

Deutsche Bank AG, Germany's largest lender, announced on May 30, 2017 that it has inked a cooperation agreement with China Development Bank (CDB) to finance the B&R projects. The first phase of the agreement lasts for about five years and is worth about US$3 billion. This agreement makes Deutsche Bank one of the first foreign lenders for the China-proposed B&R. CDB, China's largest bank for foreign investment and financing cooperation, is the world's largest development finance institution. The CDB and Deutsche Bank agreed to work together over the next five years to support the projects. The move will make Deutsche Bank one of the first global lenders to participate in the initiative. The two parties also agreed to establish a joint team to cooperate on projects promoting the Initiative, including joint lending and project finance that are beneficial to the clients of both lenders. As part of the Memorandum of Understanding, CDB and Deutsche Bank agreed to work together over the next five years with an aim of supporting projects worth US$3 billion. CDB and Deutsche Bank also agreed to establish a joint team in order to cooperate on projects that promote the B&R Initiative. Subject to applicable laws and regulations, CDB and Deutsche Bank will finance projects that are beneficial to clients of both banks, including through joint lending and project finance. This agreement will also allow the Chinese bank, China Development Bank, to benefit from the great expertise of the Deutsche Bank in conducting international projects. On the other hand, Deutsche Bank's participation in B&R will undoubtedly encourage other European banking institutions to enter into similar agreements in order to take full advantage of the B&R market.

Garth Ritchie, Head of Deutsche Bank's Corporate & Investment Bank, said expanding infrastructure links between China and Europe is a positive opportunity for the peoples and economies of both sides. He said, "We are pleased to work with China Development Bank in support of the Belt & Road Initiative. Expanding infrastructure links between China and Europe is a positive opportunity for the people and economies of both."

Werner Steinmüller, Deutsche Bank Asia Pacific CEO, added: "Deutsche Bank is proud of its unique and long-standing role in connecting the Chinese and European economies. We are confident that the depth of our network and experience in Europe will provide a critical anchor to this important China-led policy initiative."

(Continued)

(Continued)

> **German business daily** *Handelsblatt* reported that Deutsche Bank is also seeking approval to issue Renminbi-denominated bonds in China's bond market, which are widely known as Panda Bonds and are yuan-denominated bonds issued by qualified foreign capital institutions in the Chinese market.
>
> **Ministry of Commerce spokesman Sun Jiwen** said that Chinese investment in Germany totaled €11 billion (US$12.03 billion), about 1% of all foreign investment, which shows that Chinese investment in Germany is still at an early stage and has great growth.

In relation to the B&R, specific financial Institutions were created to help in realizing the Initiative like, for example, the Silk Road Fund, however all these Institutions are of public nature. Now the real task is getting the private sector also financing into the B&R projects. This seems to be a work in progress and of course requires banking sector and other institutional entities to get involved. Naturally, this will require new and innovative debt structures, denominated in renminbi, dollars, euros, and a wide range of local currencies. These will include green bonds, tax-exempt bonds issued by qualified organizations and also by third parties interested in participating into the initiative (governments interested by the Initiative). This will be briefly examined in the next chapter. We only intend to expose the general framework and it would be impossible to describe the entire functioning of the different financial markets and instruments pertaining to every single country, but it is important to understand how projects can be financed and how investors should treat those new instruments.

This all suggests that a raft of new financial expertise will be needed with specific knowledge of the B&R region. "This will include bank arrangers, lawyers, tax experts, and consultants, in addition to fund managers able to package up projects for sale internationally either to institutions or to private investors, and whose expertise will be needed to meet the complex financing requirements of the hundreds of projects that will make up the new economic corridor between East and West."[40]

---

[40] In this sense, Chris Devonshire-Ellis, Financing China's One Belt, One Road: US$8 Trillion in Capital Requirements, by Silk Road Briefing, visit: http://www.silkroad-briefing.com/news/2017/04/03/financing-chinas-one-belt-one-road-us8-trillion-in-capital-requirements/.

3.2 B&R Initiative, the Governance and the Domestic Financial Reforms

3.2.1 *B&R Initiative and the Governance Infrastructure*

The governance framework for the cross-border investments of the B&R Initiative will be critical. This is especially because the nature of the B&R Initiative encompasses multiple stakeholders with very different economic and political situations across the envisaged routes. To deal with the many potential stakeholders, China is working on establishing a formal mechanism for cooperation and coordination of the B&R Initiative across all the countries along the B&R routes. This will likely need a secretariat drawn from participating countries that will ensure that the B&R projects follow international standards and safeguards, including combating climate change. Indeed, the Initiative might require several parallel structures and innovative cooperation and financing models, linked to South and East Asia, West Asia, the Middle East and Africa.[41]

3.2.2 *B&R Initiative and the Domestic Financial Reforms*

China's B&R Initiative is becoming increasingly better financed, expanding China's influence into Europe, Asia and Africa. The projects will build up infrastructure, increase trade and finance, and boost connectivity across Europe, Asia and Africa.

According to the NDRC's (National Development and Reform Commission) Silk Road Vision Plan, this project will benefit in the following ways:

[1] Deepen financial cooperation
[2] Build a credit information, investment, and financing system as well as a currency stability system in Asia
[3] Expand the scope and scale of bilateral currency swap and settlement with other countries along the B&R region

---

[41] Sara Hsu, Research Scholar, Binzagr Institute for Sustainable Prosperity Assistant Professor of Economics, SUNY New Paltz. The views expressed in this chapter are solely those of the author(s) and not necessarily those of the Binzagr Institute for Sustainable Prosperity.

[4] Open and develop the bond market in Asia

[5] Carry out multilateral financial cooperation in the form of syndicated loans and bank credit. Encourage foreign government and companies' issuance of Renminbi bonds in China

[6] Encourage qualified Chinese financial institutions and companies to issue bonds in both Renminbi and foreign currencies outside China, and use the funds collected in countries along the Belt and Road

[7] Strengthen financial regulation cooperation, encourage the signing of MOUs

[8] Create bilateral financial regulation, and improve the system of risk response and crisis management by building a regional, financial risk early-warning system that creates an exchange and cooperation mechanism of addressing cross-border risks and crisis

[9] Increase cross-border exchange and cooperation between credit investigation regulators, credit investigation institutions and credit rating institutions

[10] Encourage the creation of sovereign wealth funds in countries along the B&R region

[11] Encourage commercial equity investment funds and private funds to participate in the construction of key projects of the Initiative.

In order to accomplish these goals, China must overcome obstacles in expanding its financial reach along the B&R region. Challenges include the following: China's banking interest rates are still not fully market-based; China's credit-scoring institutions must be implemented; the banking industry is constrained; the bond market is underdeveloped. China's credit rating and scoring institutions must be improved before China attempts to implement credit rating institutions in other countries.

China is to implement a social credit system in 2017, which will rate individuals and institutions based on past credit transactions and other data, such as legal records. Still, this system will have to be tested so that it functions properly. Since China's bank funds are already limited, bank loans to foreign institutions will be a challenge in a credit-constrained market with insufficient credit risk information.

China's own bond market is underdeveloped — especially the corporate bond market, as the financial sector has mainly emphasized bank loans and equity finance. How can China address expansion of the bond market along B&R if its domestic bond market is shallow?

Will China's planned financial reforms address these barriers to financial targets for the B&R? Some of the planned reforms may fit the B&R financial targets, while other necessary reforms are lacking. China's Financial Reform Roadmap from the CPC Central Committee's Decisions on Major Issues Concerning Comprehensively Deepening Reforms are as follows:

[i]   Further open up the financial sector by allowing small, privately owned banks to participate in the market
[ii]   Promote equity issuance registration systems, equity finance, development of regulated bond markets and increased direct finance
[iii]   Improve insurance's compensation mechanism and develop disaster insurance
[iv]   Develop inclusive finance
[v]   Encourage financial innovation trough diversified financial products
[vi]   Financial Reform Roadmap
[vii]   Improve exchange rate mechanism by accelerating interest rate liberalization
[viii]   Open up capital markets, liberalize cross-border financial transactions
[ix]   Regulate debt and capital flows in a macro prudential framework that accelerates RMB capital account liberalization
[x]   Implement financial regulatory reforms and clarify regulation responsibilities between central and local governments
[xi]   Develop a deposit insurance scheme by improving financial institutions' market exit mechanism

3.2.2.1 Sufficiency of Financial Reforms for B&R Initiative

Are these reforms sufficient for meeting the financial targets of B&R Initiative?

First, is opening the financial sector sufficient for B&R Initiative? Allowing small privately owned banks will ensure that China's domestic economy is better served. Five pilot private banks currently focus on serving SMEs. While small private banks will not be able to address all needs for private funding, encouraging private banks will certainly increase available funding in the financial market. Reforming policy financial institutions will also help improve China's domestic economy. Two Chinese policy banks are undergoing reorientation toward sustainable development. This reform may help make financial policy more environmentally and socially friendly and set precedent for lending and investment on B&R region. Most importantly, the domestic economy must be served in conjunction with B&R Initiative, as China is an important engine of growth in the region.

Second, is developing inclusive finance sufficient for B&R Initiative? In conjunction with the first reform, developing inclusive finance will help SMEs and poor individuals obtain finance within China to ensure that the domestic economy is served. This will help to encourage financial and real growth in China and ensure support for B&R Initiative. B&R Initiative should not act as a drain on China's own financial resources. B&R Initiative must not transfer resources away from China. This pattern of development would be similar to the phenomenon that occurred for many years, in which funds were transferred from China's rural to urban sectors as rural savings were used for higher-return urban projects, while rural projects were starved of funds. This should not be repeated on an international scale. Therefore, the domestic economy has to be served through new types of finance.

Third, is expanding the equity and bond market sufficient for B&R Initiative? Promoting equity finance and developing bond markets will help increase financial resources available for B&R Initiative. However, these reforms have some way to go. In the bond market, government bonds are issued by the MOF and local governments and Central bank notes and Policy Bank bonds are most actively traded. However, state-owned banks are supposed to purchase government bonds, rendering the yield curve pointless. China's corporate bond market is underdeveloped and associated with insufficient market control: issuance of corporate bonds requires excessive administrative procedures, while bonds are subject to insufficient scrutiny by ratings agencies. Non-state owned corporate bonds may face potential default. These issues must be corrected in China's planned financial reform.

Fourth, is encouraging financial innovation sufficient for B&R Initiative? Financial innovation is an important part of B&R Initiative. This can help raise private capital for B&R projects and also ensure that the domestic economy is properly served through inclusive finance. This is already happening, as newer versions of internet finance cater to underserved populations.

Innovation can also help contribute to financial deepening, which will free up more capital for use in B&R regions. However, it does not come without risks. Financial innovation brought about the shadow banking sector. Innovation caused maturity mismatches and generated liquidity risk in wealth management products. Also, the credit risk associated with underlying loans and assets that were securitized and sold as trust products later led to threatened and actual defaults. This also happens to be what caused the financial crisis in the United States.

Fifth, is exchange and interest rate liberalization sufficient for B&R Initiative? Exchange rate liberalization should be embarked upon carefully. Building a body of RMB outside China may increase pressure on China's exchange rate. Liberalization of the deposit interest rate ceilings is an important step toward interest rate marketization. This is hoped to better reflect supply and demand conditions in the market for loanable funds. However, this is a necessary but inadequate step in the right direction. Additionally, government bodies should exit the banking sector. If government bodies direct some of the lending, the banking sector will not become fully marketized, reflecting true risk and returns. Strong preference for lending to larger firms also prevents interest rate marketization. If interest rates do not reflect risk and reward internally, how can they reflect this externally?

Sixth, is cross-border financial liberalization sufficient for B&R Initiative? Financial liberalization will be a positive development, but only if risks are properly controlled. As more investors hold RMB outside of China, and as capital controls are loosened, the potential for large capital inflows or outflows increases. Recall the Asian Financial Crisis where surges in capital flows led to collapsed economies. Safeguards must be put in place to reduce capital flight where necessary. A market-based RMB exchange rate outside of China may deviate more strongly from the loosely pegged exchange rate within China, building pressures for exchange rate appreciation or depreciation.

Seventh, is accelerating financial regulation sufficient for B&R Initiative? Better financial regulations and enforcement must be put in place to prevent fraud and excessive risk. China does not have a strong accounting and auditing system for firms that can guard against fraud. Fraud is a big problem among many Chinese firms. If this is already a domestic problem, how can one ensure that fraud is not extended to B&R projects? Information may reduce risk. China is just in the process of creating its Social Credit System, which has been launched in 2017. This will provide credit ratings for individuals and institutions. This system is, as of yet, untested and includes several different standards. One looming problem is that if institutions provide fraudulent data, their credit ratings will not reflect actual risk.

Eighth, is developing an exit mechanism for financial institutions sufficient for B&R Initiative? Financial institutions experiencing higher levels of NPLs or other distress require a sound exit mechanism. Currently, the bankruptcy mechanism for any type of firm is weak. Applications for bankruptcy can be rejected by Chinese courts, which generally have more power in bankruptcy proceedings than US courts. This must be changed to avoid a "too big to fail" situation — firms in financial distress also need to be considered for winding down or reorganization. Currently, there is little recourse for distressed firms. The PBOC implemented deposit insurance in May 2015 in order to ensure that once deposit interest rate ceilings are lifted, depositors are protected from risky competitive behavior engaged in by banks.

Furthermore, the lack of underlying institutions presents a barrier to both financial reform and to realizing the financial goals of B&R Initiative. The lack of enforced property and legal rights may undermine the reform process, since it reduces ability to reinforce collateralized loans and debt contracts in general. Creditors may not seize collateral unless allowed by the court, and there are thin markets for collateral. Creditors' and debtors' rights need to be clearly protected. If borrowers do not have sufficient property rights, they cannot use assets as collateral in the first place: will lending abroad further constrain lending to smaller borrowers?

3.3 OBOReurope: An EU Initiative to Help in Developing the China's B&R Initiative

OBOReurope is a platform of cooperation that promotes the B&R strategy in Europe. The interest of the EU in attracting Chinese investment is evident and the new bilateral investment agreement under negotiation will serve this scope. However, the B&R Initiative needs to be better explained to the European investors who can be interested in investing in determined infrastructure projects.

OBOReurope was designed to raise awareness of the "B&R" Initiative in the European Union and to share the opportunities offered by the B&R Initiative to European companies and stakeholders. Naturally, OBOReurope aims to become the benchmark for relations between Europe and the B&R region.[42] This initiative although it is seen as a fundamental strategy to reinforce the globalization policy of China and is of extreme importance for Chinese authorities, it needs to be better understood by European decision-makers.

3.3.1 *New Opportunities for China and the EU to Cooperate*

The B&R Initiative is a long-term project that will take decades to be fully realized, in fact its completion might be reached in time for the 100th anniversary of the People's Republic of China, and it would be a great achievement for China. As a result, this immense project can lead to the creation of many jobs in Europe over the next 30 years, this alone should be a good reason for the EU to pay a more close attention to this Initiative.

It is evident that this initiative is also an opportunity to strengthen the European Union by launching a new set of challenges, i.e. more openness towards Eurasia and more exchanges with China. It is sad that the UK has decided to exit the EU just at a moment when China is planning to invest more in the European market and in this initiative, however for sure there will be opportunities for the UK to reposition herself. Negotiating the so-called "Brexit" is a long process and it will take approximately 4–5 years to reach a complete agreement with the rest of the EU, and it is extremely probable that compromises will be reached on different issues. Although the UK will be able to negotiate a separate trade agreement with China, it is to be seen if China will be willing to have dual tracks with the EU on trade issues and instead would not exercise some influence on the UK to compromise more with Europe.

---

[42] In this sense: http://www.oboreurope.com/en/about-us/.

In any case, thanks to OBOReurope, European stakeholders will be able to discover and participate in the B&R Initiative, so that a new Silk Road will be rebuilt between China and Europe.

3.3.2 Greener Belt Road, and the Paris Climate Agreement

China has come to understand that green development can be a potential driver of growth not only at "home." In fact, China made great efforts in transforming its development patterns and decreasing carbon intensity. China therefore is paying more attention to this delicate issue and has become a signatory of the Paris Convention on Climate Change.[43] On October 5, 2016, the threshold for entry into force of the Paris Agreement was achieved. The Paris Agreement entered into force on November 4, 2016.

The reaffirmation of China's commitment to Paris climate agreement by Prime Minister Li Keqian, while the US President Mr. Donald Trump announced his country's withdrawal, confirms China's new concern for the environment. This pro-environmental orientation will certainly have a positive impact on the B&R Initiative.

3.3.2.1 Implication for the B&R Initiative

It must be noted that both the EU and China are driven by the same desire to develop new tools to protect environment and promote greener economy in a better manner. The EU and China not only are negotiating a new bilateral investment agreement but also have announced plans to intensify any type of cooperation on climate change and renewable energies (another area of interest for China).

---

[43] At the Paris summit in December 2015, 196 countries have met to discuss and prepare a new climate change agreement. The Paris Agreement builds upon the Convention and — for the first time — brings all nations into a common cause to undertake ambitious efforts to combat climate change and adapt to its effects, with enhanced support to assist developing countries to do so. As such, it charts a new course in the global climate effort. The Paris Agreement entered into force on November 4, 2016, 30 days after the date on which at least 55 Parties to the Convention, accounting in total for at least an estimated 55% of the total global greenhouse gas emissions, have deposited their instruments of ratification, acceptance, approval or accession with the Depositary. More information is available at: http://unfccc.int/paris_agreement/items/9485.php.

The B&R Initiative could be the first beneficiary of this new environmental alliance between China and Europe. Both blocks could accelerate their cooperation by building sustainable infrastructures along the new Silk Roads.

According to the OBOReurope, from a strategic point of view, the US withdrawal from Paris climate agreement will push all Asian states toward China and the B&R Initiative. Several regions of Asia are highly vulnerable to climate change-related phenomena. The urgency of contingent situations could push them to adhere to regional cooperation projects like the B&R Initiative.

Following the US withdrawal from Paris climate agreement, China and the EU not only emerge as a pole of stability on the world scene but also assume new responsibilities.

3.3.2.2 Conditions for a Greener Silk Road

In order for the B&R Initiative to become an example for a new greener development, and link China and Europe in this sense also, projects to be developed should fulfill the following conditions: (i) be supported by the local populations; (ii) respond more sustainability to the specificities of each region; (iii) encourage and finance entrepreneurs bringing sustainable solutions along the new Silk Road.

Naturally, all the projects connected to the B&R Initiative, especially those related to new infrastructures which are to be realized along the two routes, i.e. the land route and the maritime route (like for example new ports) will have to come into existence respecting these principles to fully correspond to this concept.

In conclusion, it is worth reporting what Chinese Central Bank Governor Zhou Xiaochuan expressed recently in relation to the B&R Initiative in the latest edition of China Finance, a leading industry magazine managed by the People's Bank of China, "Funding of projects related to the Belt and Road Initiative should be raised through a market-oriented, sustainable and mutually beneficial investment and financing system."[44] Zhou also added that "no single country can afford to finance all the

---

[44] See article by Xinhua; *Chinese Financial Watchdogs Vow Support for Belt and Road Initiative* (last updated on May 8, 2017).

projects alone, and it will take mutual efforts from countries involved in the initiative to offer long-term, sustainable financial support."

3.4 B&R-related Project in Europe after Four Years: Final Notes

3.4.1 *Numbers Are Likely To Go Up*

About four years after the launch of the B&R Initiative, the number of concrete B&R-related projects in Europe remains relatively limited and involves mostly projects that were under development already before 2013. The EU Commission has established a dedicated portal where projects and investment opportunities can be found, i.e. the European Investment Project Portal (EIPP), however these projects encompass a full series of projects and not only infrastructure projects.[45]

The B&R-related projects in the EU are still limited in number, however, some EU members, and Mediterranean governments, are particularly eager to follow up on B&R Initiative and associated financing and investment promises. The development of this project will expand infrastructural connectivity and create investment opportunities. Local governments, operators of transport hubs and companies in the logistics sector in many countries are jumping on the B&R train to capitalize on emerging business opportunities. Though the B&R Initiative in the EU is only at its initial stage, it is likely that new projects of EU relevance will be co-financed by Chinese money which will come not only from institutional entities but also from the private sector.

Considering that both China and the EU are interested in not only enhancing trade relationships but also improving connectivity, this initiative and the methods to finance B&R-related projects will grow in importance and new investment opportunities will also be created. This is why understanding how the B&R Initiative will be financed is of basic importance. After discussing the so-called "Institutional funding" of the B&R Initiative in this chapter, the next chapter examines the private sector, which naturally complements the first source and offers alternative financing sources to complete this ambitious project.

---

[45] https://ec.europa.eu/eipp/desktop/en/index.html.

CHAPTER 4

The Second Pillar of the B&R Initiative Funding: The Private Sector

Mario Tettamanti

4.1 Introduction: A Bit of History and the Concept of Label

4.1.1 *The History: The Ancient Silk Road Was Also Founded on Tax and Credit*

The links between the countries and peoples living along the arteries and veins criss-crossing Asia are nothing new. For millennia, silk roads, sometimes collectively referred to as the Silk Road, brought peoples, goods and ideas into contact with each other. Two and a half thousand years ago, Chinese writers set about a systematic approach to gathering information about the peoples beyond the deserts and mountain ranges that protect China's interior, assessing their markets, leaders, strengths and weaknesses. That found a parallel in the works of authors such as Herodotus, whose attention was likewise on the land bridge that connects east and west. There was good reason for the attention lavished then on the "heart of the world" — just as there is today. Two thousand years ago, the significance came in part because of the natural wealth — silver, gold and lapis lazuli — found in rich supply in what is now Iran, Iraq, Afghanistan and the Central Asian states. The great cities such as Samarkand, Mosul and

Merv offered great commercial opportunities, thanks to their large, rich elites. Just as important were the connections that linked the cities, towns and oases. Control of these arteries allowed empires to be built — and were crucial in their fall. Known since the late 19th century as the Silk Roads, these networks carried goods, merchants and evangelists who brought ideas about faith and salvation, enabling the spread of Buddhism, Hinduism, Judaism, Islam and Christianity — the latter taking root quicker and more successfully in Asia than it did in the Mediterranean. Trade, though, was the oil in the engine of vibrant exchange over many centuries.

Those who were able to build credit networks did particularly well. Minority groups bound over long distances by family connections, religious practices and common identities developed systems to lend, borrow and pay for goods that were sometimes thousands of miles away. In late antiquity, it was the Sogdians who dominated transcontinental trade, while more recently, Armenians played a prominent role thanks to their linguistic skills. Indeed, recent research suggests that the Silk Roads were fundamental to the development of Yiddish, a transnational language of Jewish traders plying the silk routes. Many goods were traded along these networks, in both directions, including spices, silks, minerals and human beings — sold in huge numbers in the Middle Ages. But problems also flowed through the arteries: violence and disease, most notably the Black Death, which originated in Central Asia and passed from town to town, ravaging all in its path.

Foreign investors are joining Chinese policy banks in providing funds. Control of highways and cities meant control of taxes. States and leaders with ambitions — from the age of Alexander the Great to Britain and Russia in the 19th century — were drawn to the heart of the world. Few understood this better than the Mongols, whose vast empire in the 13th and 14th centuries, extending from the Pacific to the Black Sea and Mediterranean, was not characterized by violence and chaos but by careful and deliberate investment into major urban centers. They employed what we would today call progressive tax policies, which encouraged trade within and between cities to stimulate greater revenues for the state. In the 20th century, it was the turn of the Soviet Union and United States to wrestle for influence in Afghanistan, Iran and Iraq. Attempting to control the countries lying in the "heart of the world" was a significant feature of the Cold War. Now it is China's turn to cast its eye toward the Silk Roads. The combination of opportunities and challenges offered by the "B&R" plan would have been familiar in the Chinese capital 2,500 years ago.[1]

4.1.2 *The B&R Initiative Has Already Become a Label, Indeed an Asset of Labels*

The concept of Label is important if you think that fundraising is one of the basic elements of the entire B&R Initiative exercise. Private investors are very careful about the risks inherent in the investments. An attractive Label (capable of making history) will allow, together with the guarantees of public institutions involved in this great project, to find private investors.

4.1.2.1 The "Historical and Geopolitical" Label

Adding the Silk Road label (a reference to the route by which ancient China traded with the West) to a financing exercise can give it more focus and attention from investors due to the publicity already garnered by the Silk Road initiative. Many of China's new Silk Road projects are found on the path of the old Silk Road. This visionary conception that leverages on China's historical connections has created a new opportunity to rejuvenate the economic and cultural ties built via the ancient Silk Road. It presents a win–win approach to peaceful coexistence and mutual development. The idea carries forward the spirit of the ancient Silk Road that was based on mutual trust, equality and mutual benefits, inclusiveness and mutual learning and win–win cooperation. After the fall of Constantinople to the Ottomans in 1453, trade along the old Silk Road was driven more by China's lust for silver than the West's demand for paper, silk, tea and spices. As a result, China's monetary system became enslaved to the silver peso, with more circulating in China than in Mexico itself. Such is its

---

[1] Peter Frankopan, *The Silk Roads: A New History of the World*, Bloomsbury (UK) and Knopf (USA) FT Mai, 2016.

financial and geopolitical significance that it will likely be judged along-side Deng Xiaoping's economic reforms and China's entry into the World Trade Organization in 2001 as a key stage in the country's development. Global economic power ultimately depends upon capital export and sei-gniorage, i.e. the ability to use your own national paper money and domestically denominated debt to purchase international assets and accu-mulate foreign capital cheaply. The historical Label referred to as Silk Road is also incredibly important to counter the wave of anti-globalization sentiment sweeping today's developed world. The overlap between the B&R Initiative and the Silk Road provides the opportunity to present B&R Initiative as the leading vehicle for defending and increasing global trade. The B&R Initiative is now seen as part of the China solution for the whole world, not just the developing world.[2]

4.1.2.2 The "Monetary Label": The Yuan/Renminbi

History teaches us, from the Roman denarius to the British pound to the modern US dollar, that this transition of monetary power takes time. But, somewhere out in the future, the princeling yuan sits waiting to be crowned. The Chinese capital for the B&R Initiative will largely take the form of official and quasi-official loans and development aid, denomi-nated in yuan and effectively printed by the People's Bank of China. That money will circulate in the recipient economies and be held by local cen-tral banks as a settlement currency. Also, more and more Chinese exports will be priced in yuan, thus eliminating forex risks. To put it another way, China's geopolitical ambitions require that the yuan circulates internation-ally, is trusted as a standard of value and can be used both as a payment currency for trade and an investment currency in financial markets. And the B&R Initiative will help facilitate those goals. A sizable and market-determined renminbi-denominated debt market is essential to encourage non-resident corporates and investors to hold and use renminbi. The absence of large and liquid capital markets (debt, equities, derivative and money markets) offshore has hindered the global expansion of the

---

[2]Ayumi Konishi, Director General of the East Asia department at the Asian Development Bank (ADB) in Manila.

renminbi. There is an urgent need for Mainland China to either establish a sizable debt market offshore or open up its onshore debt market as soon as possible. However, as the latter remains heavily regulated and is dominated by public debt, this is unlikely to meet investors' demands in the foreseeable future.

4.1.2.3 The "Financial Place Label": Hong Kong

Hong Kong's role in the B&R Initiative will be prominent. As the B&R Initiative covers over 60 countries, this implies complex corporate treasury operations that include such elements as cash-flow management, foreign exchange, cross-border payments, risks and liability control. Therefore, a regional corporate treasury center (CTC) would be required to centralize all treasury functions so that multinational corporations can enhance operational efficiency and reduce foreign exchange exposure and risk. Hong Kong is already a premier CTC in Asia. Hong Kong's advantage lies in its well-developed financial infrastructure including but not limited to its deep and liquid foreign exchange and money markets, absence of capital restrictions, stable and free exchange rates, and concentration of the world's leading banks. Furthermore, Hong Kong possesses a competitive tax regime, a common law system, an excellent pool of well-educated labor force and business professionals, as well as world-class transport and telecommunication infrastructure. More importantly, its proximity to Mainland China makes Hong Kong a preferred location for fulfilling B&R projects.[3,4]

4.2 The B&R Initiative Funding through the Private Sector

There are basically two important funding channels of the B&R Initiative: first (Chapter 3) is the public sector (official and multilateral); second (Chapter 4) is the private sector. The first one is already in place and almost functional, and the second one is still in the process of being

---

[3] Clifford Lee is the head of debt capital market at DBS Bank in Singapore.
[4] Michael Howell is Managing Director of Cross Border Capital.

shaped. On the public funding of the B&R Initiative, many words have been said and many pages have been already written. Concerning the attitude and the situation of the B&R's funding by the private sector, not much has been said and written, for the simple reason that much has not been done yet. Our task will therefore be to go deeper in this topic that some specialists consider crucial for the success of the B&R Initiative.

Writing about these two financing modes of the B&R Initiative funding forces have to face up different important topics like the following:

(1) **The Risks**. This issue is very important because the various RISKS inherent in the financing of the B&R project are being relegated to individual citizens as tax payers (public financing) and investors (private financing).

(2) **The Public–Private Partnership (PPP)**. It is the indispensable bond or link between the public and the private financing.

(3) **The Concept of Governance**. The management of various actors (public and private) acting in the B&R Initiative funding.

(4) **The Innovative Financing**. While mentioning the private sector way of financing the B&R Initiative, it will be indispensable to talk about the concept of innovative financing that is often not so innovative. Many of the instruments and financial products are already present in the financial market in general and the capital market in particular.

(5) **The Islamic Finance**. Under the B&R Initiative, China is considering using Islamic finance as a breakthrough to initiate extensive business communication and project cooperation in many areas with Middle East and Southeast Asian countries.

(6) **The Crowdfunding**. It is an innovative financing instrument. The questions that we need to ask concerns how much crowdfunding can be extended as a mechanism capable of supporting such a project and what component of crowdfunding technology can be used in financing government-incentivized projects.

(7) **Hong Kong, the Financial Hub**. Other issues will be touched, such as the need to have one or more financial places in Asia ready to accept the challenge of becoming the financial center, capable to support the organization of the B&R financing. Hong Kong seems very well placed (end sponsored) to take on this important role.

The second pillar of the B&R financing focuses on the more important private commercial and investment banks active in international credit. Usually based on PPP, with State and Parastatal Financial Institutions, the private banks, after agreeing the due guarantees, invest their money in specific infrastructural B&R projects. Commercial players and private money will need to step in to drive the pace of the economic expansion in B&R projects. Innovative financing tools such as structured finance, trade finance and hedging will be instrumental in spreading the risk and attracting more global capital. We expect different pools of capital to be tapped to fund the expansion plans. In particular, bond markets such as the Dim Sum and Panda, given the currency relevance, as well as Asian local currencies, given their strategic place along the B&R, could be key early access points.

4.2.1 *The Actors of the B&R Private Financing*

4.2.1.1 Commercial and Investment Banks

So far, the public sector (multilateral financial institutions) has provided the majority of the B&R infrastructure investment, particularly in Asia where the contribution is over 90%. The public sector will continue to play a key role, but the B&R needs products and services that commercial and investment banks provide, from syndicated financing and capital market financing to cash management and cross-border settlement; from project financing to transactional banking, helping boost investment and trade flows along the B&R economic corridors. This will provide market confidence and liquidity on a sustainable basis. In principle, as the Initiative seeks to build new business and market opportunities, this should attract global investors to invest in its infrastructure. Entities have also started to tap the capital markets to fund B&R projects. The big Chinese banks are also active in the Investment banking business building up financial products. Bank of China (BOC) was the first in 2015 to tap the market with its multi-tranche RMB 4 billion issuance in B&R bonds. China Construction Bank (CCB) followed in August 2015, listing its first RMB 1 billion Belt & Road Initiative infrastructure bonds on the Singapore Exchange.

4.2.1.2 The Capital Market

The capital market becomes the privileged place where financial instruments offered by the banks concerned meet the demand of the same instruments by institutional and private investors. For the capital markets, the challenge is to develop an efficient structure to match projects with different investors. Whether through debt or equity financing, making infrastructure-related financial instruments part of mainstream asset allocation would attract a broader range of private investors. Greater involvement by the private sector should also help improve the efficiency of infrastructure investment. In fact, besides government and sub-sovereign bonds, there is scope for corporate and project bonds while B&R is intended to become an internationally recognized asset class. The impact on the software of financing will also be significant: the vast amounts of money needed to meet Asia's infrastructure needs will inject fresh momentum into the region's capital markets. The B&R Initiative will trigger more issuance and investment. What is more, it could galvanize China's financial reforms, and encourage policymakers to further open the country's capital market to global participants.[5]

Global capital is critical in closing funding gaps, despite China's substantial pledges. According to the Asia Development Bank, Asia needs to add US$770 billion of infrastructure annually from now to 2020. Commercial players and private money will also need to step in to drive the pace of economic expansion in B&R projects. The nascent B&R bond or Silk Road bond market (where proceeds go into funding B&R projects) is taking shape. The Shanghai–Singapore Financial Forum (SSFF), which was formed in November 2015, provides a platform for industry participants in the two countries to access and finance B&R projects in ASEAN countries. Entities have also started to tap the capital markets to fund B&R projects. BOC led the first in 2015 to tap the market with its multi-tranche US$4 billion issuance in B&R bonds (including Singapore dollars and renminbi). CCB followed in August 2015, listing its first RMB 1 billion (US$145.2 million) Belt & Road Initiative infrastructure bonds on the Singapore Exchange. Innovative financing (see Section 4.4) tools such as

---

[5] Gordon French is Head of Global Banking and Markets, Asia Pacific, HSBC.

structured finance, trade finance and hedging will be instrumental in spreading the risk and attracting more global capital. Different pools of capital are expected to be tapped to fund the expansion plans. Reforms in Mainland China have expanded the options available to foreign and domestic investors and issuers in recent years — from "Dim Sum" bonds (renminbi-denominated, issued outside the mainland) to "Panda" bonds (renminbi-denominated, issued by non-Chinese entities but sold in Mainland China). Dim Sum and Panda given the currency relevance, as well as Asian local currencies given their strategic place along the Belt and Road, could be key early access points. This is likely to boost financial centers in Greater China, Hong Kong and Singapore initially. Further growth in the B&R bond market might then attract new bond issuers beyond existing Chinese banks, with multilateral bodies, import–export agencies, sovereigns and corporations hot on their heels. Commercial strategic partnerships are also important. For instance, China Merchants Bank (CMB) signed its first B&R strategic alliance with Standard Chartered Bank in September last year, hoping to leverage Standard Chartered's deep-rooted presence in over 65% of B&R countries to enhance its clients' access to B&R. Global interest rates continue to be low on a historical basis. This makes raising long-term debt to finance long-term infrastructure projects especially opportune. If this takes off, investors will have a plethora of investment opportunities in the coming years to fund infrastructure projects across the globe. This might also spur a "crowding-out effect" where competition for funding will drive the best opportunities forward.[6]

4.2.1.3 The Renminbi (RMB) Internationalization

The B&R Initiative offers fertile fields for RMB internationalization to grow deep roots. The routes encompass 65 countries, with a population of 4.4 billion, accounting for 65% of the global total. Their combined GDP accounts for 29% of the global total, and their trade volume amounts to

---

[6]Henrik Raber is the Global Head of Capital Markets at Standard Chartered Bank. Full article: https://www.euromoney.com/article/b12kqlnm6nyx2b/the-belt-and-road-effect-on-bond-markets?copyrightInfo=true.

more than 60% of the global total. China is the biggest trading partner for most countries along the Belt and Road routes. With the implementation of the B&R strategy and through the connectivity of infrastructure facilities, it could help promote deeper integration between cross-border RMB operations and the real economy of these countries, and will help further consolidate the foundation for steady progress of RMB internationalization.

In fact, the RMB's internationalization should benefit from the rising B&R-related finance and business flows. Strengthening the connectivity of financial infrastructure among the linked countries is part of this process, and China is ready to share its experience in cross-border payment networks, rural banking and transfers by mobile phones. Thus, the challenge will be to attract private financing to complement public funds, especially from (1) international pension funds, (2) insurance companies, (3) sovereign wealth funds and (4) private equity funds, for the cross-border investments that comprise the Initiative. The B&R will also drive massive investment (infrastructure, real estate and industrial investment), merchandise trade and cross-regional logistics and distribution — these activities need to be supported by funds and financing (banking loans, bonds issuance, currency trading). In the long run, as the Belt and Road makes progress, China and its trade and investment partners need a stable financial and monetary environment, using RMB as the currency in trade settlement; payment and reserve can effectively avoid or reduce the foreign exchange risk related to trade and investment flows.

RMB is able to become an anchor currency and be widely used in less developed countries or regions, such as Central Asia, South Asia, West Asia and North Africa. RMB's wider use can speed up its process to be an international currency, and gradually form a distinctive "RMB area" or the "RMB bloc." So far, China has expanded its bilateral local currency swap programs to 21 countries along B&R, granted RMB quotas to institutional investors in seven countries and set up RMB settlement banks in eight countries. These steps have helped RMB trade settlement increase to more than 25% of China's trade in early 2016, from a mere 5% at the beginning of 2012. RMB trade settlement is set to be boosted further as Chinese companies pursue opportunities along

B&R. New financing mechanisms, set up by China, demonstrates the leadership's strong commitment to B&R. China has encouraged commercial banks, quasi-official regional cooperation funds and private capital to participate in B&R projects, to boost limited official resources and make projects more commercial.

The B&R Initiative provides the possibility for RMB internationalization to grow deep roots, but it should also be admitted that the RMB internationalization is a "double-edged sword." On the one hand, exchange-rate fluctuations will mean greater exchange risks for enterprises, but on the other hand, the RMB cross-border settlements could also help enterprises to hedge exchange-rate risks. The development of the RMB offshore market could help enterprises lower the costs of overseas financing, the RMB futures could help investors to hedge exchange-rate risks, and the firm valuation of the RMB and the gradual progress in free convertibility under the capital account will be of immense help to Chinese enterprises in executing their "going global" plans. Development of China's financial sector both at home and abroad will be an important by-product of B&R. In particular, B&R will provide a platform for further internationalization of the RMB, a strategy which China has been actively pursuing over the last decade. Significant ground has already been made on this front. In October 2015, the International Monetary Fund (IMF) added the RMB to the basket of currencies which make up the Special Drawing Rights (SDRs). This takes the RMB into the elite class of currencies of which the only other members are the US Dollar, the Euro, the Japanese Yen and the Great British Pound. In addition, China has entered into over 30 bilateral swap agreements with jurisdictions all over the world, including a number of states on the B&R route and significant players such as the EU, Great Britain, Russia, Switzerland and Canada. Supplementing and complementing these agreements are some 20 offshore RMB clearing centers, including in hubs such as New York, London, Hong Kong, Paris, Frankfurt and Zurich. So while this financial infrastructure is continually evolving in support of RMB internationalization generally, it is widely expected that B&R will provide a further significant boost to Beijing's efforts to increase the RMB's influence across the financial world. With the sheer scale of numbers being thrown around in the context of B&R-related

investment, it is expected that both outflows and inflows of RMB capital will be significantly boosted, which will have a very positive impact for Chinese importers and exporters.[7,8]

4.2.1.4 Syndicated Loans

As infrastructure financing requirements are large, loans more often than not come under a syndicate of banks. This is due to the limits on single-party exposure for each bank which are typically required by risk management policies. The US dollar is the predominant currency for syndicated loans, alongside local currencies. This trend is observed across all Asia-12 economies. By sector, electric power accounts for the lion's share of loans in most countries. The exception is China, where both nuclear power and rail transport account for a higher share than electrical power. Chinese lenders are starting to syndicate participation in B&R projects to international private sector investors and lenders. "We are seeing a shift among the Chinese institutions in the B&R projects toward syndication to international pension funds, insurance companies, sovereign wealth funds, private equity funds and others. Institutions are increasingly seduced by the promise of long-term returns of 6 to 8 per cent on B&R infrastructure. Even some government agencies appear keen. IE Singapore, the state-owned trade development board, has agreed to a partnership with China Construction Bank to finance B&R projects, with about $22bn in funding envisaged. B&R calls for an improvement on the region's infrastructure, with a call for greater energy and power interconnections and to establish a secure and efficient network of land, sea and air passages across the key routes. Additionally, the initiative calls for greater policy co-ordination (such as opening free trade areas and improving co-operation in new technologies) and financial integration (such as carrying out multilateral financial cooperation in the form of syndicated loans and supporting foreign countries to issue RMB denominated

---

[7] Kent Calder, Director of the Reischauer Center for East Asian Studies at Johns Hopkins School of Advanced International Studies.

[8] Lu Xinhong, Associate Researcher at China Center for International Economic Exchanges.

bonds). Furthermore, whilst the B&R is firmly rooted in the Silk Road's thousand year old heritage, it also clearly looking to the future — greater e-commerce interconnectivity and advancing the construction of fibre optic cables is encouraged."[9]

4.2.1.5 Project Financing and Special Purpose Vehicles (SPVs)

Project finance is typically a form of financing for projects of medium- to long-term nature with intensive capital demand. The merit of the project is derived from future cash-flow generation prospects rather than from the financial strength of the project developers/owners.

Financing infrastructure projects through the project finance route offers various benefits such as the opportunity for risk sharing, extending the debt capacity, the release of free cash flows and maintaining a competitive advantage in a competitive market. Project finance is a useful tool for companies that wish to avoid the issuance of a corporate repayment guarantee, thus preferring to finance the project in an off-balance sheet manner. The project finance route permits the sponsor to extend their debt capacity by enabling the sponsor to finance the project on someone's credit, which could be the purchaser of the project's outputs. Sponsors can raise funding for the project based simply on the contractual commitments.

Room to grow private financing for infrastructure projects comes in a range of forms: equity financing, commercial bank loans, project financing, bonds and funds. Since infrastructure projects involve many stages, different phases of the project tend to attract different types of investments or financing tools. Commercial banks have played a key role in infrastructure financing. But they are challenged by the inherent asset–liability mismatch it generates. Banks typically have substantial short-term liabilities, but infrastructure financing often involves long-term assets.

In spite of some advantages, project finance is quite complex and costly to assemble. The cost of capital arranged through this route is high

---

[9]Carolyn Dong, Foreign Legal Consultant Head of Energy of China (Finance & Projects) DLA Piper.

in comparison with capital arranged through conventional routes. The complexity of project finance deals is due to the need to structure a set of contracts that must be negotiated by all of the parties to the project. This also leads to higher transaction costs on account of the legal expenses involved in designing the project structure, dealing with project-related tax and legal issues, and the preparation of necessary project ownership, loan documentation and other contracts.

To obtain private project financing, the set-up of a Special Purpose Vehicle (SPV) is a prerequisite. The SPV is the entity which takes legal responsibility for the project, and outlines clearly the contractual obligations, pledging of cash flows to creditors and how to distribute risks among the contract partners. In China, local governments have relied heavily on Local Government Financing Vehicles (LGFVs) to finance various infrastructure projects. The key lesson learned in the case of China's LGFVs is that there needs to be clearly defined financial obligations of the LGFVs and the scope of central government's responsibility in order to protect public sector finances.

4.2.2 *How to Motivate and Unlock the Private Sector Investment*

There are two major ways to motivate private sector financing. The first way is the short-term solution of governments and multinational investment banks providing loan guarantees for private sector lenders. Loan guarantees are structured in such a way that if a big project fails, the governments or multinational investment banks providing the guarantee will absorb the debt obligation. Hence, the loan from the investors' perspective is the same as one issued to a government. Loan guarantees would help motivate private sector financing; meanwhile, the emerging new multilateral development banks such as the Asian Infrastructure Investment Bank can use their flexibility and innovation to contribute to tackling global infrastructure financing challenges.

The second solution, which is more sustainable, is the process of giving technical support to government institutions, which can then help contribute to the success of individual infrastructure projects. Such support could include the process of helping projects gain the necessary planning and environmental permits or working with governments to create multilateral regulatory frameworks.[10]

4.2.3 *The Conditions to Attract the Private Sector Investment*

There are a number of necessary conditions for private sector financing to work alongside public money. These include transparency around the way the money is allocated, an appropriate balance between the public funding and the private funding, clear returns, a strong regulatory system that is able to work across borders and conduct that everybody can recognize as being close to market principles. Without these conditions, the private sector may be reticent to invest, dampening the spill-over effects.

There are seven factor to attract the private financing. They are as follows:

[i] **Bankable and technically feasible projects**. Detailed feasibility studies and robust business cases are important to attract investors who will often require high-quality information on which to base their investment decisions. The effect of poorly thought through and ineffective business cases is profound, resulting in investors, developers and institutions losing confidence in a government's ability to be an effective business partner. To address this, it requires professional de-risking at the project level, an area in which Atkins has expertise. Early state involvement is key to maximize a project's benefit, providing more certainty in revenue projections and project input cost, which reflects the complexity in design and construction and the engineering delivery risk.[11]

[ii] **Appropriate risk allocation**. At the early stage of a project, institutional and public bodies should not expect the private sector to bear the risk. By providing the right funding to proper project

---

[10]Nathan Hayes is currently an Economist at Timetric's Construction Intelligence Centre.

[11] Chris Birdson Atkins is one of the world's most respected design, engineering and project management consultancies.

preparation and guarantees can help mitigate the risks to attract private sector investment.

[iii] **Innovative funding**. Governments need to be more open toward achieving a balanced funding mechanism between tax payer pay and user pay. The willingness to pay is key to attracting private investment. Local currency bond markets are also important to funding Asia's growing infrastructure needs as they minimize currency risk.

[iv] **Affordability**. Can the host government, tax payers or end users afford to pay for the charge over the lifetime of the concession? Linking back to the innovative funding models, should the public money rather be used to support project life affordability, than be spent on the investment side and crowd out the private sector?

[v] **Institutional capacity in host countries**. A system to identify, select and prioritize major projects can effectively shorten the lead-in times of the pipeline. Public sector bodies must ensure they have sufficient capacity within government departments involved in infrastructure delivery, especially if procurement is via PPP. Atkins Acuity has strong expertise in this area and has worked with World Bank and Asian Development Bank for capacity building in some Southeast Asian countries.

[vi] **Governance and transparency**. Transparent and consistent policies and processes are required across all sectors to provide confidence to investors. A solid regulatory framework, a reliable and consistent judicial system, and clear and transparent governance are all important considerations.

[vii] **"Project delivery risk."** Overrun on major infrastructure projects is a significant project delivery risk. Not only does it have an implication on project cost, but also has implications on the credibility of the host country, which may result in difficulty in raising investment in the future or at an unnecessarily high premium that affects the affordability of the project. At Atkins, we believe that technology has a major role to play.[12]

[12] Anoop Singh is Distinguished Fellow, Geoeconomics Studies at Gateway House: Indian Council on Global Relations, 2016.

4.2.4 *Significant Potential Risk and Return Need to Be Considered in Financing the B&R Initiative*

New channels of investment are needed, but the main obstacle for the private sector **IS NOT** a lack of available financing: pension funds, insurers and other long-term institutional investors with large pools of capital find it difficult to identify investable projects.

Private investors will commit large-scale, long-term financing **ONLY** if contracts are based on incentive-driven risks and returns with a solid legal framework that helps mitigate political threats. Specialists believe a market-oriented, multi-tier system of financing is the way to provide sustainable funding for cross-border Belt & Road infrastructure projects.[13]

4.2.4.1 Political Risks

Geopolitics and territorial dispute. The geopolitics of the B&R region is complicated; some areas suffer from territorial disputes and even local wars; and there is great uncertainty in policy and implementation.

Domestic political instability. Many countries along the B&R have unsettled political conditions with frequent rotation of political parties, which will impact policy and project implementation.

Religious extremism and terrorist threats. Religious relations in Eurasia are complicated, and religious extremism, terrorism, separatism and other activities remain rampant, threatening the safety of the projects.

4.2.4.2 Economic Risks

Big changes in market conditions. The current world economy is still unstable, and changes in macro-economy, industry and market environment will all have impacts on investment. One major risk for companies is the possibility of the countries defaulting on foreign lending.

---

[13] Marsh & McLennan companies list the opportunities and risks associated with these projects in select countries. The New York-based firm specializing in insurance brokerage and risk management notes that the B&R Initiative is strongly influencing the flow of Chinese outbound investment.

Different regulatory and cultural systems: Laws and regulations in the countries along the B&R differ from one another, and regulatory systems in many developing countries remain incomplete, which, along with custom and cultural differences, tends to result in operational frictions.

4.2.4.3 Operational Risks

Great uncertainty in project profitability: Infrastructure projects require large-scale investments and high-standard management, and have long operating cycles and huge uncertainty in profits. Innovative financing structures can help mitigate the risks that would otherwise be present through the public in countries covered by the B&R Initiative, and such an inclusive approach to achieving and private sectors' concerted efforts is coherent with China's ideology of inclusive growth. The large-scale infrastructure needs of the B&R could change how global capital is mobilized to unlock infrastructure investment, if private sector investors are willing to provide financing.[14]

4.3 Collaboration between the Public and Private Sector

4.3.1 *Public–Private Partnership: A Brief Introduction*

PPP is a long-term contract between a government entity and a private party for the provision of public service and/or development of public infrastructure in which responsibilities and rewards are shared. The partnership between private and public sectors has a long history. For example, during the 16th and 17th centuries, European sovereigns, particularly in France, began concession programs in canal construction, road paving, public transportation, etc. The industrialization in Europe during the 19th century marked the golden age of concessions in Europe. The creation of railways took place under concessions in all European

---

[14] Henrik Raber is the Global Head of Capital Markets at Standard Chartered Bank. He joined the Bank in July 2009 as Regional Head of Capital Markets for Europe, Africa and Americas, and took on the role of Global Head of Debt Capital Markets in March 2010 before assuming his current role in mid-August 2014, prior to Standard.

countries. Compared to public provision and privatization, PPP promotes the in-depth collaboration between the public and the private sectors by sharing risks, revenues and responsibilities. The unique advantages of PPPs include: increased efficiency in project planning, delivery, operation and management, additional resources and investment from the private sector and access to advanced technologies. In China, PPP has been identified as an effective mechanism to improve the efficiency and quality of public infrastructure projects and is being implemented as a major reform of public financing and governance (budgeting) policy of local governments. China hopes that PPP will mobilize private capital to plug the shortfall, and a variety of funding options are on the table to encourage private interests, from standard non-recourse bank financing accompanied by equity injections to project-bond issuance in onshore as well as offshore formats. There is a need to further the PPP framework in China and in many of the countries that are part of the B&R project.

4.3.2 *Tailoring the PPP or Closing the Financial Gap*

Investment in planned and ongoing B&R projects could total roughly US$240 billion in the coming years. However, the total investment needs in Asia are much larger than that. It is estimated, that just South Asia and Southeast Asia will need at least US$3.6 trillion over the period 2010–2020 in domestic infrastructure investment if they are to meet the needs of their growing population and of the trend toward urbanization. How can this large investment volume be financed? The solution to this financing challenge can only be a combination of public and private, domestic and international financing sources, tailored to the specific circumstances of countries and projects. Regional and cross-border projects face particular challenges, due to diverse financial and institutional capacities.

4.3.2.1 Domestic Finance — Local Bond Markets

Local currency markets in countries along the "belt and road" routes could get a crucial boost from the Initiative. Emerging Asian local-currency bond markets have developed rapidly. Outstanding volumes of such bonds have soared from US$836 billion at the end of 2000 to US$8.78 trillion in late 2015, according to the Asian Development Bank. However, countries with less-developed financial markets face difficulties with regard to the size of their domestic capital markets and the maturity of available financial instruments. There are large disparities in financial development across countries, requiring specific measures for developing domestic capital markets. Belt and Road-related spending can trigger the much-needed breadth, depth and liquidity to many of Asia's smaller markets. The effect of the bond issues of development banks and other issuers tapping these local markets can widen the local credit market, attract global investors and expand the development of long-term capital markets in the region. Bond markets in emerging countries should also be seen as an investment opportunity for an aging population in emerging countries in the region. The stable income provided by bonds can be an attractive investment for individuals and pension funds. Thus, the "Belt and Road" Initiative could help to transform Asian financial markets in the near future, expanding the opportunities for recycling Asian savings into long-term investment. However, this will not happen automatically. Governments and international institutions will have to work hand in hand to improve the market infrastructure in the region, a task that has been ongoing in recent years, but is by far not completed in many countries. A challenging task will be to bring about more cohesion among countries by harmonizing regulation in areas like taxation, foreign exchange regulation and credit ratings.

4.3.2.2 Commercial Finance

Financing by commercial banks is appropriate for revenue-generating projects (e.g. energy, ports). But in the energy sector a lack of transmission lines is often a bottleneck. Therefore, a combination of public and private financing is warranted in most cases. However, project lending by banks has a significant mismatch of maturity of assets and liabilities and is therefore suitable mainly for financing the construction phase of projects, with long-term investors as potential holders of debt in the long-term operational period of infrastructure projects. There is not much private finance outside the energy and communications sectors. PPPs are suitable for projects with lower returns where the viability gap is to be funded by the public sector. However, the institutional capacities for developing and managing PPPs are underdeveloped in many cases, particularly in less-developed countries with weak institutions. The use of corporate or project bonds for infrastructure and industrial investments is often constrained by the immaturity of the domestic capital markets. Corporate bonds and project financing structures therefore tend to receive sub-investment grade ratings, keeping institutional investors away from corporate bonds. This is reinforced by the underdevelopment of regional bond markets, inhibiting cross-border capital flows and a higher degree of liquidity in the market. The commercial banks suggested ways of (1) leveraging PPPs, (2) syndicated loans, (3) infrastructure bonds, as well as creating integrated financial services for industrial parks and economic corridors along the B&R.

4.3.2.3 Institutional Investors

Institutional investors meet obstacles in the areas of regulation, where regulatory restrictions relating to foreign ownership and to the risk classes in which they can invest considerably limit their scope for financing. They are also constrained by a lack of market infrastructure and insurance mechanisms that reduce commercial and political risks for private investors.

4.3.2.4 Trade Finance

Trade finance is a major pillar of cross-border trade, particularly for small and medium-sized enterprises which have limited access to finance. Trade Finance will be an important tool to facilitate cross-border trade and the integration in regional and global value chains. A growing part of the increasing trade in the region will be settled in Renminbi and will thus help boost the internationalization of the Chinese currency. However, as long as the Chinese capital market is not liberalized to a larger degree, the liquidity and stability of Renminbi debt will be constrained and countries will hesitate to incur Renminbi debt to a larger degree.

The B&R and the PPP model

(One Belt One Road: PPP Alchemie — Is the Silk Road Paved in Gold? Neil Cuthbert Senior Partner United Arab Emirates, neil.cuthbert@ dentons.com)

With many OBOR projects being regularly launched, issues and questions will arise as to how best to structure them. Some of the more difficult large-scale projects will be funded through government-to-government grants, others will utilize the traditional export credit models, such as buyer credits and supplier credits, and, some will use the increasingly popular "EPC+F" structure (engineering, procurement and construction plus financing). However, many will utilize the Public Private Partnership model (PPP) for structural, economic and legal reasons, including the following:

(1) Infrastructure gaps

Many of the nations along the Silk Route are underdeveloped nations with a need for foreign investment, with a particular emphasis on infrastructure, particularly through the Asia/South Asia segments of the route. With growing populations and failing infrastructure, many of these nations are crying out for partnerships with those who currently have the appetite for financial investment on a similar scale to China. This can be coupled with the arduous position in which many of the oil-based economies find themselves, with the stagnation of international oil prices, particularly in the Arabian Gulf and wider Middle East region. The outcome of these factors is that many of the projects in such nations which are looking to fill their infrastructure gaps are looking for equity investments of the kind which the PPP model strongly supports and which the OBOR strategy will encourage. This is of course a move away from the traditional procurement methods which used to see the engagement of Chinese enterprise solely for their construction capabilities.

(2) Investment through equity interests

The Chinese government itself is now aggressively advocating and encouraging outbound investment in the form of equity stakes in projects and assets across the globe. We have already mentioned some of these diverse investments in places such as Russia and Italy above. A further prime example of this is in the agriculture sector. Where previously China would

---

(Continued)

(Continued)

rely on importing food products at market prices to feed its large population, it is fast learning that it makes far more strategic sense to simply acquire agriculture assets in foreign lands and operate them themselves. By doing so it is effectively annexing the farm land of other countries as part of its own agriculture sector (which suffers as a result of a very small proportion of mainland China being productive agricultural land). The OBOR strategy and PPP model complement each other considerably in this respect.

(3) *Legal impediments*

In many of the nations along the Silk Route the mandatory position for one reason or another is for the host nation to have ownership (or at least strict control) over its own infrastructure. Without the resources to go it alone, the PPP model is an obvious choice for them to meet their infrastructure needs without ceding rights they wish to retain. By awarding a concession they can attract foreign know-how and investment while maintaining ownership (or the right to ownership at a later time). In certain regions (for example, parts of the Middle East and Africa) we are now seeing that PPP laws and regulations are being implemented and developed in order to support and facilitate the PPP model. In some cases the legal impediments are being broken down in a way which will support the use of the PPP structure. This will, in turn, support OBOR growth.

(4) *Joint ventures*

PPPs are one of the more convenient and workable project models for contractors who are looking to get into joint ventures with foreign entities. Increasingly in recent times, Chinese enterprises are looking to commit to countries beyond just contracting work. They are now looking to invest with, and in, the nations which are looking to them for their expertise. By becoming a partner to governments, rather than mere employees, there is scope for significant mutual benefits to arise. Governments are seeking investors who are willing to commit to their countries for longer terms, and Chinese enterprises are looking to become part of the decision-making process rather than being hindered by it as they historically have been in some countries. PPPs strongly support these objectives. Although it must be recognized that there is a possibility that doing business in partnership with host governments

(Continued)

142

China's Belt and Road — The Initiative and Its Financial Focus

(*Continued*)

can increase risk-sharing on the part of the private sector (for example, in the case of political risk which would otherwise exclusively lie with the host government), the goal is that in the longer term through constructive collaboration, these risks can be reduced across the board for both partners.

(5) *Project financing*

Significant development of late in the project financing arena means that governments, financial institutions and the private sector are becoming more and more comfortable with project financing PPPs. Although numerous PPPs have suffered wobbles in the early days where participants failed to plan and understand the structure adequately, this model is slowly but surely being refined and made more robust to the point where PPPs are now regularly achieving a successful financial close, including many involving Chinese interests. Chinese companies are becoming increasingly comfortable with this model, helped in a small part by the explosion of PPP projects within China over the last 24 months. The further development and refinement of project financing techniques will be an important factor in the successful implementation of OBOR projects.

(6) *Project financing and Special Purpose Vehicles (SPVs)*

Project finance is typically a form of financing for projects of medium to longterm nature with intensive capital demand. The merit of the project is derived from future cash-flow generation prospects rather than from the financial strength of the project developers/owners. To obtain private project financing, the set-up of a Special Purpose Vehicle (SPV) is a prerequisite. The SPV is the entity which takes legal responsibility for the project, and outlines clearly the contractual obligations, pledging of cash flows to creditors and how to distribute risks among the contract partners. SPV models have been employed in many NJA economies for the financing of infrastructure projects, but the experience of China is the largest in scale and has caught most attention. In China, local governments have relied heavily on Local Government Financing Vehicles (LGFVs) to finance various infrastructure projects. Although many LGFVs have been associated with financing difficulties leading to the recent imposition of a lending limit on regional and local governments in China, not all LGFVs are in financial trouble. The successful ones have been instrumental in delivering the

(*Continued*)

(*Continued*)

---

necessary infrastructure backbone to different parts of China. Despite its vast geographical size, China commands 6th place among NJA economies in the WEF's global infrastructure ranking. For those LGFVs in trouble, local banks have been encouraged to be flexible in refinancing existing infrastructure projects. The key lesson learned in the case of China's LGFVs is that there needs to be clearly defined financial obligations of the LGFVs and the scope of central government's responsibility in order to protect public-sector finances. Bonds gaining prominence: Hard-currency share still substantial but shift toward local currency visible If we consider the wider Asia-Pacific region, infrastructure bonds accounted for a sizeable 20% of global issues over the period 2000–2013, compared with 41% in North America, 21% from Europe (including 4% of emerging Europe) and 15% from Latin America. The vast majority of infrastructure bonds have been issued in local currency (LCY). Of the USD 590 bn in infrastructure bonds issued since 1990 by companies in five large NJA countries, 18 88% were issued in LCY, with a sharp rise in the LCY share since 2001.

(7) *Types of PPP*

Given the importance of the PPP structure in the OBOR context, and the expected uptake of the PPP model in facilitating OBOR projects, it is worthwhile to touch on what exactly is meant by the term "public-private partnership." It does not have a fixed legal meaning per se, nor is there one clearly defined framework for a project to be deemed to fit within the PPP model. The general premise is that it is a term used to describe a wide variety of arrangements involving the collaboration and cooperation between the public and private sectors. There is no single or "standard" form of PPP project or structure. A PPP project can essentially take whatever form the parties desire in order to meet the objectives of the project in question. Below we describe some of the common variations of the PPP model which have evolved over the years and of the use of the broader PPP structure.

(8) *BOT (build-operate-transfer)*

Under a BOT mandate the contractor will take the asset right from the construction phase through a fixed operating life, typically for a period of 20–25 years, following which the asset is transferred to the host government. BOTs tend to be favoured by governments as design,

---

(*Continued*)

(Continued)

construction and operating risk are all transferred to the private sector. Similarly, for the private sector there are incentives towards efficiency in terms of both time and cost. They can also have certainty around revenue streams with a single offtaker/customer in the form of the relevant government. On the downside, the private cost of financing a BOT is often seen as an impediment vis-à-vis the publicly funded models which can be cheaper on the back of the availability of cheap public finance.

(9) *BTO*

Conceptually the key difference between a BTO and BOT project is that the relevant asset is transferred to the government from the time construction is completed. Following transfer of the asset the private party still maintains rights to operate the asset for a fixed period of time in order to recover its investment and make a profit. The BTO model is often employed over the BOT model where there are legal or regulatory impediments to the private party owning the assets over a long period of time.

(10) *BOO*

The BOO structure is similar to BOT and BTO; however, at the end of the relevant concession period the private party does not automatically have to transfer the asset to the government. Likewise the obligations of the government will usually cease at the conclusion of the concession period. At this point the private party can assess the relevant options at the time, which includes extending the contract in place, negotiating a new contract, selling the asset or ceasing operation altogether where the asset is no longer able to produce a meaningful output. As a general rule BOOs are more common where the project is deemed to be a higher risk project and/ or where significant future investment is likely.

(11) *ROT (rehabilitate-operate-transfer)*

This is similar to the BTO arrangement; however, it involves the rehabilitation or upgrade of an existing facility rather than the construction of a new facility. Following rehabilitation or upgrade, the concessionaire operates the facility in the same way as a BOT and then transfers it back to government.

4.4 Innovative Financing, Alternative Project Funding and the Opportunities for Public–Private Partnership

4.4.1 *Innovative Financing*

Innovative financing is the manifestation of two important trends in international development: an increased focus on programs that deliver results and a desire to support collaboration between the public and private sectors.

Innovative financing encompasses a broad range of financial instruments and assets including securities and derivatives, results-based financing and voluntary or compulsory contributions — all of which this chapter explores in more detail. Established financial instruments, such as guarantees and bonds, constitute nearly 65% of the innovative financing market; while new products dominate many conversations about innovative financing, most resources mobilized through innovative financing use existing products in new markets or involve new investors. Our definition of the "innovation" aspect of innovative financing includes the introduction of new products, the extension of existing products to new markets and the presence of new types of investors.

Often, innovative financing instruments re-allocate risks from investors to institutions better positioned to bear the risk and, in the process, enable participation from mainstream investors. Instruments that have mobilized significant resources benefit from relatively simple financial structures and a proven track record that clearly describes the financial and social returns for investors.

4.4.2 *Innovative Financing is Critical to Creating Opportunities for Public–Private Sector Collaboration That Will Help Address Global Challenges*

Innovative financing has several benefits compared to traditional financial approaches.

Some examples are as follows:

Deploys significant, new private sector capital to either government official direct assistance (ODA) or private philanthropic contributions. Successful mechanisms often channel resources to projects that would not otherwise receive them. For example, guarantees that enable investments in public goods (such as infrastructure) and impact investing funds that support small and medium enterprises, which might otherwise struggle to access capital.

Transforms financial assets through financial structuring and intermediation to meet the needs of development programs by distributing risk, enhancing liquidity, reducing volatility and avoiding timing mismatches. Innovative financing mechanisms channel funds from people and institutions that want to make investments to projects that require more resources than traditional donors and philanthropies can provide. For example, green bonds and other thematic bonds provide capital to support investments in low-carbon infrastructure such as wind farms, sustainable forestry management and urban infrastructure. In addition, innovative financing mechanisms such as the Pledge Guarantee for Health provide bridge financing for projects and institutions during the gap period between when resources are committed and resources are disbursed.

Supports a cooperative public–private sector approach to scale socially beneficial operations that require significant capital outlays and traditionally sit squarely in the realm of the public sector. In many sectors — such as health, financial services and agriculture — private companies with the expertise to design, produce, market and distribute new products are crucial to creating social change. Innovative financing mechanisms can adjust incentives to encourage private companies to make the investments necessary to create new products and enter new markets. For example, the advance market commitment sponsored by GAVI reallocated demand risk for pneumococcal vaccines in developing countries, which allowed pharmaceutical companies to produce more vaccines at scale and dramatically lower the vaccine's cost per dose.

Definition of innovative financing[15]

> **World Bank**
>
> *"Innovative financing involves non-traditional applications of solidarity, public private partnerships, and catalytic mechanisms that (i) support fundraising by tapping new sources and engaging investors beyond the financial dimension of transactions, as partners and stakeholders in development; or (ii) deliver financial solutions to development problems on the ground."*
>
> Source: World Bank, Innovating Development Finance: From Financing Sources to Financial Solutions, 2009.
>
> **Organisation for Economic Co-operation and Development (OECD)**
>
> *"Innovative financing comprises mechanisms of raising funds or stimulating actions in support of international development that go beyond traditional spending approaches by either the official or private sectors, such as:*
>
> 1) *new approaches for pooling private and public revenue streams to scale up or develop activities for the benefit of partner countries;*
> 2) *new revenue streams (e.g., a new tax, charge, fee, bond raising, sale proceed or voluntary contribution scheme) earmarked to developmental activities on a multi-year basis; and*
> 3) *new incentives (financial guarantees, corporate social responsibility or other rewards or recognition) to address market failures or scale up ongoing developmental activities."*
>
> Source: OECD, Innovative Financing to Fund Development: Progress and Prospects, 2009.

4.4.3 Alternative Project Funding

The trend of seeking private investment to build infrastructure assets without huge public capital expenditures began in the 1990s in the United Kingdom and then spread steadily throughout the West. In Asia,

---

[15] Innovative Financing Initiative is an initiative of the Global Development Incubator, www.globaldevincubator.org.

however, a lack of confidence in emerging regulatory frameworks, inconsistent risk allocation and the need for a dependable pipeline of credible projects greatly inhibited private investment. With B&R, however, China has the opportunity to break new ground, as the country looks to reinforce its position as the world's largest construction market and infrastructure investor. The rise of PPPs and joint ventures has expanded opportunities for firms across the construction industry, particularly in Asia. Projects that would be too big or risky for a single firm can become a good financial bet when tackled by a consortium. The key to attracting private investors in a large infrastructure project like those associated with B&R lies in the ability of project owners, planners, developers and operators to structure and execute projects in a way that allows for ownership, risk and expertise to be shared. And, the quickest way to accomplish this goal is to partner with companies that have a proven track record of enabling 3Ps to deliver the highest levels of accountability and achieve complete transparency.[16]

4.5 Hong Kong — The Right Corporate Treasury Center (CTC) for the B&R Initiative

4.5.1 *The B&R Initiative Needs an Important Financial Place*

As the B&R Initiative covers over 60 countries, this implies complex corporate treasury operations that include such elements as cash-flow management, foreign exchange, cross-border payments, risks and liability control.

Therefore, a regional CTC would be required to centralize all treasury functions so that multinational corporations can enhance operational efficiency, reduce foreign exchange exposure and risk, as well as achieve economies of scale in treasury operations. The B&R needs an international financial center and a global investment hub, a sort of ideal platform for capital formation and financing for global investors under

---

[16] David Cheung, Vice President of Key Accounts, Asia at Aconex. December 2016.

the B&R Initiative, with a diversity of financing channels in place, including Equity listing, Syndicated loans, Private equity funds, Dim Sum bonds and Islamic bonds.

The B&R needs a financial place that can provide countries with the capital required for infrastructure construction under the Initiative. In addition, this financial place will be able to provide a wide range of financial services such as asset management, risk management, offshore RMB business, corporate treasury services and insurance services to countries along the B&R.

The B&R Initiative, which is to promote the internationalization of the renminbi, needs a sizable and market-determined renminbi-denominated debt market. This is essential to encourage non-resident corporates and investors to hold and use renminbi. The absence of large and liquid capital markets (debt, equities, derivative and money markets) offshore has hindered the global expansion of the renminbi. There is an urgent need for Mainland China to either establish a sizable debt market offshore or open up its onshore debt market as soon as possible.

4.5.2 *Is Hong Kong Ready for This Role?*

Hong Kong's vast and diverse investor base includes 201 authorized institutions, 158 insurance and reinsurance companies, and 594 Hong Kong-domiciled SFC approved funds. It is perhaps noteworthy that in 2014, more than 70% of the combined fund management businesses with some US$2.3 trillion in asset were sourced from overseas investors. Hong Kong is already a premier CTC in Asia. Hong Kong's advantage lies in its well-developed financial infrastructure. More importantly, its proximity to Mainland China and its position as a premier offshore renminbi center makes Hong Kong a preferred location for fulfilling B&R projects. For all these reasons, Hong Kong is the first choice by far in Asia for many corporations, especially Chinese firms, to raise funds. Hong Kong, is well placed to help international companies explore the B&R Initiative's potential by playing the role of a "super-connector" and facilitator. As the Initiative aims to help in building new and upgrading existing facilities, it will create business opportunities for various sectors including finance and investment, professional and infrastructure services, dispute resolution, maritime and logistics services and other business support services.

Hong Kong's professional and infrastructural development services sectors are unique in Asia in terms of their international business orientation, depth of service, expertise and professionalism. Hong Kong excels in such professional services as accounting, legal, investment environment and risk assessment, construction and project management, making it an ideal place for the provision of consultancy, legal and accountancy services as well as the operation and management of projects along the B&R.

As more Chinese mainland companies are "going out" to invest in regions along the B&R, Hong Kong can provide related professional services to enhance its role as a platform for mainland companies "going out."[17]

4.6 Concept of Connectivity in Order to Close the Financial Gap

4.6.1 *Maximizing Financial Connectivity*

Financial connectivity is essential. It empowers you to trade anywhere, with anyone. In FINTECK (finance and technology), connectivity enables to expand globally and to stay relevant to your customers. It is time for the FINTECK industry to progress beyond traditional A-to-B transaction processing. Financial institutions possess enormous amounts of valuable information, but they typically only expose or exploit the absolute minimum data required when processing payment transactions.[18]

4.6.1.1 Connectivity Means Consistency

Consistent financial connectivity is not a commodity. In order to meet market demands, you need to provide your customers with maximum financial reach for minimum effort. Offering a range of disparate

---

[17] By Henrik Raber, Global Head, Capital Markets, Standard Chartered. The article was "revisited" by the authors of this chapter.

[18] By Zhong Nan in Dalian, Liaoning province, chinadaily.com.cn (June 2017).

payment methods is one thing; normalizing the interface on the technical side, and for the user, to deliver a seamless payment experience, is quite another.

4.6.1.2 Connectivity Means Efficiency

As payments become increasingly strategic, thinking of a transaction as simply an instantaneous operation is a major oversight. Connectivity helps you look at your payment data from a business perspective, enhancing marketing and sales, as well as an operational perspective, informing risk management and financial optimization. Analyzing rich data about geolocation, web browsers, operating systems and hardware devices gives you the power to identify where the most fraud comes from and to plan mitigating measures accordingly. From a sales perspective, rich data helps you spot technical or usability issues that lead to checkout flows being abandoned by customers, empowering you to fix the problem, increasing your conversion rate. Taking a step further, dealing with inevitable exceptions such as declined transactions, order cancellations, refunds and disputes becomes painless.

4.6.1.3 Connectivity is a Commodity

Today's financial ecosystem demands a new approach, whereby formerly competitive institutions must collaborate to succeed. Customers have become accustomed to being offered multiple payment options and leveraging multiple payment schemes and acquirers is now essential. While having access to many payment partners increases the range of capabilities you can offer your customers, implementing them all in a deep and consistent manner within existing technology is often impeded by legacy infrastructure challenges.

4.6.1.4 More Financial Connectivity is Urged

Senior officials from international financial institutions have urged governments and companies to accelerate the pace of financial connectivity and build closer relations with the private sector to participate in infrastructure projects related to the Belt and Road Initiative. Deputy Managing Director of IMF, Zhang Tao, said measures including cross-border payment and mobile banking products, as well as relaxing financing supply restrictions would encourage financial institutions to provide more support to the real economy in markets related to the initiative. Modern technologies can provide relatively cheaper methods to low-income households to use basic financial products and people who do not have access to the banks. Regarding the development of the Belt and Road Initiative, the IMF will establish a new skills training center in Singapore and other countries involved in the initiative soon. The IMF has already set up one skills training center in Dalian last month (May, 2017) in partnership with the People's Bank of China. To avoid taking on too much risk in countries that have limited access for big-ticket infrastructure project financing, Zhang said all international investors should target countries with stable financial markets, ensure there is sufficient capital flowing in and have flexible policies to manage currency and foreign reserves. Vice-President of the Asian Infrastructure Investment Bank (AIIB), Danny Alexander, said PPPs are another way to finance the Belt and Road Initiative and the bank will help related parties to spread this model in Asia, Southeast Asia and Middle East. AIIB announced earlier this month that it has approved three applicants including Argentina and Madagascar to join the bank, bringing the bank's total approved membership to 80.

4.6.2 *Connectivity to Achieve a Large Investment Demand*

The key to financial connectivity is the mutual opening of financial and capital markets, including accelerating local currency settlement for infrastructure development, strengthening bilateral or multilateral currency swaps, and prudently widening the scope for such swaps. It also included increasing support to each other in such areas as overseas mergers and acquisition, overseas market development, technology upgrades, resource and energy acquisition and intellectual property rights, and expanding investments in each other's assets with foreign exchange reserves.[19]

---

[19] Norman Sze, Deloitte China.

4.6.2.1 It Is Important to Harness the Power of Financial Technology (Fintech)

A good example is the rapid growth of mobile banking, which has boosted the economic well-being of hundreds of millions of citizens — from Bangladesh, to Kenya, to Peru. Here in China — in cities like Beijing and Hangzhou — people can live without cash by using online payment platform such as Alipay and Wechat. Another example is the rapid increase in cross-border payments based on virtual currencies. For many companies and households, this is a faster and cheaper way of transferring money overseas. These benefits are significant — but so are the challenges, including the risk of money laundering and terrorist financing. Fintech providers, financial regulators, central bankers and international organizations will need to work together to ensure that financial systems are safe and inclusive. More broadly, IMF analysis shows that having a more inclusive financial system makes it safer — and more beneficial —to relax restrictions on capital flows across borders. By liberalizing their capital account over time, countries can attract more foreign investment, increase the liquidity of local financial markets, and reduce their cost of capital. In other words, by developing deep, well-regulated financial markets, countries can better mobilize domestic and international resources for investment, while reducing the financial stability risks that come with large capital inflows.

4.7 Alternative B&R Funding: The Islamic Finance

Islamic finance is a centuries-old practice that is gaining recognition throughout the world and whose ethical nature is even drawing the interest of non-Muslims. Given the increased wealth in Muslim nations, expect this field to undergo an even more rapid evolution as it continues to address the challenges of reconciling the disparate worlds of theology and modern portfolio theory.[20]

Islamic finance's emphasis on equity and investment in the real economy provides "a stable and productive banking sector." "Rather than

---

[20] http://www.investopedia.com/terms/m/modernportfoliotheory.asp.

providing a lucrative financial alternative to investing in the real economy, Islamic banking complements and strengthens the latter." "It ensures that financial capital does not lead to artificially bloated asset prices. Instead, it is made to work in the real economy, on real projects." With so much damage caused by highly complex and risky financial structures untethered to assets, it is hardly surprising that more and more investors are attracted to Islamic finance's emphasis on real assets and greater certainty.[21]

4.7.1 *Islamic Finance Part of the B&R Funding Strategy*

Initiating investment and developing economic trade communications with Islamic countries is one of the important components of the B&R strategy, and this is detailed in the "Vision and Actions on jointly building the Silk Road Economic Belt and 21st-century Maritime Silk Road" published by the government on March 28, 2015 (*Vision and Actions*).

Compared to traditional financial products, Islamic finance has developed significantly due to its high flexibility of business, low risk, low debt requirements and the need to use real estate as collateral. In 2014, Sharia compliant financial institutions represented approximately 1% of total world assets, at around US$2 trillion. The latest study shows that, by 2020, the value of the global Islamic financial market will rise to US$3.25 trillion. As a background to the strategic execution of the B&R, state-owned and private enterprises in China are also trying to make use of Islamic finance, as against traditional finance, to serve their own overseas development. Chinese banks are strengthening their cooperation with Muslim countries, and are busy developing their overseas business and outbound investment. Islamic finance is rapidly becoming an established channel for China to enlarge its overseas economic influence.

Under the B&R, China is considering using Islamic finance as a breakthrough to initiate extensive business communication and project cooperation in many areas with Middle East and Southeast Asian countries. It is considering opening outbound Islamic financing institutions,

---

[21] Kamal Munir, is Associate Professor of Strategy and Policy at Cambridge University's Judge Business School.

and participating in the investment in these regions or developing enterprises which operate through Islamic financing products. This is not only safer for funds and better for comprehensive income, but also improves the long-term benefits. Following the initiation of the B&R, it is now developing the practical stages, and there will be a significant increase in the use of Islamic financing tools and investment in major construction projects. If the Chinese government could enhance its cooperation with Muslim countries through Islamic finance, it will significantly progress in the development of the Silk Road project.[22]

4.7.2 *China and the Islamic Finance: Already Collaborating*

In the past two years, Agricultural Bank of China, Bank of China and Industrial and Commercial Bank of China have issued conventional bonds listed on NASDAQ Dubai, reflecting their appetite to expand business in the Middle East and benefit from growing trade and investment ties between China and the Gulf. The expectation (and hope) is that *sukuk* issuances by Chinese state-owned enterprises and private companies will follow in the not too distant future and Dubai will be ideally positioned to act as the hub through which both Islamic and conventional investments into China can be routed from the wider Gulf region.

Through B&R, which is overseen by China's National Development and Reform Commission, Ministry of Commerce and the State Council, China is, among other things, taking a significant step on the path to using Islamic finance to build business relationships and foster increased

---

[22] Du Baozhong is a senior legal counsel in the Beijing office of Yingke Law Firm. He had been working for the Department of Treaty and Law in China's Ministry of Commerce for 13 years. Du, as the delegation member of Chinese Government, has participated in the working group meetings held by the Commission on International Trade of the United Nations several times. He is specialized in foreign direct investment, outbound investment, international trade, private equity, venture capital, mergers and acquisitions, foreign-related arbitration, labor law, etc.

Li Xuan is working as a trainee in the International Legal Affairs Department of the Beijing office of Yingke Law Firm, and also acts as the coordinator of Yingke Brussels Office. She used to work in-house in an international shipping company, responsible for marine insurance and admiralty laws.

cooperation on projects with the Middle East and the Muslim majority Southeast Asian countries.

Islamic finance is gaining prominence as a channel for China to expand its economic influence abroad (as Chinese domestic banks continue to develop their overseas businesses and outbound investments) and strengthen ties with Muslim majority countries, and as a means for Chinese entities to raise financing offshore through previously untapped markets. To put things into context, the value of assets held in Sharia compliant financial institutions is currently estimated as representing approximately 1% of total world assets (about US$2 trillion) and the value of the global Islamic financial market is expected to increase to around US$3 trillion by 2020. China wants a slice of this pie, and Dubai is one of the best equipped financial centers in the world to provide it.

4.7.2.1 Dubai — The Hub for the Islamic Finance

The UAE, through Dubai, is already recognized as a regional financial hub for the Middle East, North Africa and sub-Saharan Africa. It has also made great strides in the past 10 years toward achieving its target of becoming the capital of the global Islamic economy. Already, Dubai, through Nasdaq Dubai, has overtaken Malaysia and London as the world's leading center for international *sukuk* listings. The UAE's banks (both conventional and Islamic) are also some of the best capitalized in the Middle East.[23]

About Islamic finance (*WORLD ECONOMIC FORUM*) "What is Islamic Finance"

> The most obvious difference when compared with Western banks is that Islamic finance is forbidden to charge interest. Under Sharia law, money is only a way of defining the value of something and has no value in itself. Therefore, money isn't allowed to generate more money by being put into a bank account or lent to someone else.
>
> Instead, banks make their money by sharing the risk of their investments with investors, operating on a profit-loss basis.

(Continued)

---

[23] Debashis Dey: The author is a Partner at White & Case in their Dubai office.

(*Continued*)

So rather than making money by offering loans or mortgages and charging an interest rate on them, a sharia-compliant bank would use its depositors' money to acquire assets, and then share any profits made on those assets with the depositors.

Because the bank is sharing the risk of investments with its depositors, high degrees of uncertainty — known as ghar — are not allowed. All possible risks must be identified to investors, and all relevant information disclosed. Another condition of Islamic finance is that these investments must be made in things that exist in the real world, such as properties or businesses although the businesses must not be associated with gambling, alcohol or tobacco. These investments must be made on an ownership basis, to avoid the risk of future unavailability.

What is a Sukuk?

A Sukuk is a sharia-compliant bond. Whereas Western bonds offer to pay bondholders a rate of interest over a set period of time, Sukuks offer a fixed rate of profit. Sukuks come in a variety of forms, with Al-Ijara being one of the most common structures. The Al-Ijara structure is essentially Islamic finance's version of a lease. Under an Al-Ijara Sukuk, ownership of the asset is transferred to the bondholder and the asset is leased back to the issuer, with the bondholder charging a "rent" for use of the asset during the time period of the bond. At the end of the time-period, when the bond reaches maturity, ownership of the asset transfers back to the issuer.

Source: WORLD ECONOMIC FORUM, www.weforum.org/agendov/2017/05/what-is-islamic-finance

4.8 Alternative B&R Funding: The Crowdfunding

4.8.1 *Government Incentivized Crowdfunding for the B&R Initiative*[24]

Local, state and federal governments have started exploring the potential of crowdfunding in transforming conventional financing methods used

---

[24] See Chang Heon Lee, J. Leon Zhao and Ghazwan Hassna, Department of Information Systems, City University of Hong Kong, Kowloon, Hong Kong SAR.

previously to fund public projects and services. While crowdfunding has been applied to improve government financing methods in recent years, little is known about how this new model can be extended and applied in international collaboration among government incentivized projects. The utilization of crowdfunding in public sectors offers many advantages, little is known about how crowdfunding can be extended or adapted in the government or public sector. However, few studies have investigated how crowdfunding can be extended into the public sector to support local, state and federal government-initiated public projects. Thus, this section studies what roles crowdfunding can play as a financial intermediary to support government-incentivized projects launched under B&R Initiatives. We conjecture that crowdfunding can offer an efficient mechanism to improve participatory budgeting, facilitate private–public collaboration and achieve transparency. Particularly, in this section, we address the following questions: (1) How can crowdfunding be extended as a mechanism to support government-incentivized projects? (2) What components of crowdfunding technology can be used in financing government-incentivized projects?

4.8.1.1 How Can Crowdfunding Help Support Government-incentivized Projects?

Considering the capabilities that crowdfunding has demonstrated during the last few years, and taking into account the emerging needs and goals of the governments today, we believe that crowdfunding can play a vital role in providing an alternative source of funding for government-incentivized projects. Furthermore, it can offer a mechanism for boosting the participatory budgeting approach by empowering citizens, enabling high levels of transparency over the budgeting and financing processes and encouraging public–private collaboration.

4.8.1.2 Boosting Participatory Budgeting

Previous research suggests that sound public participation practices can aid governments to be more open, transparent, and responsive.[25] Further, such

---

[25] Anwar Shah, *Participatory Budgeting*, The World Bank, 2007. Available at: http://siteresources.worldbank.org/PSGLP/Resources/ParticipatoryBudgeting.pd.

practices can enhance the citizen opinions of government performance.[26] Citizens usually value what the public receives from the government when they are actively engaged in the process of participatory budgeting. In other words, the budget participation feature of crowdfunding plays a critical role where governments typically lack resources, such as human and knowledge resources. This flexibility utilized in government-incentivized crowdfunding can provide the opportunity to engage diverse participants — including the citizens, the private partners and the government.

4.8.1.3 Encouraging Private–Public Collaboration

We conjecture that crowdfunding can serve a crucial function in promoting public–private engagement, essentially stimulating not only a constructive relationship but also a partnership with citizens, communities and governments.[27,28] Previous studies show that governments frequently lack sufficient resources to produce public or community services, and the incentives of the market may not align with those of the communities. Crowdfunding encourages not only simultaneous public–private engagement but also makes the selection procedures of such projects more efficient. However, in the early stages of expansion, civic crowdfunding had promising potential to support PPP, and more broadly to enhance private–public collaboration due to its potential impact on the engagement of diverse entities from both private and public sectors.

4.8.1.4 Improving Transparency of Budgeting and Financing Processes

It is widely acknowledged that crowdfunding has evolved to improve transparency in term of information disclosure and exchange since information

---

[26] Yves Sintomer, Carsten Herzberg and Allegretti Röcke, Participatory Budgeting in Europe: Potentials and Challenges, *International Journal of Urban and Regional Research*, Vol. 32, No. 1, 2008, 164–178.

[27] Othmar M. Lehner, Crowdfunding Social Ventures: A Model and Research Agenda, *Venture Capital*, Vol. 15, No. 4, 2013, 289–311.

[28] Angelo Miglietta, Emanuele Parisi, Matteo Pessione, Flavio Servato, Crowdfunding and Local Governments: A Financial Opportunity for a New Liaison with Citizens. In: Toulon-Verona Conference "Excellence in Services", 2014.

visibility is closely associated with accountability of crowdfunding. For government-incentivized projects, budget is an essential information element that lays out a government's economic priority. Budget transparency refers to the full information disclosures about government allocation and is viewed as a fundamental requirement for public accountability.[29]

4.8.1.5 Crowdfunding for the B&R Initiative

In the context of the B&R Initiative, many projects will be required to build specific parts of the planned infrastructure. To execute such projects, governments will be facing two scenarios: governments already have the necessary funding to finance these projects, or they are not able to fund them due to lack of funds. For the first scenario, the most significant challenge for governments is to make sure that the funds go to the right project at the right time. In the second scenario, considering that governments do not have the funds to support these projects, conventional approaches to obtaining funds for such projects include either seeking funds from international financing institutes (e.g. the Silk Road Infrastructure Fund, Asian Infra Investment Bank, or New Development Bank) or searching for an alternative way of collecting funds to fulfill this need. In both scenarios, transparency and accountability are required in addition to a high level of citizen participation in decision-making. One of the most important aspects of crowdfunding as a sub-domain of crowdsourcing is the utilization of the collective intelligence of the crowd. Crowdfunding in this regard can be seen as a collaborative activity involving the collection and utilization of ideas and insights from crowds. In B&R Initiative contexts, governments can utilize the power of crowdfunding and the collective intelligence to generate more creative and innovative ideas for projects that can support the initiative. Crowdfunding can play a role in encouraging citizens' involvement in the context of B&R Initiatives by empowering citizens from the different participating countries to have more control over these processes while providing a high level of transparency. Based on this argument, we present here

---

[29] Catharina Lindstedt and Daniel Naurin, Transparency Is Not Enough: Making Transparency Effective in Reducing Corruption. *International Political Science Review*, Vol. 31, No. 3, 2010, 301–322.

four different approaches in which crowdfunding can be applied to support projects in the B&R Initiative. Approaches are categorized based on the type of project initiator (i.e. public vs. private) and the type of collected funds (i.e. purely from the crowd vs. partially from the crowd with matched funds from the government).

4.8.1.6 Supported-pull Approach: Supported Citizen-To-Citizens Crowdfunding

Citizens or third parties may suggest and list projects that contribute to the B&R Initiative and seek funds from the crowd exactly as in the previous approach. Citizens from the participating countries will select projects that most reflect their interests and needs. When projects reach a specific amount of accumulated funds representing the citizens' interest in those projects, governments may decide to support those projects by providing matching funds that enable those projects to reach their goals.

4.8.1.7 Culture-sensitive Platform Design

In the context of B&R Initiative, crowdfunding might remove the distance-related tension so that citizens from different countries can contribute to the projects from other countries in the same initiative. The initiative aims at linking 65 countries belonging to three continents (i.e. Asia, Europe and Africa) with distinctively different languages and cultures. Even though crowdfunding can help bridge the distance-related gaps, language and cultural differences may create a barrier to fully utilizing the power of crowdfunding. Extant literature suggests that culture can have serious implications for website adoption, usability, trust, satisfaction, and loyalty.[30,31] In our B&R context, culture may create different challenges to the acceptance, adoption, and use of the online crowdfunding platform in general and

---

[30] Dianne Cyr, Carole Bonanni, John Bowes and Joe Ilsever, Beyond Trust: Website Design Preferences Across Cultures, *Journal of Global Information Management*, Vol. 13, No. 4, 2005, 25.

[31] Dianne Cyr, Milena Head, Hector Larios and Bing Pan, Exploring Human Images in Website Design: A Multi-Method Approach. *MIS Quarterly*, Vol. 33, No. 3, 2009, 539–566. Available at: http://www.jstor.org/stable/20650308.

in the browsing, selection and funding of crowdfunding projects listed on the platform in particular. Citizens coming from different cultures may behave in different ways regarding the adoption and use of the platform. A solution for such arising challenges can be the adoption of the recommendations provided by previous literature in the domain of web design.[32] Among the recommendations is the localization of the website design to respond to the cultural sensitivity. In this process, not only idiomatic language translation is required, but also other details such as time zones, currency, culturally desired colors, the name of the product or service, the roles different genders can play and the examples related to the geography.

4.8.1.8 Social Inequality and Crowdfunding

As civic crowdfunding may democratize financial markets, there might be unintended or unforeseen consequences resulting from this funding phenomenon. It is important to examine whether public crowdfunding could improve or worsen social inequality. There are concerns that civic crowdfunding could further broaden social inequalities, i.e. wealthy communities may benefit disproportionately from civic or public projects, while poor neighborhoods may not obtain social benefits from the combination of government funding and private financial support. Recent research shows that the distribution of civic projects such as infrastructures and community development is deeply skewed and unevenly distributed such that a majority of funding transactions for civic projects are more concentrated in metropolitan areas than in rural areas.[33]

---

[32]Yu-Ming Li, Yung-Shao Yeh, Increasing Trust in Mobile Commerce through Design Aesthetics. *Computers in Human Behaviour*, Vol. 26, No. 4, 2010, 673–684.

[33]Chang Heon Lee (CHL), J. Leon Zhao (LZ) and Ghazwan Hassna (GH), *Financial Innovation*, 2016. CHL and LZ developed the central idea of the research and contributed to the conceptualization of the study. CHL and GH have been involved in drafting the manuscript. All authors read and approved the paper. This article is distributed under the terms of the Creative Commons Attribution 4.0 International License which permits unrestricted use, distribution, and reproduction in any medium, provided you give appropriate credit to the original author(s) and the source, provide a link to the Creative Commons license, and indicate if changes were made.

CHAPTER 5

Global Implications of the "B&R" Initiative and Its Impact on the EU Economy

Cristiano Rizzi

5.1 China as an Essential Partner in Global Governance

It is evident that China is now playing a more important role at the international stage in particular thanks to its growing economic importance. China is now seeking for a more proactive role in developing the B&R Initiative and trying to involve third countries to participate in this project because in doing so China will enhance its relationships with those countries. This at the same time implies assuming new responsibilities and also a leading role in developing a new growing model which needs the contribution of the rest of the world to be successfully implemented and to work properly. China, in fact, is imposing itself as a new model of sustainable economic growth, but this needs the indulgence of a more close cooperation not only with international organizations like the World Bank or the International Monetary Fund to adjust its policies and achieve its targets but also with the international community and its trade partners to put in place its plans. In doing so, China is becoming an essential partner in the global governance. Its influence on the rest of the world is a natural consequence of the development of its economy, and the gradual implementation of the B&R Initiative will only highlight the necessity for a greater integration at the international level. This can create some friction on some determined issues, but definitely with the participation of China in solving other problems, like climate change, which is having a global impact, it will be easier to reach a win–win situation with the rest of the world.

5.1.1 *The Weight of the B&R Initiative in Rebalancing the World Economy*

China's plans, and especially the B&R Initiative, inevitably will have an impact on the world economy. It is not difficult to imagine that China's growing economic importance will influence the world economy, and with its Initiative China is going to enhance trade relations with the countries along the Silk Road (both land and maritime). It can be affirmed that China's Initiative also represents a new model of economic cooperation which will contribute to rebalancing the world economy, but it is not a response to America's moves in the Asia-Pacific or to Russia's Eurasian Union (EEU).[1] China is simply trying to reinvigorate trade relationships, not only with neighbors, but in a more wide vision, its plan is also to reinforce connections with the EU. Furthermore, B&R Initiative should be seen as a tool in the rapprochement between Asian and European economies.

It is interesting to note that Western economies, and in particular the US, for some scholars, were responsible for the global economic and political imbalances that led to the global financial crisis. China should work to "rebalance" these imbalances through the B&R Initiative. However, it is clear that to save the West is not the scope of this Initiative. "China's priority should be to cooperate with developing countries, in particular with the countries along the Silk Road, and take on its responsibilities as the largest developing country so as to push for a partial reform of global

---

[1] This is also the opinion expressed by Li Ziguo, Deputy Director of the "One Belt, One Road" research centre, which is affiliated to the Ministry of Foreign Affair's China Institute of International Studies (CIIS).

governance and international cooperation."[2] This is something which is already happening. As we mentioned in the previous chapter, projects have been proposed and financial institutions, such as the AIIB, are actively involved in financing the B&R Initiative. Moreover, the B&R Initiative can be seen as a strategic bridge between China and the countries involved in the B&R, but in particular with the EU. In fact, the EU is focusing more and more on Asia and China for economic reasons, and partially disengaging from the US–Europe relations. It is of particular significance that the UK, which is the US's closest ally, even if it has left the EU, has joined the AIIB because it is evident there will be more opportunities of strength also trade ties with China. In response to this and because other European countries are involved in the B&R Initiative, China is actively promoting its Initiative and working to overcome the obstacles of distance and connect in a more solid manner with Europe. EU and Chinese representatives discussing the new bilateral investment agreement between the two blocs should keep in mind this Initiative and adjust the final outcome of their negotiations in order to favor investments connected to the B&R Initiative.

5.1.2 *Overcoming Obstacles*

It is not surprising if some projects encounter obstacles. The development of the B&R Initiative implies full cooperation with the authorities of the hosting countries in order to eliminate legal obstacles and problems of administrative nature. As the B&R Initiative is not a foreign aid program, but rather a commercial project which requires participating countries to make a long-term commitment and contribute investment, China has to work with them to find the smartest solutions to implement its plan and realize all the infrastructures needed to complete this ambitious project.

To this end, the Chinese leadership has called for better coordination among participating countries, and the "B&R Forum" held in Beijing in May 2017 is a clear example of these efforts; however, in order to achieve this China needs to articulate clearly the mutual economic benefits of the

---

[2]This is the opinion of Zheng Yongnian, a scholar from Singapore, who contributed to the article published by the European Council on Foreign Relation, "One Belt, One Road": China's Great Leap Outward," June 2015.

Initiative and demonstrate through existing projects that the B&R Initiative will create jobs, improve trade connections and improve living standards. This is of paramount importance for China; in fact if China cannot succeed in "marketing" its Initiative in this sense, reaping the benefit will be difficult. For instance, Chinese companies leading the investments or seeking to participate in different projects need to gain more experience and knowledge in operating and investing in B&R countries, and they also need to navigate in new and different jurisdictions, not to mention also understand specific local rules and laws governing this specific sector, i.e. infrastructure sector. In order to overcome all these obstacles, cooperating with local professionals in the legal area is also a must for Chinese companies willing to contribute to this Initiative.

5.1.3 *China — A New Type of Rising Power?*

It is evident that China, with the implementation of the B&R Initiative, is showing off its muscles, especially in financial terms. However, this should not threaten third countries. On the contrary, China has shown its interests in strengthening relationships, especially trade relationships, with its neighborhood, and in doing this China is also allocating its enormous financial resources. Although it seems appropriate to argue that the implementation of B&R can be compared to a kind of "rise" of China, it is certainly a "peaceful rise." This in any case is not a completely new concept in terms of methodology, i.e. constructing new infrastructures. *De facto,* China is already conquering third countries through the acquisitions of desired foreign companies in order to expand its presence abroad and penetrate new markets. This trend was extensively explained and examined in a dedicated work titled *Chinese Expansion in the EU — Strategies and Policies of the Two Blocks and the Role of the U.S.*[3]; however with this new move China aims at connecting herself with the countries along the B&R in a more deep and constructive manners, and not just to enhance trade relationships with them. Also, this project aims at creating a more interconnected world in particular in Asia, like it was

---

[3]Cristiano Rizzi, Paolo Rizzi, Lex Smith and Li Guo, *Chinese Expansion in the EU — Strategies and Policies of the Two Blocks and the Role of the U.S.*, American Bar Association, August 2016.

for the EU before the UK decided to leave it. It is natural that other countries see in this initiative a "rise" of China because in doing this China is using its capitals and financial resources, and China is also making use of all its connections and especially of its influence in order to make sure this project can go ahead and produce all the results China hopes to harvest. This initiative will benefit not only China but also all the third parties involved. China is assuming a leading role in developing this Initiative not only because it is its own project but also because as a developing country herself China is interested in completing these infrastructure projects which will have a huge impact in poorer countries connected to the B&R. Considering all these, it is not surprising at all if China is assuming a greater importance; however, this Initiative should not be confused with the new Marshall Plan[4] (which was limited to some countries), this Initiative is open to anyone who wants to participate, and it is presented as an unconditional plan to assist in the development of China's neighbors, regardless of their current relationship with China.

5.1.4 *The Importance of the B&R Initiative for the EU: Introduction*

The B&R Initiative represents an opportunity for Europe not only to enhance relations with Asian countries and in particular with China, but also to boost its economy. No doubt the entire Europe will benefit from this Initiative, and we have already introduced the "OBOReurope" (3.3). Here we want to stress that Europe, because of experiencing economic difficulties over the past years and because the crisis is not completely over, is looking for a new stimulus, and the B&R is definitely an opportunity to grasp. Besides, in spite of its depressed economic situation, the EU member states have plenty of funds available for investments, and they are looking for more profitable opportunities; this is also one of the reasons why a number of the EU members joined the AIIB.[5] Given the growing

---

[4]The Marshall Plan for the reconstruction of Europe after WWII placed harsh political conditions on the countries it covered and excluded pro-Soviet European countries, which led to the division of Europe.

[5]The AIIB project had only gathered 21 countries, China included, when the "memorandum" was signed on October 24, 2014. But after the declaration by British's Chancellor

importance of China and its influence at the global level, the EU countries (and the EU itself with the new bilateral investment agreement) see the AIIB as an opportunity to deepen their relationship with China. The natural consequence of participating in the AIIB for European countries is that they should be able to promote projects among local companies also, so that the cooperation with China for the realization of infrastructure projects might be facilitated (working together with local authorities and administrative bodies it is a must).

The B&R Initiative has huge potential to strengthen EU–China relations, but all the parties involved must work together and coordinate their efforts in order to benefit from it. In the next section, we have shown how China and the EU are developing their relationships with a view to include all possible opportunities deriving from the Initiative.

5.2 The B&R Initiative is Reshaping the Relationship with the EU

It is worth remembering that 2015 marked the 40th anniversary of the establishment of China–EU diplomatic relations. In 2014, Xi Jinping made his trip to Brussels — the first time a Chinese president has visited the EU headquarters in 40 years. Xi proposed to jointly forge four major China–EU partnerships for peace, growth, reform and civilization, and called for carrying out cooperation at the China–EU level, the Asia–EU level and the global level. President Xi already had in mind to reinforce the relationship with the EU, and thus this Initiative presented the opportunity to further deepen this partnership. Indeed, to enhance ties with the EU, it is crucial to boost China's own global influence and build up an inter-polar world that serves the mutual interests of Beijing and Brussels.[6]

George Osborn on March 12, 2015 that the UK wished to join the bank as a founding member. This provoked an avalanche wave of additions, including Germany, France, Italy, and later on, Luxembourg, Denmark, and Switzerland. The full list of non-Asian countries who have adhered to the bank is available at: https://www.aiib.org/en/about-aiib/governance/members-of-bank/index.html.

[6] See in this sense, Zhao Minghao, in IAI *(Istituto Affari Internazionali)* Working Paper 15|37- October 2015, *China New Silk Road Initiative*, p. 8.

The B&R Initiative has major political and economic implications that the EU cannot ignore. The EU is interested in cooperating with China in developing this project because it meets the objectives of the European Union: the *EU–China 2020 Strategic Agenda for Cooperation*[7] mandated both sides to strengthen their cooperation in "developing smart, upgraded and fully interconnected infrastructure systems," as well as "to explore models of infrastructure cooperation, including project bonds, project shareholding, joint contracting and co-financing, and further coordinate the cooperation among China, the EU and its member states." It is noteworthy that trade and investment remain at the core of China–EU relationship. The EU needs new stimulus in order to leave the prolonged crisis behind, and investments in infrastructure projects connected to the B&R represent a unique opportunity. On the other hand, China has also embarked on an ambitious transition to a new model of economic development, based more on consumption and innovation, and enhancing infrastructures should be seen as collateral consequence; this is why the B&R Initiative is an integral part of China's new plan.

5.2.1 *The European Fund for Strategic Investments (EFSI) and Its Relation with the B&R Initiative*

In the ambit of the Strategic Agenda for Cooperation, the EU has made headway in defining a roadmap of China's participation to the European Fund for Strategic Investment (EFSI)[8] which is also linked to China's B&R Initiative. This should facilitate the participation of China in the realization of infrastructures projects in the EU, but not only in this area, due to the nature of the EU EFSI.

---

[7] *EU–China 2020 Strategic Agenda for Cooperation:* The EU–China Strategic Agenda for Cooperation provides a list of key initiatives which should be achieved. The document is the outcome of a Summit meeting of the two blocks held in November 2013. The text of this document is available at: http://eeas.europa.eu/archives/docs/china/docs/eu-china_2020_strategic_agenda_en.pdf.

[8] The European Fund For Strategic Investment (EFSI) is an initiative launched jointly by the European Investment Bank (EIB) and the European Investment Fund (EIF) and the European Commission. Visit: http://www.eib.org/efsi/what-is-efsi/index.htm.

The EFSI is one of the three pillars of the Investment Plan for Europe[9] (see next section) that aims to revive investment in strategic projects around the continent to ensure that money reaches the real economy. EFSI is a €16 billion guarantee from the EU budget, complemented by a €5 billion allocation of the EIB's own capital. The total amount of €21 billion aims to unlock additional investment of at least €315 billion by 2018. EFSI is implemented by the EIB Group and projects supported by it are subject to usual EIB procedures.

China and EU should actively expand practical cooperation and align China's B&R Initiative with the European Strategic Investment Plan, to inject new driving energy into the development of China–EU relations.

5.2.1.1 Non-EU Countries' Participation

Though the EFSI was specifically studied for helping the EU members and thus is focused on EU, in order to maximize the impact of the EFSI, it was made open to contributions by third parties, including entities outside the EU, provided EU regulations are fully respected. Therefore, non-EU countries can co-invest in EFSI projects, either directly or via co-investment platforms. Subject to the agreement of the Steering Board, non-EU countries can also contribute with cash directly to the EFSI, but this shall not give them any right in the EFSI's governance or decision-making processes. The European Commission is in contact with several non-EU countries about potential co-investments in projects in the context of the Investment Plan.

EFSI financing can flow to entities from certain non-EU countries, but only as part of cross-border projects that involve EU countries. These are countries falling within the scope of the European Neighborhood Policy including the Strategic Partnership, the Enlargement Policy, and the European Economic Area or the European Free Trade Association or to an Overseas Country or Territory.[10]

---

[9] *Investment Plan for Europe* involves three main elements: (i) the European Fund for Strategic Investment (EFSI), (ii) Ensuring that investment finance reaches the real economy; iii) Improving the investment environment. Visit: http://www.consilium.europa.eu/en/policies/investment-plan/.

[10] Reference must be done to the European Commission Fact Sheet titled "Investment Plan for Europe: One Year of the European Fund for Strategic Investments (EFSI)," June 1, 2016, available at: http://europa.eu/rapid/press-release_MEMO-16-1967_en.htm.

5.2.1.2 China's Involvement in the EU Investment Plan

At the High-level Economic and Trade Dialogue (HED) in China on September 28, 2015, China made a commitment in principle to the Investment Plan. The Commission and the EIB are working closely with the Chinese authorities to determine the technical details of the contribution, including the choice of appropriate investment vehicles. The HED agreed to put in place a working group with representatives of the European Commission, the EIB and Chinese counterparts.

China was the first non-EU country to announce its contribution to the plan, although it was unclear what the best technical option to facilitate its involvement was. Work at the HED level is now advancing, but a precise scheme of how China will contribute is not ready yet and discussion are in progress.[11]

Although China was the first non-EU country in announcing its interest, other foreign investors have shown interest in the EFSI scheme since talks began with Beijing. According to the officials involved, investors from the US, Canada and the Middle East are already taking part in the Juncker Plan, although they did not give details on the specific figures or projects.

5.2.1.3 Concrete Possibility for EU–China Collaboration on Infrastructure Financing

It must be underlined that with the new Juncker Commission and its plans to establish an EFSI, another concrete possibility for EU–China collaboration on infrastructure financing was born. China became the first country that announced its willingness to participate in European Commission President Jean-Claude Juncker's plan,[12] clearly eying opportunities for Chinese participation in investments in the infrastructure sector also, which represents a key pillar of the plan. The Silk Road Fund (SRF) was nominated as the conduit for a potential Chinese contribution. China

---

[11]*Ibid.*

[12]In order to improve investment and financial environment in the EU area and to create a framework for enhanced investments, the European Commission has initiated the Investment Plan for Europe, known also as "The Juncker Plan."

could finally see some tangible opportunities for its "B&R" Initiative on the EU level.

5.2.1.4 Latest Update on the Cooperation between the EU and China on the Investment Plan for Europe

The European Commission and China have concluded technical work allowing Beijing to start pouring up to €10 billion under the Juncker Plan, i.e. the "Investment Plan for Europe."[13] Brussels and Beijing set up a working group in September 2016 in order to find the best solution to channel the big sum of money that China was ready to offer. According to EU officials, the figure would range between €5 and €10 billion.

HOW DOES THE EFSI WORK?

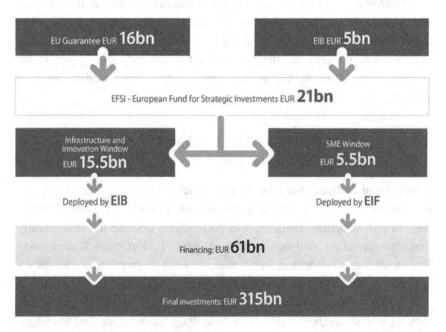

Source: European Investment Fund's website.

---

[13] See article by Jorge Valero, *Brusseles Clears Way for China to Poor Billions into Juncker Plan*, available at: https://www.euractiv.com/section/innovation-industry/news/brussels-clears-way-for-china-to-pour-billions-into-juncker-plan/.

5.2.2 Some More Details About the Investment Plan for Europe

The European Commission and the European Investment Bank proposed the Investment Plan for Europe in November 2014, as an initiative to fight economic weakness which was generated by the financial crisis that started in 2008. The main purpose is to re-launch investment and restore EU competitiveness and increase growth. The investment plan focuses on removing obstacles to investment, providing visibility and technical assistance to investment projects, and making smarter use of new and existing financial resources. To achieve these goals, the plan is active in three areas:

- mobilizing investments of at least €315 billion in three years
- supporting investment in the real economy
- creating an investment-friendly environment[14]

One major pillar of the plan is the Fund for Strategic Investment, i.e. the EFSI. The EFSI is helping to finance infrastructure and innovation projects as well as small- and medium-sized enterprises (SMEs) and mid-cap companies. Mobilization of private capital is a key feature of the EFSI. It is worth mentioning that the European Commission and the EIB Group officially kicked off this part of the Investment Plan for Europe in summer 2015.

5.2.2.1 Investment Plan: Finding Investment Opportunities

The EFSI is available for economically viable projects, including projects with a risk profile.

It focuses on sectors which support sustainable growth and employment in the EU:

- strategic infrastructure (digital, transport and energy)
- environmentally sustainable projects (renewable energy and resource efficiency)

---

[14] https://ec.europa.eu/commission/priorities/jobs-growth-and-investment/investment-plan_en.

- urban and rural development and social projects
- education and training, research, development and innovation
- investments boosting employment, in particular support for smaller businesses and midcap companies[15]

Noteworthy financial instruments under the Investment Plan are integrated into the European Investment Bank Group.

5.2.2.2 First Steps for Investors, and Opportunities for Potential Beneficiaries

The EFSI helps to identify and unlock investment projects[16] of European significance, gives investors greater confidence to invest in riskier projects such as large-scale, long-term investment projects in infrastructure, acts as a credibility label for investment and enables non-EU countries to also co-invest in EFSI projects.

To make the most of EFSI opportunities, potential beneficiaries can use

(1) **European Investment Project Portal (EIPP)** — It is the online marketplace where worldwide investors and EU project promoters can meet and find investment opportunities[17];

(2) **European Investment Advisory Hub (EIAH)**[18] — It is Europe's gateway to investment support: the European Investment Advisory Hub ("The Hub") aims to strengthen Europe's investment and business environment. The Hub offers a single access point to a 360-degree offer of advisory and technical assistance services.

The Hub is a joint initiative by the European Commission and the European Investment Bank, and is part of the Investment Plan for Europe.

---

[15] https://ec.europa.eu/commission/join-investment-plan_en#investors.

[16] The following EU website helps in finding projects: http://www.eib.org/efsi/efsi-projects/index.htm.

[17] https://ec.europa.eu/eipp/desktop/en/list-view.html.

[18] This is the European Investment Advisory Hub — Europe's gateway to investment support: http://www.eib.org/eiah/.

The European Fund for Strategic Investments

The European Fund for Strategic Investments drives the investment plan for Europe. The EFSI aims to overcome current market failures by addressing market gaps and mobilizing private investment.

The EFSI will support strategic investments in key areas such as infrastructure, education, research and innovation, as well as risk finance for small businesses.

Supporting investment in the real economy

New opportunities available for:

- **Institutional investors in the EU and abroad**
- **Project promoters**
- **Small and medium-sized enterprises**

5.2.3 *China Uses Investment Plan for Europe to Boost Involvement in the EU*

The interest of China in participating in the Investment Plan for Europe was manifested only after a few months of talks between the two sides with China deciding to contribute €10 billion to the EFSI. As soon as China's contribution is confirmed and the modalities clarified, this will make China the largest contributor to the Juncker Plan since it was launched in autumn 2016. To date, the biggest national contribution has come from the United Kingdom, with €8.5 billion. The EU and Chinese authorities have agreed that Beijing will contribute to the EFSI via its SRF, a public fund.

This means China will have to fulfill the same rules applicable to private (EU) investors; in addition, China will have to meet all EU rules on public procurement, labor law or environment regulations when investing under the scheme. "There will be no special treatment for Chinese investment," the EU Commission Vice President Jyrky Katainen affirmed during his visit in September 2016 with Chinese authorities to discuss China's participation in the Investment Plan for Europe through the EFSI.[19]

---

[19] Reference must be done to the article by Jorge Valero, *Brusseles Clears Way for China to Poor Billions into Juncker Plan*, available at: https://www.euractiv.com/section/innovation-industry/news/brussels-clears-way-for-china-to-pour-billions-into-juncker-plan/.

5.2.3.1 Project Selection Set to Start: Brief Overview

It is now up to the Chinese government to start selecting projects among those already filtered by the EFSI.[20] Approval of EIB projects by the EIB Board of Directors is a requirement for financing negotiations with project promoters which, if successful, will lead to the financing agreements being signed.

EFSI financing is the tranche of an operation that benefits from the support of the European Fund for Strategic Investments. This amount will sometimes differ from the total EIB financing amount of the same operation. Signed projects (see EFSI project List at EIB website)[21] are listed with the actual amounts agreed in the contract, which may differ from the amounts initially authorized by the EIB Board of Directors.

Total investment related to EFSI refers to the total financing amount expected to be attracted for any particular EFSI project. This amount might come from public or private sources, and it includes EFSI financing provided by the Bank.

Pre-Approvals: These are umbrella operations that have been approved under EFSI but which cannot be counted towards the EFSI objective until concrete "sub-projects" have been signed.

Investment Platforms are a tool for pooling investment projects with a thematic or geographic focus. They can bring together co-investors, public authorities, experts, social partners and representatives of the civil society and other relevant actors. Investment platforms and operations which are included in an investment platform are marked with an * in the tables below.

Source: European Investment Bank's website (EFSI project List).

China is eager to invest in the EU, and this is also demonstrated by the interest China is putting in concluding the new bilateral investment agreement which is still under negotiation; however, it seems that the participation of China in this Investment Plan for Europe should facilitate Beijing's

---

[20] A complete list of the signed project, approved projects, and of the pre-approvals can be available at: http://www.eib.org/efsi/efsi-projects/index.htm.

[21] http://www.eib.org/efsi/efsi-projects/index.htm.

B&R Initiative because it is likely that China will invest more in infrastructure projects to better connect the EU market with China.

5.2.3.2 EIF (part of the EIB) Transactions Under EFSI

This European initiatives, i.e. the EFSI and the EIF, were created to foster the depressed European economy, but these two initiatives, though focused on Europe, are not limited to EU members as it has emerged. First, it is necessary to underline that as part of the EIB Group, EIF is committed to the implementation of EFSI and "it is expected that the investment volume to be triggered under the EFSI SME Window by summer 2018 will amount to EUR 75bn. This entails an estimated fifteen-fold leverage, meaning that every EUR 1 guaranteed by EIF would generate EUR 15 of investment in the real economy, at the level of SMEs and mid-caps."[22]

5.2.4 *EIB Group Cooperation with China to be Strengthened with new €500 Million Silk Road Fund Equity Investment Initiative*

It is a matter of fact that a broader access to investments and participation on the respective initiatives is a key issue to strengthen business relation between the EU and China.

The 12th EU–China Business Summit took place on June 2, 2017 in Brussels, Belgium. This business summit was co-organized by BusinessEurope and the China Council for the Promotion of International Trade (CCPIT), and formed the most significant business platform for discussion on the economic relationship between China and Europe.[23]

---

[22] In this sense the EIF, see: http://www.eif.org/what_we_do/efsi/how_does_EIF_contribute/index.htm.

[23] Under the Patronage of the Directorate General for Trade of the European Commission and the Ministry of Commerce of the People's Republic of China, the 12th EU-China Business Summit was held on June 2, 2017 in Brussels, Belgium. It was organized by BusinessEurope and the CCPIT, in cooperation with the European Union Chamber of Commerce in China (EUCCC) and the EU–China Business Association (EUCBA). With some 500 participants from both China and Europe, the summit offered the best opportunity to meet fellow business and political leaders. For more details visit: http://www.eu-china-business-summit.eu/.

At the EU–China Summit, the EIF and the SRF signed a Memorandum of Understanding (MoU) that outlines new strategic cooperation to support equity investment across Europe. Once operational, the China–EU Co-Investment Fund (CECIF) is expected to provide €500 million, jointly backed by the EIF and the SRF, to support equity investment.[24]

"The European Investment Bank Group works with Chinese partners to support transformational investment around the world that reflects our shared recognition of the importance of sustainable development. The new *China–EU Co-Investment Fund* will build on the strong spirit of partnership between Europe and China and I wish all involved the best of success," highlighted Jonathan Taylor, European Investment Bank Vice President responsible for East Asia.[25] It is worth noting that the European Commission and China's National Development and Reform Commission have played an important role in supporting discussion and negotiations which led to the signature of the Memorandum. This is also the result of China's commitment made at the High-Level Economic Trade Dialogue in 2015 to examine opportunities to contribute to the Investment Plan for Europe and thus enhance cooperation with the EU on investment issues.

12th EU–China Business Summit (June 2, 2017)

> This is an extract from the Joint Business Declaration, and it stresses the points the EU and China have decided to focus on and develop together:
>
> *Organized in parallel to the EU–China Political Summit, the 12th EU–China Business Summit brought together the highest level of Business and Political Leaders from the EU and China. The President of BusinessEurope Emma Marcegaglia and the Chairman of the China Council for the Promotion of International Trade (CCPIT) Jiang Zengwei, hosted the Business Summit. Their Excellencies Premier of the People's Republic of China Li Keqiang, and President of the European Commission Jean-Claude Juncker, attended and addressed the participants.*

(Continued)

---

[24] In this sense, *EIB Group Cooperation with China to be Strengthened with New EUR 500 Million Silk Road Fund*, the content of this document is available at: http://www.eif.org/what_we_do/equity/news/2017/eib_silk_road_fund_initiative.htm?lang=-en.
[25] *Ibid.*

(Continued)

Under the theme "strengthening the pillars of global trade and investment," the 12th EU–China Business Summit served as an important platform for discussion on topical issues in EU–China relations, including the digital economy, climate change and sustainability, and connectivity.

In a changing international environment with many questioning the benefits of trade and open markets, participants called on China and the EU to remain committed to free and fair trade and avoiding protectionism. They called on the EU and China to continue to engage in key multilateral fora like the WTO — World Trade Organization — and pursue policies that open and improve market conditions, foster innovation and enhance the competitiveness of companies.

Participants emphasized the importance of advancing the on-going negotiations for an EU–China Bilateral Investment Agreement. The investment agreement is key to provide legal certainty and to open new avenues for EU and Chinese companies to do business together. They also agreed that closer cooperation between the EU and China is required in the fields of digital economy, climate change, sustainable development and connectivity to maximize trade and investment opportunities.

Both China and the EU are committed to implement the Paris Agreement and fight climate change. Participants recognized the need for European and Chinese companies to share best practices and work together in developing new technologies and solutions that promote sustainability.

The Digital economy presents significant opportunities and challenges for companies in China and Europe. Participants recognized the need for China and the EU to work together, developing a framework that is conducive to business and supports efforts from companies to adjust to digitization. In this context, the facilitation of cross-border flows is of crucial importance. 8. Participants recognized the importance of improving connectivity and strengthening networks between China and Europe. This could spur trade and investment and lead to increased cooperation between Chinese and European companies.[26]

---

[26]This is an extract of the "Joint Business Declaration at the 12th EU–China Business Summit, Brussels, June 2, 2017, document available at: http://www.eu-china-business-summit. eu/content/uploads/2017/06/CH-BS-020617-Joint-Business-Declaration-final-V2.pdf.

5.2.4.1 Differentiated Interests of China

China is interested in cooperating with the EU in different areas and not only in developing together projects linked to the B&R Initiative, and these latest developments clearly demonstrate the proactive role China is taking in strengthening its relationship with the EU particularly in the investment sector conducting negotiations for the conclusion of the new bilateral investment agreement, and also to strengthen financial connections with the EU. This Memorandum expresses the interest of China particularly under this aspect. "The *China–EU Co-Investment Fund (CECIF)* will bring together unique financial and technical expertise from the European Investment Fund and the Silk Road Fund. This exciting new initiative will strengthen investment into private equity and venture capital funds to support growing companies across Europe in the years ahead," confirmed Pier-Luigi Gilibert, Chief Executive of the EIF.

5.2.4.2 The New Fund Likely to Be Supportive to
Both the Investment Plan for Europe and
Projects Connected to the B&R

The establishment of the CECIF in the coming months, with the signature of this Memorandum, will create new opportunities for China to invest or participate in projects not necessarily related to infrastructures; for this, China has the option to choose from the list of the projects approved by the EFSI Project List; however, the opportunity to choose other investment types will help in better connecting China and the EU.

It is noteworthy that according to the Memorandum, the SRF and the EIF intend to establish cooperation under the framework of the CECIF for the purpose of developing synergies between China's B&R Initiative and the Investment Plan for Europe. Through CECIF, SRF and EIF will jointly invest into private equity funds and venture capital funds that support SMEs and midcaps in Europe and beyond, which have connections with China or are likely to develop such connections.

The new initiative, i.e. the CECIF, reflects the broad cooperation between the European Investment Bank Group and Chinese partners supporting climate-related investment across China, development of green bonds in cooperation with the People's Bank of China and working with

China-based international financial institutions. It is up to the players now to initiate choosing the projects and promote them among potential investors (Chinese and European). Only time will tell us how successful this initiative is and will determine its contribution to both the B&R Initiative and to the Investment Plan for Europe.

5.2.5 *EU–China Partnership Moving Forward: Other Outcomes of the Brussels Summit*

The outcomes of the summit between the EU and China held in Brussels on June 2, 2017 were not limited to the issues just mentioned above, but a series of political and programmatic decisions were made in order to further develop the EU–China bilateral relationship, a partnership that has a global impact considering the themes treated.

5.2.5.1 Climate Action

Climate change is an extremely important theme and after the retreatment of the US from the Paris Agreement, the EU and China have become two fundamental supporters. At the summit, the EU and Chinese leaders reaffirmed their commitment to implementing the 2015 Paris Agreement on climate change, and, as major energy consumers and importers, highlighted the importance of fostering cooperation in their energy policies.

At the joint press conference the President of the European Commission Jean-Claude Juncker said, "As far as the European side is concerned, we were happy to see that China is agreeing to our unhappiness about the American climate decision. This is helpful, this is responsible, and this is about inviting both, China and the European Union, to proceed with the implementation of the Paris Agreement."[27]

It is noteworthy that the EU and China are planning to work together with Canada to advance the implementation of the Paris Agreement and accelerate the clean energy transition.

---

[27] See the press release of the European Commission http://europa.eu/rapid/press-release_IP-17-1524_en.htm.

5.2.5.2 Improving Business Relations and the Investment Environment

We have already discussed the initiatives taken to improve business relations; however, here it is worth underlining that the EU and China are committed in establishing a more solid and interrelated system and they need to cooperate more closely to grasp the opportunities deriving from the enhanced framework but also dealing with the challenges that remain.

In his keynote speech, President Juncker said, "Our relationship is founded on a shared commitment to openness and working together as part of a rules-based international system. I am glad that we can meet here today and say this, loud and clear. It is one that recognizes that together we can promote prosperity and sustainability at home and abroad. We applaud the ambition of China's reform path. We recognize that reforms have been made and that plans have been established. But we would like to see implementation speed up — so that your policies are in line with your world vision."[28]

Related to this aspect, the EU Commissioner Cecilia Malmström in her speech stressed that, "Sound economic development, trade and investment also require respect for the rule of law, with independent lawyers and judges who can operate freely and independently. To conduct business — and for their daily lives — people need to be able to access free and independent information, communicate and discuss. This is a fundamental human right which also applies in the age of the Internet. Limits to online freedom also affect peoples' lives and the business climate."[29]

Investments are to be fostered via the EIF, which is part of the European Investment Bank Group, and China's SRF. We have already discussed this theme, and here it is sufficient to remember that the two parties have signed an MoU with the aim of jointly investing in private equity and venture capital funds that will, in turn, invest in SMEs located primarily in the EU. However, synergies with the SRF will facilitate the participation in projects connected to the B&R Initiative.

---

[28] *Ibid.*
[29] *Ibid.*

5.2.5.3 Competition Policy

Another important achievement was the agreement on competition policy. The European Commissioner Margrethe Vestager,[30] in charge of competition policy, and He Lifeng, Chairman of China's National Development and Reform Commission, signed "Memorandum of Understanding to start a dialogue on state aid control."[31] The state aid dialogue creates a mechanism of consultation, cooperation and transparency between China and the EU in the field of state aid control.

The dialogue will be used to share with China the European experience in enforcing state aid control. It will also be used to learn more about the implementation of the newly adopted Fair Competition Review in China, which is designed to prevent public policies from distorting and restricting competition while maintaining fair market competition and promoting a unified market.[32] This new state aid cooperation dialogue will further the EU's and China's mutual interest and joint work to promote fair global competition. It is part of the Commission's broader strategy to address the distortion that national subsidies policies put on the promotion of a global level playing field where companies can compete on their merits. The European Union has a strong interest in promoting fair and competitive markets globally, and to this end it welcomes the adoption of

---

[30] Commissioner Vestager, responsible for competition policy, commented, "Decisions by one country to grant a subsidy to a company that operates globally may affect competition elsewhere. The European Commission is pleased to start a discussion with China on how to best handle state intervention in the economy." See: http://europa.eu/rapid/press-release_IP-17-1520_en.htm.

[31] The MoU on a dialogue in the area of the State aid control regime and Fair Competition Review System, between on one side, "The Directorate-General for Competition of the European Commission" and on the other side "The National Development and Reform Commission of the People's Republic of China" (June 2, 2017) is available at: http://ec.europa.eu/competition/international/bilateral/mou_china_2017.pdf. More on the framework between China and the EU on this theme available at: http://ec.europa.eu/competition/international/bilateral/china.html.

[32] See European Commission — press release State aid: *Commission and China Start Dialogue on State Aid Control*, Brussels, June 2, 2017, available at: http://europa.eu/rapid/press-release_IP-17-1520_en.htm.

the Fair Competition Review System and looks forward to working with China in this context.[33]

5.2.5.4 Energy Cooperation

Following the EU–China High Level Energy Dialogue, EU Commissioner for Climate Action and Energy, Miguel Arias Cañete and Nur Bekri, Vice-Chairman of the National Development and Reform Commission and Administrator of the National Energy Administration of China signed the "Work Plan 2017–2018 of the Technical Implementation of the EU–China Roadmap on Energy Cooperation."[34] This Roadmap,[35] agreed in June 2016, commits both sides to tackling common energy and climate challenges, including security of energy supply, energy infrastructure and market transparency. "The Roadmap lays the foundations for sharing best practices with regard to energy regulation, demand and supply analysis, energy crisis and nuclear safety, as well as grid design and the integration of renewable energy into the electricity grid."[36]

5.2.5.5 Connectivity (Projects Connected
to the B&R Initiative)

The second meeting of the "EU–China Connectivity Platform"[37] enabled progress on (i) policy exchange and alignment on the principles and the priorities in fostering transport connections between the EU and China, based on the Trans-European Transport Network (or "TEN-Ts frame-work") and the B&R Initiative, and involving relevant third countries;

---

[33] *Ibid.*

[34] The document is available at: https://ec.europa.eu/energy/sites/ener/files/documents/workplan_2017-2018_of_the_eu-china_roadmap_on_energy_cooperation.pdf.

[35] EU–China Roadmap on energy cooperation (2016–2020), this document is available at: https://ec.europa.eu/energy/sites/ener/files/documents/FINAL_EU_CHINA_ENERGY_ROADMAP_EN.pdf.

[36] In this sense, European Commission — press release, *EU–China Summit: Moving Forward with our Global Partnership*, Brussels, June 2, 2017: http://europa.eu/rapid/press-release_IP-17-1524_en.htm.

[37] *Joint Agreed Minutes of the Second Chairs' Meeting of the EU–China Connectivity Platform*, available at: https://ec.europa.eu/transport/sites/transport/files/2017-06-01-joint-agreed-minutes-second-chairs-meeting-eu-china-connectivity-platform.pdf.

(ii) cooperation on promoting solutions at the international level with a focus on green transport solutions; (iii) concrete projects based on agreed criteria including sustainability, transparency and a level-playing field. "The two sides appreciated the results of the Belt and Road Forum for International Cooperation held in Beijing in May (2017) and stressed that the collaboration on the Belt and Road Initiative and on Trans-European Transport Networks should be strengthened to promote sustainable infrastructure development and connectivity."[38] Some projects connected with the EU–China Connectivity Platform have been presented but not financed yet.[39]

5.2.5.6 Customs

European Commissioner for Economic and Financial Affairs, Pierre Moscovici, and the Minister of Customs of China, Yu Guangzhou also signed a "Strategic Framework for Customs Cooperation for the years 2018–2020,"[40] setting out the priorities and objectives for the EU–China customs cooperation for the years ahead. The framework's priority areas of focus are protecting citizens and combating illegal trade through effective customs controls, at the same time speeding up and reducing administrative burdens on legitimate trade. The Framework provides for an effective communication and cooperation mechanism between the customs authorities in the EU and China. It allows them to assist one another to ensure the proper application of customs legislation and to prevent, investigate and combat any breaches. Also, the framework is aimed at supplying chain security while facilitating reliable traders, the enforcement of Intellectual Property Rights, and the fight against financial and

---

[38] In this sense, the *Joint Agreed Minutes of the Second Chairs' Meeting of the EU–China Connectivity Platform.* See previous footnote.

[39] The List is available at: https://ec.europa.eu/transport/sites/transport/files/ten-t-rel-projects-may-2017.pdf. See also: https://ec.europa.eu/transport/sites/transport/files/ten-t-rel-projects-nov-2016.pdf.

[40] The European Commission and the General Administration of Customs of the People's Republic of China have reaffirmed their commitment to trade security and facilitation by signing the Strategic Framework for Customs Cooperation 2018–2020 during the EU–China summit held in Brussels on June 2, 2017. More information available at: http://ec.europa.eu/taxation_customs/business/international-affairs/international-customs-cooperation-mutual-administrative-assistance-agreements/china_en.

environmental fraud. The agreement signed on June 2, 2017[41] also introduces an important cooperation on matters concerning e-commerce,[42] an emerging part of the industry which has been on a steep rise in terms of the value and market share.

5.2.5.7 Trade and Agriculture

On Trade and Agriculture also the two parties signed agreements. Commissioner Malmström and her Chinese counterpart, the Minister of Commerce, Zhong Shan, signed important documents covering the protection of intellectual property rights and geographical indications.

The administrative arrangement related to EU–China cooperation on the "protection and enforcement of intellectual property rights" aims to ensure smooth cooperation between the European Commission and the Ministry of Commerce of China in the implementation of the new phase of the program "Intellectual Property: A Key to Sustainable Competitiveness." This program has, since 2013, been the European Commission's main instrument to address legal challenges faced by EU businesses in China. These include, for example, patents, trademarks and industrial designs. The new phase, funded under the Partnership Instrument,[43] will run from September 1, 2017 until 2021.

---

[41] The official document from the Council of the European Union titled *"Strategic Framework for Customs Cooperation 2018–2020 between the European Union and the Government of the People's Republic of China,"* n. 9548/17, Brussels, May 22, 2017, is available at: http://data.consilium.europa.eu/doc/document/ST-9548-2017-INIT/en/pdf.

[42] See point 5 of the document, *Strategic Framework for Customs Cooperation 2018–2020 between the European Union and the Government of the People's Republic of China.* Establish customs cooperation in cross-border e-commerce. The ever-increasing volume and importance of cross-border e-commerce is at the center of attention of the international customs community. In this context, the focus would be to: (i) in sharing in-depth knowledge and best practices. This can take the form of case studies and recommendations on customs supervision and facilitation practices; (ii) ensure efficient controls including on security, safety and intellectual property rights, whilst facilitating legitimate e-commerce in a manner that is non-discriminatory towards other trade modes; (iii) enhance risk management cooperation in cross-border e-commerce; (iv) cooperate in the World Trade Organization (WTO) and in the WCO E-Commerce Working Group. See in this sense: http://data.consilium.europa.eu/doc/document/ST-9548-2017-INIT/en/pdf, pp. 10, 11.

[43] Through the Partnership Instrument (PI), the EU cooperates with partners around the world to advance the Union's strategic interest and tackle global challenges. The PI will

Commissioner Malmström, on behalf of the European Commissioner for Agriculture, Phil Hogan, and on the Chinese side, Zhong, also signed an agreement committing both the European Union and China to publish a list of 100 European and Chinese "geographical indications." This publication opens the process for protecting the listed products against imitations and usurpations and is expected to result in reciprocal trade benefits and increased consumers' awareness and demand for high-quality products[44] on both sides.

"The Chinese market for agri-food products is one of the world's largest, and is getting larger every year, fueled by a growing middle class population that has a taste for European food and drink products, often as a result of their international travels. The country also has a rich tradition of geographical indications of its own, many of which are still largely unknown to European consumers but which should now become more widely available thanks to the agreement."[45]

---

fund activities that carry EU agendas with partner countries forward, translating political commitments into concrete measures. The PI is one of the funding instruments that enable the EU to take part in shaping global change and promote its core values. It is one of several instruments included in the EU's budget for 2014–2020 as a means of financing the Union's external action. The PI will finance activities in a number of areas of key interest to the Union. This funding will support the external dimension of EU internal policies — in areas such as competitiveness, research and innovation, as well as migration — and help to address major global challenges such as energy security, climate change and environmental protection. As one of its main orientations, it will contribute to the external projection of the Europe 2020 Strategy. The PI will also deal with specific aspects of the EU's economic diplomacy with a view to improving access to third-country markets by boosting trade, investment and business opportunities for European companies. It will encourage public diplomacy, people-to-people contacts, academic and think tank cooperation and outreach activities. For more information on the Partnership Instrument visit: http://ec.europa.eu/dgs/fpi/what-we-do/partnership_instrument_en.htm.

[44] More information on this specific theme is available at: http://europa.eu/rapid/press-release_IP-17-1507_en.htm.

[45] In this sense, European Commission press release, *100 European Geographical Indications Set To Be Protected in China*, Brussels, June 2, 2017, document available at: http://europa.eu/rapid/press-release_IP-17-1507_en.htm.

5.2.5.8 Research and Innovation

The EU and China have agreed to boost their cooperation also in the field of research and innovation with a new package of flagship initiatives targeting in particular the areas of food, agriculture and biotechnologies, environment and sustainable urbanization, surface transport, safer and greener aviation and biotechnologies for environment and human health.[46] These initiatives will translate into a number of topics for cooperation with China under Horizon 2020,[47] the EU's funding program for research and innovation.[48]

It is worthy of mention that the European Commission's science and knowledge service, the Joint Research Centre (JRC), under the

---

[46]This is one of the outcomes of the 3rd EU–China Innovation Co-operation Dialogue that took place on June 2, 2017 as one of the key events of the 19th EU–China Summit, and co-chaired by Carlos Moedas, Commissioner for Research, Science and Innovation, and Wan Gang, China's Minister of Science and Technology. At the EU–China Summit, Commissioner Moedas and Minister Wan signed an Administrative Arrangement renewing the Co-funding Mechanism for the period 2018–2020 to support collaborative research and innovation projects under joint flagship Initiatives and other areas. This round of the Innovation Co-operation Dialogue also discussed progress on framework conditions and innovation cooperation. In particular, the two sides agreed to promote open science and to exchange best practices in open access to publications and research data, and have confirmed the principle of reciprocity in access to Science Technology and Innovation resources. See: http://ec.europa.eu/research/iscp/index.cfm?pg=china.

[47]Horizon 2020 is the biggest EU Research and Innovation program ever with nearly €80 billion of funding available over seven years (2014–2020) — in addition to the private investment that this money will attract. It promises more breakthroughs, discoveries and world-firsts by taking great ideas from the lab to the market. Horizon 2020 is the financial instrument implementing the Innovation Union, a Europe 2020 flagship initiative aimed at securing Europe's global competitiveness. Seen as a means to drive economic growth and create jobs, Horizon 2020 has the political backing of Europe's leaders and the Members of the European Parliament. They agreed that research is an investment in our future and so put it at the heart of the EU's blueprint for smart, sustainable and inclusive growth and jobs. Horizon 2020 is open to everyone, with a simple structure that reduces red tape and time so participants can focus on what is really important. This approach makes sure new projects get off the ground quickly and achieve results faster. More info available at: https://ec.europa.eu/programmes/horizon2020/en/what-horizon-2020.

[48]More information on the framework for cooperation between the EU and China in innovation is available at: http://ec.europa.eu/research/index.cfm?pg=newsalert&year=2017&na=na-020617.

responsibility of Tibor Navracsics, Commissioner for Education, Culture, Youth and Sport, and the Chinese Academy of Sciences signed an overarching Research Framework Arrangement,[49] building on their longstanding and fruitful cooperation in the field of remote sensing and earth observation. The objective of the agreement is to expand collaboration between the EU and China with the scope to develop new scientific approaches in key areas, such as air quality, renewable energy, climate, environmental protection, and digital economy, the last one having a paramount importance for the future development of the economies of both the EU and China.

5.2.5.9 Tourism

The European Union and China signed an Arrangement on the implementation of the 2018 EU–China Tourism Year.[50] In particular, on July 12, 2016, at the 18th EU–China Summit, the year 2018 was designated as the "EU–China Tourism Year" (here-after ECTY). The ECTY falls under the scope of the EU–China Summit, the High Level Strategic Dialogue, the High Level Economic and Trade Dialogue and the High Level People to People Dialogue. The European Commission's "Directorate-General for Internal Market, Industry, Entrepreneurship and SMEs" (DG GROW) and China National Tourism Administration (CNTA)

---

[49] On June 2, 2017, the JRC, represented by Director-General Vladimir Šucha, and the Chinese Academy of Sciences (CAS), represented by its President, Professor Bai Chunli, signed a Research Framework Arrangement. The ceremony took place in the framework of the EU–China Summit 2017. The new framework arrangement will focus on areas linked to the EU–China Strategic Agenda 2020 for Cooperation, and in particular on air quality, renewable energy, climate, environmental protection, digital economy, regional innovation policy, smart specialization and support to evidence informed policies. More information on this topic is available at: https://ec.europa.eu/jrc/en/news/expanding-scientific-cooperation-china-jrc-and-chinese-academy-sciences-sign-research-framework.

[50] Arrangement on the Implementation Of The 2018 EU–China Tourism Year between Directorate-General for Internal Market, Industry, Entrepreneurship and SMEs of the European Commission and China National Tourism Administration of the People's Republic of China, the document is available at: http://ec.europa.eu/docsroom/documents/23581.

are responsible for the implementation of the ECTY. Good progress is being made on preparation of the tourism year, which should promote lesser-known destinations, improve travel and tourism experiences, and provide opportunities to increase economic cooperation. This initiative also provides an incentive to make quick progress on EU–China visa facilitation and air connectivity.

5.2.5.10 Maritime Affairs

Finally, representatives from the European Union and China also signed, in the margins of the Summit, a Joint Press Statement on the 2017 EU–China Blue Year.[51] As part of this EU–China Blue Year, a series of activities on ocean matters are taking place. These activities aim to foster closer ties and mutual understanding between European Union and China and highlight a strong China–EU maritime relationship.

5.3 How China's B&R Initiative Impacts on the EU

It is evident that the EU and China have a brilliant future to share, and this is not only highlighted by the good relationship they are developing which include the new bilateral investment agreement[52] still under negotiation, but also because the B&R Initiative will create new opportunities to develop even stronger trade relationships. The two blocs have to work together to fully exploit opportunities created by their strengthened relationship and to further open their respective markets. The B&R Initiative will only facilitate this process. However, there is some concern about the increasing weight China is gaining and the EU seems to seek assurance that the Middle Kingdom not exclusively pursue its geostrategic interests. The EU is already committed to opening and enhancing trade relations with China. However, it is understandable that the EU also

---

[51] "EU–China Blue Year," Joint press statement, Brussels, June 2, 2017, "The European Commission and The Government of the People's Republic of China on 2017 EU–China Blue Year," available at the following website: https://ec.europa.eu/maritimeaffairs/sites/maritimeaffairs/files/eu-china-blue-year-2017_en.pdf.

[52] European Commission, Overview of FTA and other trade negotiations, available at: http://trade.ec.europa.eu/doclib/docs/2006/december/tradoc_118238.pdf.

wants to ensure that China trades fairly, respects intellectual property rights and meets its WTO obligations, and also invests according to the EU regulations.

5.3.1 State-of-the-Art of the Ongoing Negotiation between China and the EU on the New Bilateral Investment Agreement

Just as a background, negotiations of a comprehensive EU–China investment agreement were formally launched at the EU–China Summit on November 21, 2013 in Beijing. The aim of this agreement is to remove market access barriers to investment and provide a high level of protection to investors and investments in EU and China markets. It will replace the 26 existing Bilateral Investment Treaties between 27 individual EU member states and China by one single comprehensive investment Agreement.

The 13th round of negotiations took place in Beijing on May 15, 2017.[53] The successful conclusion of these negotiations may be of great importance even beyond the EU–China investment relations. This holds value in at least two respects. Firstly, a successfully concluded bilateral investment agreement may pave the way for a future EU–China free trade agreement. And secondly, looking beyond the bilateral relationship, the negotiations between the EU and China may make an important contribution to the establishment of a more liberal global investment framework.

5.3.2 EU's Reservation About China

China repeatedly has expressed that it wants to share "growth, development and connectivity" and "collaborate more closely on concrete projects" with the EU, but the European Commission's Vice President Jyrki

---

[53]Visit: http://trade.ec.europa.eu/doclib/docs/2017/june/tradoc_155625.pdf. As soon as the new bilateral Investment Agreement will be executed between the two blocks, it will provide for progressive liberalization of investment and the elimination of restrictions for investors for each other's markets. It will also provide a simpler and more secure legal framework to investors of both sides by securing predictable long-term access to EU and Chinese markets respectively, and it will provide for strong protection for investors and their investments.

Katainen made some different points at the Beijing Forum on the B&R.[54] In his speech, the European Commission's Vice President said that any scheme connecting Europe and Asia should adhere to a number of principles including market rules and international standards, and should complement existing networks and policies. It is worth noting that the EU's reservations about China came to a head last year when EU lawmakers voted against[55] China's application for "market economy status" under the WTO rules, which if granted, would reduce possible penalties in anti-dumping cases. It is undeniable that the progresses China has made since its entrance into the WTO are remarkable; however, it seems that the international community does not consider China ready to be granted this status yet. The sore point is with regard to the steel industry: China's huge production capacity has flooded world markets and threatened the robust industrial base, which the European Commission considers essential for jobs, growth and competitiveness.[56]

5.3.2.1 How China Is Overcoming the Situation: The "16+1 Mechanism" (Brief Introduction)

Notwithstanding these difficulties, China is interested in expanding its presence in the EU and has been increasing her presence in Eastern and Central Europe through other strategies. For example, in 2012, China created the so called "16+1 mechanism" which is a platform where the Chinese prime minister meets, usually once a year, with the leaders of 16 countries including EU members such as Poland, Hungary, Bulgaria,

---

[54] "Belt and Road Forum for International Cooperation," May14–15, 2017, Beijing. Visit: http://www.xinhuanet.com/english/special/201705ydylforum/index.htm.

[55] Brussels, May 12, 2016 — with an 83% overwhelming majority, the European Parliament today passed a Resolution against dumping and the granting of MES to China. The Resolution is an important signal that the EU will not grant "Market Economy Status" (MES) so long as China fails to meet its WTO obligations. http://www.aegiseurope.eu/news/european-industry-applauds-european-parliament-vote-against-granting-china-market-economy-status.

[56] More details on this point and about China's overproduction capacity available at: http://www.euractiv.com/section/trade-society/news/eu-lawmakers-reject-granting-china-the-market-economy-status/.

Slovenia and the Baltics states, as well as non-EU members including Serbia, Albania and Montenegro. The formation of 16+1 cooperation framework, no doubt, is one of the most important achievements of China's diplomacy. "16+1 Cooperation Framework" in particular refers to different mechanisms and arrangements between China and 16 Central and Eastern European countries which were formed after Premier Wen Jiabao's historic visit to Poland in 2012. On September 6, 2012, the Secretariat for Cooperation between China and Central and Eastern European Countries was established in China's Ministry of Foreign Affairs, and the Deputy Minister of the Ministry of Foreign Affairs served as the Secretary General. Notably, this platform has become a launch pad for the B&R Initiative, and has helped China to build or rebuild close relations with Eastern European countries. After some complaints from Brussels, the European Commission was eventually admitted as an observer in the 16+1 group.

The box below highlights the characteristics of this framework; however, it must be stressed that this platform only represents a part of the strategy China has in mind for the EU. As already mentioned, the new Bilateral Agreement and the B&R Initiative will complete the China's policies toward the EU. In particular, the B&R Initiative's main focus is on the infrastructure sector and major B&R Initiative infrastructure projects are now starting to take shape in the EU, not without controversy, as briefly illustrated in the next paragraph.

Characteristics of the 16+1 Cooperation Framework

To better understand 16+1 cooperation framework, it is imperative to outline the main characteristics of the 16+1 framework. The 16+1 cooperation framework is quite special, neither group nor international organization can encapsulate its characteristics.

1. Equal partnership. *Although China is much larger than Central and Eastern European countries in term of area, population and the size of economy, China has sought to build partnership with Central and Eastern European countries on an equal footing. 16+1 cooperation framework, in which each country is equal partner, can serve as the platform to enhance*

(Continued)

(*Continued*)

every country's interests. The 16+1 cooperation framework as China's brainchild is based on principle of voluntarism. When China set up the Secretariat for Cooperation between China and Central and Eastern European Countries in Ministry of Foreign Affairs, for the sake of coordination, the 16 central and eastern European countries can, based on the principle of voluntarism, designate a counterpart department and a coordinator to take part in the work of the secretariat. Concerning the different mechanism of 16+1 format, each country from CEE can chose to join voluntarily. China does not impose its will on Central and Eastern European countries, Central and Eastern European countries are regarded as equal partners in the 1+16 cooperation framework.

2. Loose institutionalization. *In the last 3 years, the 16+1 cooperation framework has evolved in the direction of loose institutionalization. Institutional arrangement in different mechanism is not tight-knitting, each country or entity can decide whether or not join the relevant mechanism for cooperation on voluntary basis. China-CEEC Summit i.e. China-CEEC Leaders Meeting at prime minister level is held yearly. China-Central and Eastern European Countries Economic and Trade Forum held on an annual basis. Before the summit, national coordinators meeting is held to coordinate positions and make preparation for the summit. It should be noted the progress has been made in institutionalization of cooperation mechanisms in various areas, usually, institutionalization in different areas takes the form of association, forum or networking which can facilitate contacts between China and CEEC. Hungary hosted China–CEEC Association of Tourism Promotion Institutions and Travel Agencies. Serbia will set up China–CEEC Federation of Transport and Infrastructure Cooperation. The executive office of China–CEEC Joint Chamber of Commerce will be stationed in Warsaw. The secretariat of China–CEEC Contact Mechanism for Investment Promotion Agencies will be established in Beijing and Warsaw. Bulgaria is going to host the China–CEEC Federation of Agricultural Cooperation. Czech Republic will host China–CEEC Federation of Heads of Local Governments. Romania made the initiative to set up China–CEEC Center for Dialogue and Cooperation on Energy Projects. Belgrade Guideline demonstrated support for establishment of China–CEEC Federation of Logistics Cooperation and China–CEEC Think Tanks Exchange and Cooperation Center.*

(*Continued*)

(*Continued*)

3. Comprehensiveness of cooperation. *16+1 cooperative framework covers different fields from political dialogue, economic cooperation, to people-to-people exchanges. If we take stock of the areas of cooperation between China and CEEC, it can be said the areas of cooperation is quite comprehensive. The priority of the cooperation is given to connectivity, trade and investment, financial cooperation, cooperation in sciences and technology, people-to-people and cultural exchanges.*

In the area of political dialogue, 16+1 framework serves as a platform between China and CEEC. In the past, high-level visits between China and CEEC was not frequent, Central and Eastern European countries were not in the favorite list for high-level visit in China. Premier Wen's visit in Poland was Chinese premier's first visit within 25 years, it means that no Chinese premier paid a visit to Poland in one quarter of century. When 16+1 framework emerged, China-CEEC Summit provides an opportunity for high-level political dialogue at prime minister level.

Connectivity is the common concern for both China and CEEC. Cooperation in connectivity has borne fruits. China signed cooperation agreements on the railway connecting Belgrade and Budapest with Hungary and Serbia. China's initiative to build a China–Europe land–sea express line based on the Budapest–Belgrade Railway and the Greek port of Piraeus to enhance regional connectivity was well received by relevant parties among CEEC.

Trade and investment is high agenda in 1+16 framework. Last decade has seen rapid growth of trade between China and Central and Eastern Europe. The trade volume between China and CEEC in 2014 reached 60.2 billion USD, which is 5 time more than the trade volume in 2004. During Bucharest Meeting, China and CEEC set the goal of doubling trade volume over the next five years. There are some visible investment cases in CEEC, for example, Wanhua Industrial Group acquired full control over Hungarian chemicals company BorsodChem in the transaction of 1.69 billion U.S. dollars in February 2011. LiuGong Machinery Corp. finalized its agreement to acquire Poland's Huta Stalowa Wola (HSW S.A.) and its distribution subsidiary Dressta Co, Ltd in January 2012. China Railway Signal & Communication Corporation has signed a deal to buy a majority stake of 51 percent in the Inekon Group from its founder Josef Hušek. Inekon, a Czech tram producer, will thus receive a marked financial boost

(*Continued*)

(Continued)

---

and a strong foothold in the Chinese market. Rizhao Jin He Biochemical Group (RZBC) announced in Budapest in 2014 that it had chosen Borsod County in Hungary as the site of a new citric acid factory, with sales planned for the European market. China's loan reached Macedonia, Serbia and Montenegro. From 12 measures to Bucharest Guideline and Belgrade Guideline, trade and investment has been high on agenda. Belgrade summit decided to hold the China–CEEC Ministerial Meeting on Promoting Trade and Economic Cooperation once every two years. Several measures to enhance the trade and investment have been taken in the 16+1 framework.

4. Multi-functional arrangement. *Despite 16+1 framework was a Chinese initiative, it has become a common enterprises between China and CEEC. The 16+1 framework has multiple functions. On the one hand, 16+1 framework serves as the instrument for strengthening bilateral relations between China and CEEC; on the other hand, 16+1 framework can contribute to the development of China–Europe relations. As the Belgrade Guidelines for Cooperation between China and Central and Eastern European Countries pointed out "China–CEEC cooperation has provided new driving force to China–CEEC traditional friendship, built a new platform for mutually beneficial cooperation and served as a new engine for deepening China–Europe relations for mutual benefit and win-win cooperation" [7]. When the 16+1 framework took shape in 2012, some misgivings were voiced by some officials from EU and some member states; some observer even mentioned China's tactics of "divide and rule" in its policy towards Europe, even the press communiqué of the first China–CEEC summit mentioned that China–CEEC relationship is an important part of China–EU relations as a whole. With the passage of time, it is evident that 16+1 framework does not pose any threats to China–EU relations. China responded with action to EU's concern over China's policy. As Polish scholar noticed that China modified its approach, consulting the European Commission and CEE about its proposals in advance in second summit held in Bucharest[8]. Bucharest guideline stressed that "China–CEEC cooperation is in concord with China–EU comprehensive strategic partnership. [9]"As former Albanian president Rexhep Meidani made comment on the new institutionalized cooperation format, "Central and Eastern*

(Continued)

(*Continued*)

Europe's cooperation with China doesn't undermine EU policy, on the contrary. Some concerns raised from the bureaucracy of Brussels are without sense. Apart from EU–China policy, which is a general framework for all 28 states, in fact each EU member pursues its own bilateral policies towards China. Similarly, the eleven CEE countries members of EU or five potential candidates are also eager to use China's rising interest in the CEE region"[10]. Although 16+1 framework is a Chinese initiative, it does get the active response from CEEC. In the last couple of years, the political will of the cooperation through 16+1 framework has increased. As Mr. Sikorski pointed out that "the more ties there is between our region and China, the better it is for the EU–Chinese relationship"[11].

5. Well-planned framework. *The institutionalized framework of 16+1 has become goal-oriented practice. In the last three years, the 16+1 initiative has been transformed into institutionalized framework for cooperation between China and CEEC. In spite of the informal nature of the framework, the 16+1 framework is well planned. From second summit on, 16+1 framework has resulted in the formulation of guidelines for cooperation. The Bucharest Guidelines for Cooperation between China and Central and Eastern European Countries and Belgrade Guidelines for Cooperation between China and Central and Eastern European Countries were passed by the heads of government of China and Central and Eastern European Countries in 2013 and 2014, respectively. The Belgrade Guidelines even attached an annex containing the information about implementation of the measures of the Bucharest Guideline. If we observe the evolution of 16+1 framework, usually current summit reviews the progress made in previous year and works out plan for the next year. Whether the guidelines on a yearly base will become custom in the future remains unknown. It was* stated *in Belgrade Guidelines that formulation of medium-term agenda for cooperation between China and Central and Eastern European Countries will start in 2015.*

Source: China–CEEC Think Tanks Network.[57]

---

[57] Document available at: http://16plus1-thinktank.com/1/20151203/868.html.

5.3.2.2 Infrastructure Projects

It is clear that infrastructure projects are the core of the B&R Initiative, and China is willing to engage more in these projects; however, some problems have already manifested, and a more close cooperation with local authorities is necessary to overcome such obstacles. Chinese presence will only increase in all the countries hosting B&R-related projects, so cooperation with local authorities is necessary also to understand procurements rules.

In November 2013, China, Serbia and Hungary signed an MoU for the construction of a high-speed railway line between Belgrade, the capital of Serbia, and Budapest, the capital of Hungary, to facilitate transportation of Chinese exports from Greek ports to European markets. The €2 billion (US$2.5 billion) project, financed by soft loans from China's Export–Import Bank and built by state-owned China Railway and Construction Corporation (CRCC), represents one of the first projects connected to the B&R Initiative, and it is already having an impact on China's relations with certain European countries. This project will serve as a staging ground for greater Chinese access to Western Europe, for both commerce and infrastructure projects, however it is also necessary to underline that some problems has already manifested and Hungary is currently under investigation[58] for possible violations of EU transparency requirements in public tenders in relation to the project.

It is worthy of mention that the Hungaro-Serbian project is an important part of China's strategy to extend its Maritime Silk Road (MSR) into Europe via land routes. The maritime terminus of the MSR is the Greek port of Piraeus, which is partially owned by China's state-owned shipping

---

[58] EU investigates Chinese plans for Belgrade to Budapest rail link. China's plans to build a 350 km, US$2.89 million high-speed railway between Belgrade and Budapest are under investigation by the authorities in Brussels on the grounds that they may fall foul of EU laws which stipulate that transport projects of this magnitude should be put out to public tender. An MoU committing the governments of China, Serbia and Hungary to the development of the international rail link was signed at a summit in Belgrade in December 2014 and was immediately hailed as a flagship scheme within President Xi Jinping's "One Belt One Road" dream of resurrecting the old Silk Road trade routes between Asia and Europe. http://www.eurasianbusinessbriefing.com/eu-investigates-chinese-plans-belgrade-budapest-rail-link/.

giant China Ocean Shipping Company (COSCO) and is now the main entry point for Chinese goods to Europe, though Beijing has also shown interest in developing and utilizing other Greek ports in Thessaloniki and Igoumentsia, as well as several Adriatic ports, including Bar in Montenegro and of course the port of Venice[59] which represents ideologically the final part of the Silk Road. The Venice project is of particular interest for China also for historical reasons (Marco Polo started his journey from here) and because there are Chinese companies willing to provide not only the needed capital but also to participate in the construction. However, it is to be seen if Chinese companies will win the bureaucracy and the complex legal framework and if it can adapt with the EU regulations for participating in such projects so as not to incur any embarrassing position which would impede the participation to the project(s).

As can be seen, the Chinese presence in the EU is already an important presence and the most skilled Chinese investors have foreseen the development of trade relations with the EU; for this reason, some significant investments are now clearer and their connections with the B&R Initiative have become evident. For instance, the Athens's Piraeus Harbor is another major piece of infrastructure that has become representative of China's interest toward Europe. Since 2016, the Greek harbor has been controlled by COSCO which acquired 51% of the Port Authority and will be able to acquire a further 16% by 2021, following substantial investments. The idea is quite simple, and just to underline China's strategy it is necessary to stress that through the "Maritime Silk Road" and the extension of the Suez Canal, China will be able to reach the Mediterranean Sea and will use Piraeus as a platform for Chinese companies and goods.

---

[59] VOOPS — Venice Offshore Onshore Port System — refers to a Construction of Offshore Terminal for energy and container, onshore container terminal and transfer vessels. Given its location, the Port of Venice could play a relevant role as a gateway and logistics service provider to the whole of the North of Italy and more specifically to Eastern Lombardy, and other international destinations, such as Central and Eastern Europe (e.g. Southern Germany, Austria, Switzerland). The estimated project cost is €2197 million. Starting date: January 2018. More details on this project available at: https://ec.europa.eu/eipp/desktop/en/projects/project-19.html. Also visit the European Commission portal for Investment: "European Investment Project Portal" (EIPP) at: https://ec.europa.eu/eipp/desktop/en/index.html.

COSCO intends to turn Piraeus into one of the largest container transit ports in Europe.

5.3.3 Building a Part of Europe's Vision in the Communication Networks: Some Resistances

The examples mentioned above clearly show China's willingness not only to participate but also to finance these projects providing opportunities, in this specific case, for Serbia and Hungary, in order to keep their economies afloat. These projects are of strategic importance to better connect them to the rest of the EU. However, the EU has been neglectful in developing such projects because it concentrated on reinforcing relations with China through also the new Bilateral Investment Agreement. A more substantial involvement of the two blocs, i.e. the EU and China, in this area, will facilitate the development of the B&R Initiative.

It is evident that China's determination to proceed with these railways projects will facilitate the EU's own development strategy of Central Eastern European (CEE) countries. The EU in fact plans to develop corridors all across the EU as key projects for European integration, as they aim to facilitate the efficient flow of goods, people and capital. China's intention is to connect all these projects to the B&R Initiative and gain access to Europe's interior markets. Yet, Chinese projects do not receive universal support in CEE countries. For example, the Serbian business community has a less-favorable view of Chinese investment and projects, as business elites feel threatened by Chinese competition, especially if the Chinese investors besides money want to bring everything to realize the project. The success of the realization of infrastructure projects will greatly depend on the grade of cooperation between third countries and China, and naturally a significant role will be played by the rules to be applied to those projects.

Despite these difficulties, China's infrastructure projects in these countries are, at least, diminishing Brussels's ability to dominate regional proceedings. With the development of the B&R Initiative, it is clear that the massive presence of "Chinese elements" in projects with a European matrix, will have an impact that the EU cannot ignore.

China is following a strategic plan to establish a transportation infrastructure network in the region of the Balkans in order to connect those projects with the broader B&R Initiative. This is in order to bolster Chinese exports to Europe and support its "going out" policy for SOEs. However, China's vision should be accompanied by more intense diplomatic work with the countries involved in the B&R Initiative, and especially with the EU, to prevent the projects in the infrastructure sector from being disrupted by unforeseen regulatory issues. It is of basic importance that every initiative/project in connection with the B&R Initiative respects local rules, and when coming to Europe, with the rules of the EU this in order not to interfere with the established order and functioning of the EU.

5.4 The B&R Initiative and the Accelerated Internationalization of the Chinese Yuan

One of the objectives of the B&R is financial integration between China and the countries along the B&R. Naturally, in developing the B&R Initiative China intends to use its own currency financing the different projects. This will help the internationalization of the Chinese yuan and the financial integration China is seeking. Indications that the yuan is on its way to becoming an "international" currency heightened after important currency trading centers such as London, Paris, Frankfurt, Sydney and Dubai expressed interest in becoming offshore yuan-trading centers. However, it is in relation to the B&R Initiative that the Chinese currency will gain more international attention, and the Initiative will definitely push the internationalization process of the Chinese yuan. The interest of international commercial counterparts, like for example the EU and the US, toward a more convertibility of the Chinese yuan is evident, and China is also interested in gradually letting its currency fluctuate. However, this process needs to be closely monitored by the PboC. The use of the yuan should further favor interexchange of goods and services (not only between the countries along the B&R) but liberalization should be guided by the respective interests, and China is perfectly aware that letting the yuan float more freely will have an impact on both outbound direct investment and inbound direct investment.

5.4.1 *Internationalization of the Chinese Currency: A Corollary of China's Financial Power*

The implementation of the B&R Initiative with the use of the enormous resources China has accumulated, is allowing China to reinforce its position internationally in financial terms also. In fact, as a corollary, with China exporting its financial power through the B&R Initiative, the internationalization of the Chinese yuan will be not only facilitated but also accelerated.[60] So far, China has expanded its bilateral local-currency swap programs to 21 countries along the B&R, granted renminbi quotas to institutional investors in seven countries and set up renminbi settlement banks in eight countries. These steps have helped Chinese yuan trade settlement increase to more than 25% of China's trade in early 2016, from a mere 5% at the beginning of 2012.[61] Chinese yuan trade settlement is set to be boosted further as Chinese companies pursue opportunities along B&R.[62]

The internationalization of the Renminbi will bring important long-term benefits not only for China but also for its commercial partners. China's currency is already being used increasingly as the currency for cross-border settlement,[63] and if a substantial portion of China's assets and trade were denominated in Renminbi, consequently fluctuations in the dollar (or euro)–CYN exchange rate, would have implications for domestic stability and also for third-world country imports. According to the International Monetary Fund (IMF), continuing to move to a more market-based exchange rate system should be a priority for China.[64] The Fund stressed in its Report that "a more flexible exchange rate will strengthen liquidity management by reducing the need to sterilize reserve

---

[60] China's commitment to global financing certainly will help the IMF to decide to include the Chinese yuan in the definition of the SDRs as of October 2016.

[61] L. Shen, "One Belt, One Road gains traction," *Standard Charted Economic Trends*, December 2, 2016, available at: www.sc.com.

[62] See article at: https://www.sc.com/BeyondBorders/one-belt-one-road-traction/.

[63] *China 2030: Building a Modern, Harmonious, and Creative Society*, 2013, The World Bank and the Development Research Center of the State Council.

[64] International Monetary Fund, Country Report No. 13/211, People's Republic of China, July 2013, p. 28.

purchases, facilitate further gradual capital account opening, and help ensure that investment decisions pay due regard to exchange rate risk."[65]

5.4.2 *The B&R Initiative Facilitates Financial Integration with Countries Along the Silk Road*

It important to underline again that the financial integration is another important drive for the implementation of B&R. This project will help in the internationalization of yuan and encourage Chinese companies to issue yuan bond to fund projects related to the B&R Initiative. As more and more trade will get channelized through the route, the demand for Chinese currency will increase, which will further help increase its weightage in the IMF and Special Drawing Rights. Also with most of the projects (in initial phases at least) to be financed by Chinese financial institutions like China Investment Corporation, China Development Bank and China-dominated institutions like Asia Infrastructure Investment Bank and BRICS New Development Bank, it is being commented by many observers that this would help China in faster internationalization of its currency. Thus, it quite apparent that China has a grand vision for promoting B&R — a vision which will seek for a greater role for China (both political and economic) in the international community.

5.4.3 *China's Efforts to Establish the Renminbi as an International Currency Will Take Time*

The pace of internationalization of the Renminbi will of course be determined in part by international conditions. According to the World Bank, to the extent that alternative reserve currencies, notably the dollar and the euro, are subject to instability and mismanagement, reliance on the Renminbi will increase more rapidly. And now with the development of the B&R Initiative, this process will be accelerated. China in fact is ready to use its huge reserves to make this program move ahead. However, for the Renminbi to become a global currency it will take time and cooperation with other institutions like the IFM is needed to reach this target.

---

[65] *Ibid.*

A more market-based exchange rate would mean less reliance on exports and a rebalancing of the economy from manufacturing to services. All of these changes would be beneficial in their own right, in addition to being consistent with a greater international role for the Renminbi.[66]

"China's efforts to establish Chinese yuan as an international currency would support global economic stability, which, given China's size and openness, is an essential ingredient of stability in China" (in this sense, World Bank, *China 2030*, p. 402).

---

[66] *China 2030*, p. 401.

CHAPTER 6

EU Infrastructure Priorities Connected to the B&R Initiative, and the Necessity for Coordinated Efforts with China in Developing the B&R Initiative

Cristiano Rizzi and Mario Tettamanti

Engaging with the B&R Initiative will put under scrutiny whether the EU can be regarded as a true "Union" and single entity, or just a collection of individualistic entities. When China launched the B&R Initiative, most EU member states increased their activism toward China to gain more attention and opportunities, and of course attract Chinese investment into the infrastructure sector.

It is worth noting that in September 2015, the United Kingdom's Foreign and Commonwealth Office (FCO), in cooperation with the China–Britain Business Council, published the first comprehensive strategic document on how London could benefit from the B&R Initiative, both by helping its private sector to jump on Beijing's bandwagon and by attracting Chinese companies to the United Kingdom. Further complicating the puzzle, China has been actively linking up B&R with its investment strategy in Central and Eastern Europe (CEE), whose cornerstone is the sub-regional "16+1" framework, which was launched in 2012 (see Section 5.3.2.1).

There is an increasing concern that the agreements recently passed for the implementation of infrastructure projects in the framework of the "16+1 mechanism" might be a breach of the EU legislation. In this context, on September 28, 2015, the EU and China have signed the Memorandum of Understanding (MoU), setting up a "connectivity platform" which aims to create an environment conducive to transnational infrastructure investment/transport services improvement in all regions and countries linking China to Europe, taking fully into consideration the aspects previously mentioned and caring about — above all — the overall EU's strategic interests.

However, the real question is how to integrate the B&R Initiative with the EU initiative in this area, namely in realizing infrastructure projects which can benefit both the parties. This chapter will explain the Connectivity Platform (CP) which represents not only the European response to the B&R Initiative but also a point of contact to develop synergies.

6.1 The EU Connectivity Platform and the TEN-T Policy, and their Relationship with the B&R Initiative

Transport is an enabler of growth and prosperity by providing connectivity between regions and countries. Both the EU and China have come to understand that improving their infrastructures and connecting the different regions of their territories is the best solution to enhance internal economic growth and that if the concept is extended behind the limit of their territory, it can contribute in boosting international trade and relations. For this reason, the EU and China have been developing, over the past years, connections and infrastructure networks in their own territories: in particular, the EU has developed the Trans-European Transport Network (so-called "TEN-T")[1] to ensure the good functioning of the Single Market through an infrastructure planning aiming at ensuring smooth and seamless transport for goods and people. And now China is implementing its B&R Initiative. As underlined at the beginning of this book, this Initiative

---

[1] Trans-European Transport Network (also known as "TEN-T"), European Commission, 2015, *Investment Plan for Europe Goes Global: China Announces its Contribution to Invest in the EU*, press release, 28 September.

encompasses the *Silk Road Economic Belt* and the *21st Century Maritime Silk Road* which aim to ensure seamless transport connections between Asia and Europe. Given that China and the EU are at the beginning and the end of these links, in fact China's intention to revive the ancient Silk Road is not just limited to boosting trade and economic relations with the EU and all the countries along the Road, and they are both developing transport initiatives with their neighbors, coordinated efforts between the two parties is essential in order to ensure compatibility between their relevant plans and policies and the completion of their respective plans.

6.1.1 *The Connectivity Platform: Connecting the EU and China's B&R Initiative*

The "EU–China Connectivity Platform" is highlighted as Europe's most advanced response to Beijing's moves to foster its economic development and implement the B&R Initiative. It is worthy to note that the EU–China CP which was launched in September 2015 is an initiative undertaken by the European Commission that seeks to enhance synergies between China's B&R Initiative and the EU's connectivity initiatives such as the TEN-T mentioned in the above section. The CP aims to promote cooperation in areas such as infrastructure, equipment and technologies.

The first formal working group meeting of the CP took place in January 2016 and highlighted a remarkably broad yet structured agenda.[2] The main outcomes of the meeting were as follows:

Identify and map the transport corridors between the EU and China;
- Identify a list of pilot projects and priority actions;
- Create an expert group (EIB–CDB) that will work on financing options for those projects;

---

[2]The first Working Group meeting of the CP took place on January 20–22, 2016 in Brussels. Focus was on made on: (i) Infrastructure planning (B&R and TEN-T), and possible cooperation (including in third countries), (ii) Explanation relating to our respective regulatory framework: public procurement, competition, environment, technical standards; (iii) Financing cooperation; (iv) Border crossing facilitation; (v) Cooperation on standards (in rail). For more details see: https://ec.europa.eu/transport/sites/transport/files/themes/international/european_neighbourhood_policy/european_eastern_partnership/doc/tenth-eastern-partnership-transport-panel/eu-china_connectivity_platform_by_dg_move.pdf.

- Work on transport facilitation issues in the identified projects and corridors — in the areas of standards, customs, interoperability, logistics, etc.;
- Discuss ways to encourage industry participation and ensure a level playing field for private operators;
- Identify pilot projects on low-carbon and smart transport solutions and enhance cooperation in inland waterways.

Two items should be highlighted: the first is the substantial focus on infrastructure planning and how to achieve the highest possible level of synergy between the EU and China in implementing common policies and realizing projects of common interest. Discussion between the two parties is also necessary in order to ensure that Chinese actions do not undermine EU initiatives such as the TEN-T, as well as investigate opportunities for possible cooperation, including in third countries.[3] Second, emphasis is placed on the need to foster better understanding of the EU's regulatory framework, including on public procurement (this is particularly important for a third country like China if they want to participate in realizing determined infrastructure projects within the EU), competition policy, and on environmental and technical standards, with the EU's aim being to ensure compliance with the EU regulations. This more normative angle is of paramount importance in order to minimize B&R-related risks and, in the longer run, to spur China toward greater systemic conformity when operating with EU companies.

It must be underlined that the "Connectivity Platform" between the EU and China should be considered as the most effective vehicle to frame collaboration. One of the main aims of the "Connectivity Platform" is to guarantee that transport markets could rely on free, fair and undistorted competition based on regulatory convergence, a level playing field and sustainability and promote cooperation in transport areas such as infrastructure, equipment, technologies, standards, engineering and construction.

---

[3] In this sense, Francesco Saverio Montesano and Maaike Okano-Heijmans, economic Diplomacy in the EU–China Relations: Why Europe Needs Its Own "OBOR," *Clingendael*, June 2016. https://www.clingendael.nl/sites/default/files/Policy%20Brief%20Economic%20Diplomacy%20in%20EU%E2%80%93China%20relations%20-%20June%202016.pdf.

It took almost another year for the two sides to agree on the modalities of the CP. One of the reasons for the delay was the EU's insistence with respect to the common market rules.

6.1.1.1 The Connectivity Platform (CP) as a Centerpiece of EU–China Relations

The CP has become a procedural centerpiece of the EU–China relations, and it serves as the default venue for discussions between the EU and China concerning infrastructures projects.

Working level meetings continue and will soon be complemented by high-level meetings involving the EU Commissioner. From the EU side, the CP is perceived as a way for the EU to defend shared interests of the member states. "Such relevance plays out in two main ways. First, the Platform should serve as a powerful tool for intelligence gathering with regard to China's ongoing and foreseen investment plans. Second, it should also be used as a signalling platform — that is, as a way to get consolidated European standpoints across, hence communicating how the economic diplomacy 'game' should be played in Europe."[4] Naturally, all these exercise a certain pressure for opening up the Chinese market itself, especially in the fields of public procurement, food and services. With regard to this second point, it is worth restating how the objective of getting China to conform to EU norms and standards is very explicit, and has already been featured in bilateral discussions for quite some time.[5]

6.1.1.2 Advancing Foreign Policy

The CP is a tool that has the potential to further develop foreign policy and refine EU economic diplomacy. In fact, proactively developing a platform that is devoted to strengthening trade and investment with China provides a boost to the EU–China partnership. The European economic diplomacy toward China should, however, be more comprehensive and the CP should represent only one piece of different tools.

---

[4] *Ibid.*
[5] *Ibid.*

In communicating with Chinese counterparts, it is crucial to ensure that the EU can convey its messages in a clear and coherent way if they want to reach common objectives. As already mentioned in this chapter, there exist several areas of cooperation, which include sustainable development, pollution control, smart green urbanization, social healthcare; the CP expresses one area only, though an area of paramount importance for both China and the EU. It is also necessary to underline that the Chinese B&R Initiative is designed to serve Chinese interests and the CP is more focused on the EU's interests. Therefore, the EU initiative should not only become a catalyst of European interests but also an instrument to converge the interests of both the EU and China.

6.1.1.3 Improving Infrastructures That Link the EU and China: The Vision of the EU

The European Commission stressed the importance of improving infrastructures as a link to better connect the EU with China, in a dedicated document which highlight the "Elements for a new EU strategy on China.[6] The EU Commission has stressed that infrastructure links between the EU and China would boost the economic prospects for all concerned. The EU–China CP should create synergies between EU policies and projects and China's B&R Initiative, as well as between respective sources of funding, in the field of transport and other kinds of infrastructure.

In EU's vision, "China needs to fulfill its declared aim of making its 'B&R' Initiative an open platform which adheres to market rules and international norms in order to deliver benefits for all and to encourage responsible economic behavior in third countries. Cooperation in this field should be based on full respect for relevant policies, and applicable regulations and standards, including with regard to public procurement, and guarantee a level playing field for economic operators from both sides. This should also apply to those countries outside the EU which have

---

[6]European Commission, High Representative of the Union for Foreign Affairs and Security Policy, Joint Communication to the European Parliament and the Council — Elements for a New EU Strategy on China, Brussels, 22.06.2016, Join (2016) 30 final, document available at: http://eeas.europa.eu/archives/docs/china/docs/joint_communication_to_the_european_parliament_and_the_council_-_elements_for_a_new_eu_strategy_on_china.pdf.

pledged to apply EU standards. The aim should be to help build sustainable and inter-operable cross-border infrastructure networks in countries and regions between the EU and China. Joint work on a pipeline of priority investment projects should involve close coordination with the countries concerned, not least to ensure compatibility with their fiscal constraints. EU–China co-operation on connectivity should fully benefit Asian partners, including Afghanistan, Pakistan and countries in Central Asia, by contributing to their integration in international trade flows."[7]

6.1.2 *What Is the TEN-T Policy and Program? And Who Is Responsible?*

The TEN-T is a European Commission policy[8] directed toward the implementation and development of a Europe-wide network of roads, railway lines, inland waterways, maritime shipping routes, ports, airports and railroad terminals. It consists of two planning layers:

 (i) The Comprehensive Network: Covering all European regions;
(ii) The Core Network: Most important connections within the Comprehensive Network linking the most important nodes.

The TEN-T policy supports the completion of 30 Priority Projects, representing high European-added value, as well as projects of common interest and traffic management systems that will play a key role in facilitating the mobility of goods and passengers within the EU (see Figure 1).

---

[7] *Ibid.* III.4 Connectivity and people-to-people links, p. 9.

[8] *Following a 2013 review of TEN-T policy, nine Core Network Corridors were identified to streamline and facilitate the coordinated development of the TEN-T Core Network. These are complemented by two Horizontal Priorities, the ERTMS deployment and Motorways of the Sea; both established to carry forward the strategic implementation of the objectives of the Core Network, in-line with the funding period, 2014 to 2020. Oversight of the Corridors and the implementation of the two Horizontal Priorities lies with European Coordinators; high-level personalities with long standing experience in transport, financing and European politics, nominated by the European Commission. First generation Work Plans for each Corridor and Horizontal Priority were presented in 2014, outlining exact objectives for each Corridor and Horizontal Priority, within the framework of the TEN-T Core Network.* https://ec.europa.eu/transport/themes/infrastructure/about-ten-t_en.

The Core Network Corridors
Trans-European Transport Network

Figure 1:   Infrastructure: TEN-T Connecting Europe.

Source: European Commission, Mobility and Transport.[9]

---

[9] https://ec.europa.eu/transport/themes/infrastructure_en.

What it is important to underline is that the infrastructure development of the TEN-T is closely linked with the implementation and further advancement of EU transport policy. When, in the past, TEN-T policy was merely perceived as a funding instrument for major projects, it has now grown into a genuine policy which:

- reinforces the network approach, thereby establishing a coherent basis for the identification of projects and for service provision in line with relevant European objectives, and
- sets standards for all the network — existing and planned parts — which integrate EU legislation in force and lead the way infrastructure-wise to achieving key policy objectives. Existing standards include, in particular, those set in the fields of railway policy, transport telematics or safety. New policy approaches are enabled in fields such as clean power for transport and other innovative areas, the link between TEN-T and urban mobility or sustainable and high-quality services for freight and passengers.[10]

It is noteworthy that the EU funding for projects is provided by the Connecting Europe Facility (CEF),[11] with relevant member states obliged to align national infrastructure investment policy with European priorities. Other sources of funding and financing include the European Structural and Investment Funds (ESIFs) and the European Fund for Strategic Investment (EFSI).

"The ultimate objective of TEN-T is to close gaps, remove bottlenecks and eliminate technical barriers that exist between the transport networks of EU Member States, strengthening the social, economic and territorial cohesion of the Union and contributing to the creation of a single European transport area. The policy seeks to achieve this aim through the construction of new physical infrastructures; the adoption of innovative digital

---

[10] See: https://ec.europa.eu/transport/themes/infrastructure/ten-t-guidelines/transport-policy_en.

[11] The CEF for Transport is the funding instrument to realize European transport infrastructure policy. It aims at supporting investments in building new transport infrastructure in Europe or rehabilitating and upgrading the existing one. https://ec.europa.eu/inea/connecting-europe-facility/cef-transport.

technologies, alternative fuels and universal standards; and the modernizing and upgrading of existing infrastructures and platforms."[12]

The European Commission's Directorate-General for Mobility and
Transport (DG MOVE) defines the TEN-T policy and monitors and controls
the overall program execution. The TEN-T Executive Agency turns it into
action by managing the individual TEN-T projects on behalf of the European
Commission. This direct management approach has resulted in fewer delays
and more influence on the projects themselves. The transport ministries of
the member states remain fully involved in their TEN-T projects, because of
their strategic importance also at the national level. Often, the national
implementing bodies are charged with carrying out the construction.[13]

6.1.2.1 Scope of the EU–China Connectivity Platform in This Context

The MoU on the "EU–China Connectivity Platform" signed during the
EU–China High Level Economic Dialogue was intended to enhance synergies between China's "B&R" Initiative and the EU's connectivity initiatives,
in particular the Trans-European Transport Network (i.e. TEN-T policy),
and to "promote cooperation in infrastructure, equipment, technologies and
standards." Beyond the identification of potential TEN-T projects with a
financial gap which could attract financing from third parties,[14] the sharing
of information on the relevant legislations applicable in respectively the EU
and China, EU–China dialogue on investment can help to develop a more
transparent, fair and fruitful cooperation in the transport sector.

6.1.2.2 The Pillars of the TEN-T Policy

Nine core network corridors[15] have been defined, each of them involving
between four and nine different member states and featuring the full

---

[12]In this sense, European Commission, Mobility and Transport, available at: https://
ec.europa.eu/transport/themes/infrastructure/about-ten-t_en.

[13]http://ec.europa.eu/transport/infrastructure/tentec/tentec-portal/site/en/abouttent.htm.

[14]See: https://ec.europa.eu/transport/sites/transport/files/ten-t-rel-projects-may-2017.pdf.

[15]A more detailed description of these nine corridors is contained in the Report of the
European Commission, *Core Network Corridors — Progress Report of the European
Coordinators*, 2014, available at: https://ec.europa.eu/transport/sites/transport/files/

range of transport modes. These corridors represent the backbone of the EU transportation system. To make sure that the corridors are developed effectively and efficiently, each corridor is led by a European Coordinator[16] who stimulates and coordinates action along the respective corridor.

Core network corridors play a key role in the coordinated implementation of the new TEN-T policy. The corridors are based on three pillars:

- enhancing cross-border connections and removing bottlenecks;
- integrating different transport modes (multi-modality);
- promoting technical interoperability.

Smart, sustainable and fully interconnected transport is a necessary condition for the completion and well functioning of the European single market and for linking Europe with the world market. Investments in key infrastructures with strong EU added value can boost Europe's competitiveness ("Connect to Compete"). Building infrastructure offers opportunities for European companies and boosts employment while infrastructure investment generates long-term benefits through improved connectivity, thereby catalyzing smart, sustainable and inclusive growth.[17]

In order to complete this infrastructure plan, the EU has already studied and structured a dedicated framework in order to assist in financing all these projects. In the next section, we have explained briefly this framework.

6.1.3 *EU Funding for TEN-T*

As of January 2014, the European Union has a new transport infrastructure policy, i.e. TEN-T, and the CP (to catalyze infrastructure projects)

---

infrastructure/tentec/tentec-portal/site/brochures_images/CorridorsProgrReport_version1_2014.pdf.

[16]The European Coordinators and their team strive to be as transparent as possible when developing the corridor work plan. Apart from informing about the corridor work on a dedicated page per corridor on the Commissions' website (see http://ec.europa.eu/transport/themes/infrastructure/ten-t-guidelines/corridors/index_en.htm) and via press releases, the European Coordinators look for direct (bilateral) exchanges with the stakeholders, either through missions to the countries belonging to the corridor or by taking part in thematic events.

[17]Building Infrastructure to Strengthen Europe's Economy, EU Commission, document available at: https://ec.europa.eu/transport/sites/transport/files/themes/infrastructure/ten-t-guidelines/doc/building_infrastructure_en.pdf.

that connects the continent between East and West and North and South. This policy (or policies) aims to close the gaps between member states; transport networks, remove bottlenecks that still hamper the smooth functioning of the internal market and overcome technical barriers such as incompatible standards for railway traffic. The TEN-T policy aims at promoting and strengthening seamless transport chains for passengers and freight, while keeping up with the latest technological trends. This policy is vital for Europe to re-boost its economy and to generate new jobs. The budget the EU Commission planned to allocate is of €500 billion up to 2020, in combination with funds from other EU sources and the European Investment Bank, which should significantly stimulate investments and ensure a successful implementation of the new infrastructure policy. "By 2030, the completion of the TEN-T Core Network Corridors alone will require approximately EUR 750 billion worth of investments. The largest percentage of this amount will come from the national budgets of Member States. EU grants will form another significant contribution."[18]

6.1.3.1 The Needs of Innovative Financial Instruments

The implementation of the TEN-T policy and the CP will need resources to be gathered not only from member states but also from other different sources such as new financial instruments. Thus, further EU funds will be assigned to innovative financial instruments such as loans, guarantees and other risk-bearing mechanisms. These instruments are specifically designed to draw private investment into commercially viable TEN-T projects by lowering project risk profiles and engendering confidence among private investors. It is anticipated that the credibility offered by these risk-bearing schemes will create a leverage affect, thereby mobilizing investments far in excess of that which could be achieved by an entirely grant-funded approach. However, not all transport infrastructure projects can generate the levels of returns on investments sought by the private sector, even with the support of risk-bearing mechanisms. As such, grants continue to play a

---

[18] In this sense, the European Commission, Infrastructure, TEN-T: Connecting Europe, available at: https://ec.europa.eu/transport/themes/infrastructure/ten-t-guidelines/project-funding_en.

key role in financing the TEN-T, particularly for projects deemed essential to the successful implementation of the network as a whole, but which cannot offer the levels of profitability sought by investors.[19]

6.1.3.2 Funding Instruments of the EU

The following funding instruments of the EU make financial support available to projects implementing the TEN-T:

1. The Connecting Europe Facility (CEF)[20]
2. The European Fund for Strategic Investment (EFSI)[21]
3. Horizon 2020[22]
4. The European Structural and Investment Funds (ESIFs),[23] including notably:

---

[19] *Ibid.*

[20] The CEF is a key EU funding instrument developed specifically to direct investment into European transport, energy and digital infrastructures to address identified missing links and bottlenecks. Under the CEF is a funding framework to support key EU investments in transport (Trans-European Transport Networks, TEN-T), energy (Trans-European Energy Networks, TEN-E) and Broadband and Information and Communication Technologies (ICT). Under the CEF, over €24.05 billion has been made available from the EU's 2014–2020 budget to co-fund TEN-T projects in EU member states and where eligible, connections to neighboring countries. Of this amount, €11.305 billion will be made available specifically for projects located within the territories of member states that are eligible for the Cohesion Fund. For more info visit: https://ec.europa.eu/transport/themes/infrastructure/ten-t-guidelines/project-funding/cef_en.

[21] The EFSI is an initiative to help overcome the current investment gap in the EU. Jointly launched by the EIB Group and the European Commission, it aims to mobilize private investment in projects which are strategically important for the EU. The ESIFs are expected to make approximately €70 billion available for transport projects during the period, 2014–2020. €35.6 billion of this amount will be allocated to projects eligible under the under the Cohesion Fund. The remaining €34.4 billion will be made available for projects eligible under the European Regional Development Fund. Also visit: http://www.eib.org/efsi/.

[22] Horizon 2020 is the financial instrument implementing the Innovation Union, a Europe 2020 flagship initiative aimed at securing Europe's global competitiveness. For further information, visit: https://ec.europa.eu/programmes/horizon2020/en/what-horizon-2020.

[23] The ESIFs are: (i) European Regional Development Fund, (ii) European Social Fund, (iii) Cohesion Fund, (iv) European Agricultural Fund for Rural Development, (v) European

- The Cohesion Fund (CF)[24]
- The European Regional Development Fund (ERDF)[25]

A noteworthy key supplier of further financing for TEN-T projects is expected to be the EFSI (see Section 3.2.1). All the other funding instruments of the EU are of supportive role.

6.1.4 Some Final Considerations on the TEN-T and CP Policies and Its Relation with China's B&R Initiative

It is clear that ensuring a level playing field for investors still remains a condition which shall be met to ensure the objectives of the European CP. Both the EU and China have therefore subscribed to that approach and included in the conclusions of June 2016 and 2017 of the Connectivity Platform Chairs the objective of "promoting transparency and a level playing field based on market rules and international norms."

As far as the EU infrastructure sector is concerned, the EU Commission has set up a series of regular meetings with Chinese counterparts with the view to exchange information on projects and market access in order to ensure that their potential interests as well as concerns could be addressed at each meeting in the framework of the EU–China CP, as well as feed into the negotiations on the EU–China Investment agreement which represent an important piece of the puzzle in the EU–China relationships.

Maritime and Fisheries Fund, more details available at: ,https://ec.europa.eu/info/funding-tenders/european-structural-and-investment-funds_en.

[24]The Cohesion Fund allocates a total of €63.4 billion to activities under the following categories: (i) TEN-Ts, notably priority projects of European interest as identified by the EU. The Cohesion Fund will support infrastructure projects under the CEF; (ii) environment: here, the Cohesion Fund can also support projects related to energy or transport, as long as they clearly benefit the environment in terms of energy efficiency, use of renewable energy, developing rail transport, supporting inter-modality, strengthening public transport. Further details available at: http://ec.europa.eu/regional_policy/en/funding/cohesion-fund/.

[25]More information on the ERDF available at: http://ec.europa.eu/regional_policy/en/funding/erdf/.

In view of the large funding needs of European infrastructure, in particular rail, third-country investments and financing — like those foreseen in the framework of the B&R — new funding instruments can be an important and welcome contribution. This is, however, not without risks as the development and implementation of such a massive plan could also affect the coherence of the planning set — for instance — by the EU to develop in a coordinated manner its transport infrastructure through the TEN-T framework. In this context, it is of primary importance to recall that investments within the EU have to follow the existing EU legislation, in particular procurement and environment rules, technical specifications for interoperability and the TEN-T-regulation. This is to be monitored closely by the European Commission; in fact, one of its functions is to ensure that projects to be developed within the EU shall respect the EU rules and regulations.

6.2 Coordinated Efforts between the EU and China, and Projects of Common Interest

The EU and China, even before the emergence of the B&R Initiative and the implementation of the CP policy, held regular dialogues on railways, maritime, aviation, customs facilitation as well as other issues related to "connectivity." It is noteworthy that during the negotiations on the "EU–China 2020 strategic Agenda for Cooperation"[26] in 2013, the Chinese government did not advocate an inclusion of the B&R Initiative (announced in the same period) into the Agenda, although it contained a number of ambitious goals in developing fully interconnected infrastructure systems and smart supply chain logistics networks between Asia and Europe.

6.2.1 *The Need for Coordinated Cooperation between the EU and China*

A more close cooperation between the EU and China started when China officially included the EU in the B&R Initiative after the visit of President

---

[26] In particular, reference must be made to Chapter IV of the "Strategic Agenda" namely transport and infrastructure. The document is available at: https://eeas.europa.eu/headquarters/headquarters-homepage/15398/eu-china-2020-strategic-agenda-cooperation_en.

Xi to the EU in March 2014. B&R-related projects were quickly developed in Central Europe under the so-called "16 + 1 mechanism," though this has created embarrassment among the other EU members. This is why new efforts were made in order to seek a comprehensive inclusion and gain the EU Commission's support for the search of a tangible cooperation in projects related to this new "connectivity" initiative promoted by the EU.

China should encourage partnerships between its own enterprises, host countries, and the EU and its institutions, to cooperate on projects, in particular those related to ports and other infrastructures. However, Chinese enterprises should be aware of the particular EU legal framework related to competition and adapt to those rules.

Linking up the B&R Initiative with the Junker Plan, an investment program central to the EU's effort to ensure stable and sustainable growth in Europe, should create opportunities for both Chinese and European companies to help the respective countries reach their goals.

6.2.1.1 First Chinese Investments Related to the B&R Initiative: An Example

China's implementation of the B&R can be affirmed starting with the realization of some investments in infrastructure destined to link the EU with China. An example of the far-sighted Chinese strategy is its move in Greece regarding investments in the Port of Piraeus, and in Germany for the Chongqing–Duisburg railway. Certainly, China will further expand its presence in the EU, especially investing in joint projects but also acquiring the strategic infrastructures deemed of particular interest for assuring the development of the B&R Initiative.

Chinese SOEs will lead the way in realizing these "B&R-related" investments; however, it is expected that more players will participate in developing this initiative through the realization of other projects. With reference to the investment made in Greece, it must be underlined that Greece hosts one of the few large-scale "B&R-labeled" projects in Europe: a potential US$4.3 billion investment by the China Ocean

Shipping Company (COSCO)[27] at the Port of Piraeus that aims to promote Chinese commodities in Southeast and Central Europe. Consequently, the annual throughput of COSCO's subsidiary Piraeus Container Terminal (PCT) nearly quadrupled from 0.88 TEU (20-foot equivalent unit) in 2010 to 3.36 million TEU in 2015, making it the world's fastest growing container port. COSCO Shipping is now the majority shareholder, taking over the port's management and operation, and the sale gives COSCO rights to run Piraeus until 2052. The deal was signed by COSCO and the Hellenic Republic Asset Development Fund (HRADF), which is in charge of privatizing public utilities given Greece's current severe fiscal crisis. The investment will help boost Greek GDP and create new jobs.[28]

COSCO Investments in the Piraeus Port Authority

2009	COSCO invested in the port's infrastructure and has brought in other leading operators (Hewlett Packard, Maersk and the Mediterranean Shipping Company).
April 2016	COSCO gained the majority 51% stake of the Piraeus Port Authority for €350 million.
August 2016	COSCO increased its current acquisition to a 67% stake of the Piraeus Port Authority for a total €368.5 million.
2016–2025	COSCO will invest €350 million over the next decade to improve the port's facilities.

6.2.1.2 "State-of-the-Art" of the Piraeus B&R Project and the "Interference" of the Italian State Railway Group

It is worthy of mention that the Piraeus B&R project is a key driver of Sino-Greek relations and Greece is certainly an important gateway in sea

---

[27]China COSCO Shipping, which was formally established in February 2016 through the merger of China Ocean Shipping (Group) and China Shipping (Group), is now at the vanguard of the B&R Initiative.
[28]In this sense, Xieshu Wang, Joel Ruet and Xavier Richer, *One Belt One Road and the Reconfiguration of China–EU Relations*, CEPN — Centre d'economie de l'Universite Paris Nord CNRS UMR n. 7234, Document de travail du CEPN . 2017-04, March 2017. Document available at: https://cepn.univ-paris13.fr/wp-content/uploads/2017/03/DT-CEPN-2017-04.pdf.

routes between Asia and Europe. Nevertheless, there is no clear B&R strategy from Greek government or from China's side regarding Greece. After winning the bid for Piraeus port, COSCO was expected to integrate Greece's rail network in order to build a major transshipment hub and access markets in the north. However, the "rail related" bid was won by the Italian State railway group, probably because COSCO was concerned with political uncertainty in Greece aggravated by the migrant crisis. Another privatization scheme regarding the Thessaloniki Port Authority (THPA) in northern Greece which could have entered China's B&R strategy and interested COSCO was left to other bidders.[29]

It is important to note that the Chinese ownership of Piraeus port will speed up the implementation of the "China–Europe Land–Sea Express Lane," a plan for the modernization of the railway link from the port of Piraeus, through the Balkans to Hungary and onward, which will further cut transport time and narrow the distance between China and east and south Europe, in accordance with the aim of the B&R.

6.2.2 The Search for Tangible Projects Especially in the Logistic Sector

The search for tangible projects to be completed jointly by Chinese and EU companies is not an easy task, because first the Chinese counterpart cannot understand completely the EU's role in shaping the rules for China's engagement with individual EU member states. It is the EU which dictates the rules, and all member states must abide with these rules. We are not going to describe the complicated functioning of the EU in this context, but it must be understood that to initiate a project or to invest in the EU, certain rules have to be applied, and the EU Commission is the

---

[29]Greece has received three bids for the acquisition of the 67% stake in the Thessaloniki Port Authority, the second largest port in the country, the Greek privatizations agency, Hellenic Republic Asset Development Fund, informed. The bids were submitted on March 24 by the Philippines-based International Container Terminal Services (ICTS), UK-based Peninsular and Oriental (P&O) Steam Navigation Company (owned by DP World) and German private equity firm Deutsche Invest Equity Partners GmbH. http://worldmaritimenews.com/archives/216099/greece-receives-three-bids-for-thessaloniki-port/.

organ which is in charge of overseeing that those rules are followed correctly by all member states.[30]

After a first period of general slow advancement of B&R projects in Europe, the Chinese government has realized that the EU institutions hold a central role in the dialogue of the EU-wide rules regarding Chinese investment and in coordination of different projects with the EU member states. One thing which must be clarified is that for successful accomplishment of the project, it is crucial that the EU officially endorses a B&R project and that B&R project complies with the framework of the EU rules.

6.2.2.1 Cooperation Based on Open and Transparent Rules

For the EU, the opportunities for cooperation with China under B&R would materialize only if the cooperation is based on open and transparent rules. The EU's approach with B&R is based on the objective to seek a level playing field and to channel Chinese investments in accordance with EU frameworks and priorities. It is interesting to note that EU member states decided to join the AIIB in a chaotic order; however, their participation triggered a joint EU action in designing the rules governing the AIIB during the negotiation for its articles of association.

The fact that the B&R Initiative has strong political support in China and that the EU has come to understand that this Initiative is going to be implemented regardless of any kind of opposing forces, has forced the EU to adopt a proactive approach to seek engagement and try to benefit from an invigorated EU–China relationship, putting in place initiatives like the CP, which has already been discussed in the previous section.

---

[30] A brief introduction about the EU and the EU organizations is contained in the book titled *Chinese Expansion Into the EU — Strategies and Policies of the Two Blocks and the Role of the U.S.* by Cristiano Rizzi, Paolo Rizzi, Lex Smith and Li Guo, American Bar Association, August 2016, where at §2.01 is described the functioning of the major bodies of the EU. The European Commission represents the interest of the Union as a whole. More info can at: http://europa.eu/about-eu/institutions-bodies/european-commission/index_en.htm.

6.2.2.2 COSCO Is Helping in Realizing President Xi's Vision

The proactive role of COSCO in expanding its own business is also helping in pushing ahead the vision of President Xi and thus the development of the B&R Initiative. We already discussed the recent acquisition of the Piraeus port in Greece by COSCO; now, the shipping company is poised to venture into some fresh overseas investments to secure ports and hubs for the development of its own business of course, but this greatly contributes to create the real Belt and Road (B&R), in fact those ports and hubs are included in China's Initiative.

The state-owned shipping giant specifically plans to acquire a Spanish port operator for €200 million (US$228 million) and spend US$38 million to secure an inland logistic hub in Khorgos, Kazakhstan.

It is noteworthy that COSCO Shipping Ports, a COSCO group company, signed an agreement in June (2017) to acquire a 51% stake in Spanish port operator Noatum Ports,[31] securing its biggest foothold at a port in the Mediterranean.

COSCO is accelerating its expansion overseas as part of its growth strategy while playing "unwittingly" the role of a trailblazer in the B&R scheme.

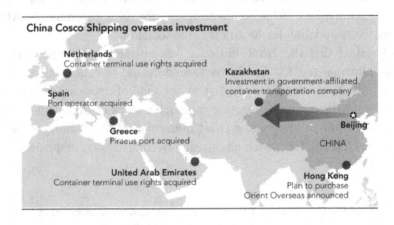

China Cosco Shipping overseas investment

Netherlands
Container terminal use rights acquired

Kazakhstan
Investment in government-affiliated
container transportation company

Spain
Port operator acquired

Beijing

Greece
Piraeus port acquired

CHINA

United Arab Emirates
Container terminal use rights acquired

Hong Kong
Plan to purchase
Orient Overseas announced

---

[31] Noatum Ports is one of the leading port and transportation operators in Spain, and it operates terminals at ports such as the Valencia port, Barcelona, and railroad terminals in Madrid for example. Noatum is owned by institutional investors, the majority of which are pension funds, advised by J.P. Morgan Asset Management Infrastructure Investment Group, and the Dutch Pension Fund Stichting Pensioenfonds ABP. http://www.noatum.com/en/company/presentation/.

COSCO Shipping Holding, a major container transportation company of the COSCO group, announced that it had offered to buy the major shipping company ORIENT Overseas International, together with Shanghai International Port Group, for HK$49.2 billion (US$6.3 billion). The takeover will create the world's third-largest shipping line by capacity as Beijing pushes to raise China's profile in global shipping.

6.2.3 Continued Chinese Expansion in the Logistic Gateways Toward the EU

As it has emerged, from what we have elucidated above, the interest of China toward major logistic hubs has already manifested with the acquisition of major ports. The interest of China in developing its B&R Initiative manifests itself in formal B&R projects which also often involves EU container terminals and railways. COSCO and other Chinese port companies have invested, or have expressed an interest in doing so, in seaports in the entire EU, for example in Belgium, the Netherlands, Croatia, Slovenia, Italy, Portugal, Spain, Latvia and Lithuania.

With regard to railways, the planned construction of a new Belgrade–Budapest railway by Chinese companies is a notable B&R-related project. In addition, several other China–Europe rail services are increasing in number and frequency.[32] Chinese local governments and companies are involved in these freight services, which connect various cities in China with destinations in Poland, Germany, the Netherlands, Belgium, France and Spain. Many of these port and rail projects date from before the

---

[32]The first freight trains from China to reach the UK arrived in England on January 18, 2017. The January 18 arrival at DB Cargo's London Eurohub terminal in Barking, east London, was an event in the logistic sector. The 34 TEU-train had travelled more than 12,000 km to Britain from Yiwu in eastern China, and was the first-ever freight service to complete the journey. Taking 18 days to pass through eight countries, the train received a VIP welcome, with Chinese lion dancers and TV crews from around the world gathering to mark its arrival. http://www.railjournal.com/index.php/freight/china-europe-rail-freight-continues-to-soar.html.

launch of B&R and have been given the B&R label since 2013. Such "repackaging" of existing projects is a general feature of B&R that can be observed in most of the EU's member states.[33]

6.2.3.1 Other Logistic-related Activities Impacting the B&R Initiative

It is interesting to note, as reported by European Think-tank Network on China — ETNC, that "some activities within the EU that are initiated by Chinese actors are relevant for, but are not formally designated part of, B&R. Several European airports have attracted Chinese investments (including Parchim in Germany and Toulouse in France) or expressions of interest (such as Kastelli in Greece). In some cases, Chinese companies provide logistical services for non-Chinese clients that do not involve direct investments in the EU and that are not visible to outsiders. For example, COSCO Logistics, a subsidiary of COSCO, designed and implemented the transport of HP components from Foxconn factories in Chongqing, central China, over land to Guangdong province."[34] They are shipped from there by sea to Piraeus, and then onward by train to assembly plants in the Czech Republic that are also owned by Foxconn. The final products are then sold by HP across Europe. COSCO Logistics has been instrumental in setting up this operation, including a cross-docking center at Piraeus for HP products.[35] Because HP is the client, this new transport corridor seems more an initiative of private American and

---

[33] In this sense, Frans-Paul van der Putten, John Seaman, Mikko Huotari, Alice Ekman and M. Otero-Iglesias (eds.), *Europe and China's New Silk Roads*, European Think-tank Network on China - ETNC Report, December 2016, at: https://www.clingendael.nl/sites/default/files/Europe_and_Chinas_New_Silk_Roads_0.pdf.

[34] Frans-Paul van der Putten, "Greece: Piraeus and the Maritime Silk Road," in Frans-Paul van der Putten (ed.), *The Geopolitical Relevance of Piraeus and China's New Silk Road for Southeast Europe and Turkey, Clingendael Report*, December 2015.

[35] COSCO Logistics, "COSCO Logistics Set Up Cross-Docking Center for Hewlett-Packard in Piraeus," COSCO Logistics website, 2013, http://www.cosco-logistics.com.cn/e_about%20us/news.jsp?newsid=95000620.

Taiwanese firms than a purely Chinese activity. While the Piraeus port activities of COSCO Shipping Ports, another COSCO subsidiary, are thus widely seen as being part of B&R, the scope of COSCO's role is much greater.[36]

6.2.3.2 The Need to Improve China–EU Rail Freight, and Not Just Shipping

The example of COSCO is extremely significant not only because it shows how the B&R Initiative can be effectively developed, but also because it combines the interests of a company with the interests of both China and the EU in enhancing trade relations and increasing the volume of goods to be transported in the respective markets. However, shipping represents only one method, and considering the importance of the railway networks in the ambit of the EU and China relations, more attention should be given to the transport of goods by trains.

Enhancing the infrastructure connecting the EU and China and all the other countries along the B&R represents a priority for China at the internal level as well. Unprecedented investment in China's rail infrastructure over the last decade means that its major cities are now all well connected. Rail links with logistics facilities are also improving, while Russia has invested billions of rubles in recent years to improve capacity and increase line speeds on the Trans-Siberian. "Kazakhstan is also engaged in a $US 2.7bn railway upgrade program, encompassing 724km of track as well as locomotives and freight wagons, with its president, Mr Nursultan Nazarbayev a long-time backer of restoring the Silk Road.

This is perhaps best reflected in the construction of the Khorgos Gateway project. Situated on the Kazakhstan–Chinese border, the future logistics and industrial hub is billed as the new Dubai, covering a colossal 5470ha. This includes the 129.8ha Khorgos Gateway Inland Container Dock, a gauge-changing station for the trans-Eurasian

---

[36] *Europe and China's New Silk Roads*, European Think-tank Network on China: ETNC Report, December 2016, available at: https://www.clingendael.nl/sites/default/files/Europe_and_Chinas_New_Silk_Roads_0.pdf.

railway, which has capacity for six trains at one time, and can process 580,000 TEUs annually."[37]

It is evident that the interest of China in developing more infrastructures and as part of the B&R Initiative, China is pushing, and largely funding, a vast program of Eurasian infrastructure investment. The China Investment Bank estimates that 900 B&R infrastructure projects worth US$890 billion ranging from rail to road, port and pipeline, are planned or underway in the 64 countries involved in the Initiative. However, it must also be understood that these projects and investments, in particular if involving Chinese capitals, must be approved by the Chinese governments. Even though B&R-related projects might be particularly favored by the Chinese government, in any case their approval must follow the normal procedure for the authorization of such outbound investments.

6.2.3.3 Chinese Interests Go Behind Railway Projects in the EU

Apart from the railway projects in European countries, the Chinese government has shown an interest in cooperating with mainly western European countries — such as the United Kingdom, France, Portugal and Spain — on B&R projects in "third countries" — that is, countries in Asia, Africa and even Latin America. China shows active willingness to cooperate with France in francophone Africa, with Spain in Spanish-speaking countries in Latin America, and with Portugal in Portuguese-speaking countries in Africa and Brazil. To an important extent, China's official approach to Europe (and elsewhere) with regard to B&R is a matter of public diplomacy. What it is important to underline is that China promotes not only the actual instances of Sino-European cooperation on connectivity, but also B&R as a tool not only aimed at

---

[37] In this sense, Kevin Smith, China–Europe Rail Freight Continues to Soar, *Rail Journal*, April 18, 2017, available at: http://www.railjournal.com/index.php/freight/china-europe-rail-freight-continues-to-soar.html.

expanding China's presence across Eurasia and Africa but with the vision of bringing innovation and as a transformative process that is inclusive and beneficial to all.

The only response for China to bring stability and prosperity not only to Chinese people but also to the rest of the world is through globalization, and the B&R Initiative seems to be an important part of the process. This is why a key component of the Chinese diplomacy is to promote its Initiative. B&R is vital not only for further development of Chinese economy but also a key element for third countries to boost their respective economies and to enhance relations with China.

6.2.4 Outbound Chinese Investments Need to Be Approved by Chinese Governmental Bodies

Chinese enterprises interested to invest in the EU, and in general in third countries, may be required to seek certain approval from government regulatory bodies. As the B&R Initiative starts to be better understood and Chinese companies are eager to cooperate in B&R-related projects overseas, they need to abide with Chinese rules for outbound investments also. This short section is intended to offer a brief overview about the processes needed to obtain the necessary authorization, though it must be clear that this is only an outline of this very first step, because further authorizations are necessary to structure specific investments in the country of destination.

6.2.4.1 Approval Process Differs Depending on the Nature of the Chinese Outbound Investment

The approval process for Chinese outbound investments differs depending on whether the enterprise is privately or state owned. Whether it is approved at local, provincial or national level depends on the size of the investment. Typically, there are four Chinese governmental bodies involved in approving the outbound investments of Chinese enterprises:

These are SASAC[38] (for SOEs only), NDRC,[39] MOFCOM[40] and SAFE,[41] although other bodies may be involved depending on the details.

---

[38] In 2003, the PRC Government decided to strengthen the regulatory regime governing state-owned asset by creating the SASAC, namely the State-owned Assets Supervision & Administration Commission, a commission directly under the State Council, which is charged with the responsibility of supervising the assets of state-owned enterprises at the national level directly subordinate to the Party Central Commission. SASAC guides and pushes forward the reform and restructuring of state-owned enterprises, advances the establishment of modern enterprise system in SOEs, improves corporate governance, and propels the strategic adjustment of the layout and structure of the state economy. SASAC is responsible for the fundamental management of the state-owned assets of enterprises, works out draft laws and regulations on the management of the state-owned assets, establishes related rules and regulations and directs and supervises the management work of local state-owned assets according to law. More information about the main functions of this organ available at the following website: http://www.sasac.gov.cn/n2963340/n2963393/2965120.html (accessed on December 23, 2013).

[39] NDRC, National Development and Reform Commission People's Republic of China (NDRC), 国家发展与改革委员会, http://en.ndrc.gov.cn//mfndrc/default.htm (accessed on December 23, 2013).

[40] MOFCOM is the Ministry of Commerce. Its main function is to formulate the strategies, guidelines and policies of developing domestic and foreign trade and international economic cooperation, draft the laws and regulations governing domestic and foreign trade, foreign investment in China, foreign assistance, overseas investment and foreign economic cooperation, devise relevant departmental rules and regulations; to study and put forward proposals on harmonizing domestic legislations on trade and economic affairs as well as bringing Chinese economic and trade laws into conformity with multilateral and bilateral treaties and agreements; to study the development trends of economic globalization, regional economic cooperation and modern distribution patterns and give proposals. The MOFCOM is the main organ to decide about the entry of foreign investments in Mainland China and its approval is always necessary for any type of FDI, but this organ has many other functions which are related to not only inward FDI but it can have an influence on outward Chinese investments. MOFCOM formulates multilateral and bilateral (including regional and free trade area) trade and economic cooperation strategies and policies, be responsible for multilateral and bilateral negotiations on trade and economic issues, coordinate domestic positions in negotiating with foreign parties, and to sign the relevant documents and monitor their implementation. To establish multilateral and bilateral intergovernmental liaison mechanisms for economic and trade affairs and organize the related work. To handle major issues in country (region)-specific economic and trade relationships, regulate trade and economic activities with countries without diplomatic relationship with China. In line with the mandate, to handle the relationship with the World Trade Organization on behalf of the Chinese government, undertake such responsibilities under the framework of the WTO as multilateral and bilateral negotiations, trade policy reviews, dispute settlement, and notifications and inquires and to coordinate trade and economic activities with foreign parties MOFCOM other functions are described at the following webpage: http://english.mofcom.gov.cn/ (accessed on December 23, 2013).

[41] SAFE, State Administration for Foreign Exchange. http://www.safe.gov.cn/wps/portal/english/ (accessed, December 23, 2013). One of the main functions is to study and

For an SOE, SASAC approval is sought as the first step. If an overseas investment is to be made by a central SOE (and therefore directly controlled by SASAC) of a value of less than that required to receive central NDRC approval, then provincial NDRC approval can be bypassed by the SOE. National NDRC approval is required for investments over USD 300 million in resources sectors or over USD 100 million in non-resources sectors. For investments below these levels, provincial level DRC approval is sufficient. When the NDRC receives an application it takes five business days to decide whether or not to accept the application. If it is accepted, it will be approved or rejected within 20 business days.

6.2.4.2 The Role of MOFCOM in Approving Outbound Chinese Investments

The Chinese investor will then need to seek the approval of MOFCOM, which is the body responsible for administering and supervising overseas investment. Central level MOFCOM approval is required for investments:

(i) *of US$100 million or more;*
(ii) *in a country which has not established a diplomatic relationship with China, or in certain other countries or regions specified by MOFCOM;*
(iii) *which are spread over multiple countries or regions;*
(iv) *involving the establishment of an overseas special purpose company.*

Provincial level MOFCOM approval is required for investments between US$10 million and US$100 million or specifically in the energy, minerals or other strategic sectors.

---

propose policy suggestions on the reform of the foreign exchange administration system, prevention of the balance of payments risks, and promotion of the balance of payments equilibrium; to study and implement policy measures for the gradual advancement of the convertibility of the RMB under the capital account and the cultivation and development of the foreign exchange market; to provide suggestions and a foundation for the People's Bank of China to formulate policy on RMB exchange rate. However, the SAFE play an important role in influencing the direction of Chinese investments abroad and this organs has several major functions, please visit the following website: http://www.safe.gov.cn/wps/portal/english/AboutSAFE/Major (accessed on December 23, 2013).

MOFCOM will also consult with the relevant overseas Chinese consulate. MOFCOM takes five business days to determine whether or not to accept an application. After accepting an application, it must approve or reject the investment within a further 15 business days. Some applications requiring central level MOFCOM approval will also be subject to a preliminary examination by provincial level MOFCOM, taking an additional 10 business days. After obtaining NDRC and MOFCOM approval, an application is made to SAFE for the transfer of foreign currency funds overseas.[42] This is usually the last step in the approval process and takes up to two weeks. Additional approval from the State Council is also required where investment is in countries or regions which do not have a formal diplomatic relationship with China, are on a list of international sanctions or where a war or riot is taking place, or in an industry of a sensitive nature. If the enterprise making the investment is from an industry with its own specific regulator then it is possible that an additional approval will also need to be required from that body.[43]

This is an extract from the book: Cristiano Rizzi, Paolo Rizzi, Lex Smith and Li Guo, *Chinese Expansion in the EU — Strategies and Policies of the Two Blocks and the Role of the U.S.*, American Bar Association, 2016.

6.3 The Importance and Strategic Significance of the Mediterranean Region for the B&R

As a matter of fact, the Mediterranean region is one of the objectives of China in constructing the B&R. The Mediterranean is a key point in developing the B&R Initiative — this is why emphasis is given to projects in this area. It is not surprising that one of the major players in financing B&R-related projects has expressed the interest of China in reinforcing relationships with countries located in this strategic part of the world.

---

[42] SAFE lifted restrictions on the amount of foreign exchange available annually to domestic investors' outbound investments and announced in 2009 that Chinese firms can seek financing from multiple sources. MOFCOM simplified and shortened the approval procedures in 2009, and the NDRC reiterated in 2011 its desire to decentralize the outward investment approval decision process.

[43] In this sense, the European Chamber of Commerce in China in its study titled *Chinese Outbound Investment in the European Union*, January 2013.

The Euro-Mediterranean's most important geostrategic point is definitely the Suez Canal (along with three natural straits: Gibraltar, Bosporus, and Dardanelles). It represents the shortest seaway from East Asia and Middle East to Europe as well as for some African states to Europe.

It must be stressed that "Mediterranean region was the world's center for many centuries. The Mediterranean Sea is a gateway for East Asian countries and a sea window to world oceans for Russia and Ukraine. The Mediterranean Sea gained its main geostrategic importance during the Second World War when the Nazi Germany, Fascist Italy and Communist Russia (Soviet Union) saw it as a tool towards regional and further world supremacy. Germany saw it as part of *Großdeutchland*, Italy as *mare nostrum* and Russia as a tool for economic expansion and export of the communist idea."[44]

The view of the Bank of China Chairman, Chen Siqing, to stress the fundamental role of the Mediterranean region in China's plans is reported in the following sections.

6.3.1 Bank of China Chief Stresses Mediterranean Region's Importance in B&R Construction

Chen Siqing[45] was invited as a guest speaker at the 3rd edition of the MED — Mediterranean Dialogues — held in Rome in 2017.[46]

---

[44] In this sense, Laris Gaiser and Dejian Hribar, Euro-Mediterranean Region: Resurged Geopolitical Importance, *International Journal of Euro-Mediterranean Studies*, December 2012, Vol. 5, No. 1, pp. 57–69.

[45] Siqing Chen is currently Chairman of the Board, Chairman of the Nomination Committee, and Member of the Remuneration Committee of the Company and the Bank. He has been Chairman of Bank of China Limited ("BOC") since August 2017 and was its Vice Chairman from 2014 to 2017. He has been Executive Director of BOC since April 2014, and was the President of BOC (2014–2017). He is also the Director of BOC Hong Kong (BVI) Limited and BOC Hong Kong (Group) Limited. He held various positions in BOC from June 2000 to May 2008, including Assistant General Manager, Vice General Manager of the Fujian Branch, General Manager of the Risk Management Department of BOC and General Manager of the Guangdong Branch. Siqing Chen served as Executive Vice President of BOC from June 2008 to February 2014. He has been serving as Chairman of the Board of Directors of BOC Aviation Limited since December 2011.

[46] Rome, third edition of the MED, (November 30, 2017–December 2, 2017). Mediterranean Dialogues (MED) is the annual high-level initiative promoted by the Italian Ministry of Foreign Affairs and International Cooperation and Italian Institute for International

Bank of China Chairman Chen Siqing affirmed that the Mediterranean region's position is unique and of strategic importance, at the crossroads of land Silk Road and Maritime Silk Road, and for this reason China needs to reinforce relationships with all the countries in the region (especially with Italy). Chen Siqing shared with an audience of some 500 participants from different countries and regions the topic of how to promote "B&R" construction projects for a more prosperous Mediterranean region. It is worth reporting Chen's vision because his view reflects the view of China as well.

Chen said the construction of the B&R has created a new platform for international cooperation and provided new energy for common development. According to the Chinese banker, the role of the Mediterranean region becomes more and more important as the B&R construction goes on.

"Here (the Mediterranean) is the key juncture of the infrastructures along the B&R. The Mediterranean's position is unique and of strategic importance, at the crossroads of land Silk Road and maritime Silk Road," he said.

In 2014, China and four Mediterranean countries decided to build "China–Europe Continental and Ocean Expressway." As of now, Chen said, China–Europe trains have already become an important means of transport in international logistics.

"In the future, we should continue to intensify the building of infrastructures in the Mediterranean region and to push forward the construction of great projects such as the Hungary–Serbia railway linking Budapest and Belgrade, as well as the shaping of a logistic and transport network linking Europe, Asia and Africa by land, sea and air," Chen said.

According to the bank chief, the Mediterranean region is one of the most popular destinations for Chinese tourists, and there is an increasing number of products moving from the Mediterranean to China.

Noting that in 2016 the Mediterranean–China import–export trade volume exceeded US$150 billion, Chen urged both sides to speed up trade and investment liberalization and facilitation, and expand financial

---

Political Studies (ISPI) in Rome. The event aims at drafting a "positive agenda" for the Mediterranean by stimulating debate and promoting new ideas, rethinking traditional approaches and addressing shared challenges at both the regional and the international level.

and commercial exchanges in order to provide new engines to regional development.

Chen also described the region as a big market for international cooperation on B&R industrial capacity.

"In the future, we should accelerate industrial capacity cooperation with countries along the B&R, promote regional development and peaceful coexistence among peoples," he added.[47]

6.3.1.1 About the "MED — Mediterranean Dialogues"

Rome MED builds upon four pillars: Shared Prosperity, Shared Security, Migration, and Civil Society and Culture. Debates on these topics are intended to complement analyses of current challenges with new ideas and suggestions to scale up economic cooperation, overcome regional rivalries and conflicts, and ensure that adequate incentives for sustainable development are set in motion.

Shared Prosperity

Under the "Shared Prosperity" pillar, particular attention is devoted to the role that business leaders and civil society can play to foster prosperity and political stability in a region where new opportunities may be seized.

Shared Security

Discussions on "Shared Security" are focused on viable strategies to avoid further turmoil, fight terrorism and promote successful post-conflict transitions and institution building, thus enhancing resilience in Mediterranean countries.

Migration

The "Migration" pillar encourages discussion about migration-related topics, including: identifying safe and legal routes for asylum seekers,

(Continued)

---

[47]See Siqing Chen's speech available at https://rome-med.org/speeches/med-2017-to-wards-a-mediterranean-prosperity/, the speech is also available at the "Belt and Road Portal" at: https://eng.yidaiyilu.gov.cn/qwyw/rdxw/38360.htm.

(Continued)

> *fostering social inclusion, and efficiently combining countertrafficking*
> *policies with respect to human rights.*
>
> **Civil Society and Culture**
>
> *The "Civil Society and Culture" pillar allows to put all these challenges*
> *into perspective by acknowledging that the Mediterranean region is a*
> *unique "melting pot" of cultures and religions, with important historical*
> *legacies and a rich natural and cultural heritage.*[48]

6.3.1.2 China's Endeavor to Foster a New Form of International Relations Will Benefit the Development of the B&R Initiative

Foreign Minister Fu Ying[49] also participated at the MED Forum. During several occasions, Fu repeatedly affirmed that China's endeavor to foster a new form of international relations and build a community with a shared future for mankind will be the overarching goals of China's foreign policy in the years ahead. This is also because, no doubt, it will help in developing the B&R Initiative. For China to expand and enhance external relations is of paramount importance. China needs to create a more favorable external environment and stronger external impetus to create a moderately prosperous society in all respects.

---

[48]This information was retrieved from the 3rd Forum of MED, available at: https://2017. med.ispionline.speakers.

[49]Fu Ying was Vice Minister of Foreign Affairs of China from 2009 to 2013, the first woman to serve in the role since 1979, and one of only two to serve in Chinese history. Born in the Inner Mongolia Autonomous Region of China, Fu went on to graduate from the Beijing Foreign Studies University and began her career as an interpreter. After the death of Mao in 1976, she became the official interpreter of the diplomatic service where she served for the next 20 years. Between 2000 and 2003 she was Director-General, Department of Asian Affairs, MFA. Prior to her appointment as Vice Minister of Foreign Affairs, Fu served as the Ambassador Extraordinary and Plenipotentiary of China to Australia (2003–2006), and to the United Kingdom of Great Britain and Northern Ireland (2006–2009). She currently serves as the Chairman of the 12th National People's Congress, Foreign Affairs Committee.

There is no doubt that the B&R Initiative will promote global economic development; however, coordinated efforts among all the subjects involved in and affected by this Initiative are necessary to reach the full potential and smoothly develop every project connected to the Initiative. Thus, it is reasonable to affirm that China will continue to seek more constructive cooperation with all the Mediterranean countries, and considering the enormous economic implications China will play a fundamental role in solving or acting as a mediator to overcome obstacles or conflicts in the region.

CHAPTER 7

Relations between China and Italy: The Development of Diplomatic Ties and the Impact of the B&R Initiative and a Brief Overview on the EU and Italian Rules Regulating Public Works

Cristiano Rizzi

China and Italy have started their relationship long time ago. The first encounters between Italians and Chinese stretch back to the Middle Ages, when Venetian merchants (among whom there was Marco Polo) began opening up trade routes — later known as the "Silk Road" — with the Celestial Empire. Since then, their relationship continued to evolve. In 2015, Italy and China celebrated the 45th anniversary of the establishment of diplomatic relations. It is noteworthy that the Italian government recognized the People's Republic of China (PRC) on November 6, 1970, almost five years before the European Community opened diplomatic relations with the PRC (which occurred on May 6, 1975). Beijing and Rome established a comprehensive strategic partnership in 2004, though no particular agreements were signed. However, this represents a turning point in bilateral relations. To give meaning and content to the strategic partnership, the two sides set up an inter-ministerial committee — led by

239

each country's Minister for Foreign Affairs — which has been the focal point for coordinating bilateral relations over the last decade.[1]

7.1 China–Italy Relations: *Status Quo*

The latest meeting at the ministerial level between China and Italy was held in Rome in June 2017 in the ambit of a comprehensive strategic partnership. China International Trade Representative and Vice Minister of Commerce Fu Ziying and Italian Vice Minister of Economic Development Ivan Stafaroto co-chaired the 12th meeting of China–Italy Joint Commission for Economic and Trade Cooperation in Rome on June 14. The two sides exchanged views on issues concerning implementing the leaders' consensus, strengthening trade and economic cooperation under the framework of "B&R Initiative," playing the role of China–Italy Joint Commission for Economic and Trade Cooperation and China–Italy Entrepreneurs Committee, strengthening cooperation in new areas like sea transport, aviation and agricultural areas, promoting investment facilitation, strengthening IPR protection, and deepening China–Europe trade and economic relations. Extensive consensus has been made.[2]

7.1.1 *Promoting Cooperation and Political Dialogue on Global Issues*

The relations between the two countries include a political and security dimension as well as a growing number of sectorial dialogues. For instance, in a joint declaration issued during Li Keqiang's visit to Italy in October 2014, the two sides made pledges to boost cooperation in areas such as justice, law enforcement, security and rule of law; however, it

---

[1] In Mikko Huotari *et al.* (eds.), Mapping Europe–China Relations. A Bottom-Up Approach. A Report by the European Think-tank Network on China (ETNC), Berlin, Mercator Institute for China Studies, October 2015, pp. 46–50. Visit: http://www.iai.it/en/pubblicazioni/italy-and-china-investing-each-other.

[2] See in this sense, MOFCOM news-room, document is available at: http://english.mofcom.gov.cn/article/newsrelease/significantnews/201706/20170602595743.shtml.

remains to be seen whether the two sides will be able to cooperate on these issues effectively, given their different political and legal systems. In addition, the two governments reached consensus on strengthening collaboration in five priority areas: energy conservation, environmental protection, food security, aviation and space.

7.1.1.1 Focus on Investments

Development of relationships is largely based on the investment opportunities Italy offers to Chinese investors. Italy is particularly attractive to Chinese investors in the following sectors: fashion, furniture and food. However, the moves of the respective parties, i.e. sellers and investors, are not always directed or promoted by institutional bodies. This can lead to a disorganized approach and opportunities are missing. Governmental action(s) is/are not always the most appropriate response; however, an initiative at the ministerial level can help in boosting trade relationships.

One of the latest governmental moves took place at the end of April 2015 when the China–Italy inter-ministerial committee took place in Beijing, coinciding with the visit to China of the new Italian Minister for Foreign Affairs, Paolo Gentiloni (now the new Italian Prime Minister). At the margin of the inter-ministerial committee, a China–Italy Business Forum for Small and Medium Enterprises — initially proposed by the Italian government — was held to discuss industrial cooperation, non-tariff barriers and market access, with particular attention devoted to the question of Chinese investments in Italy, which have increased significantly in the last couple of years.

7.1.1.2 A Brief Overview on Chinese Investments in Italy

It is worth mentioning that the most significant investments in Italy, since early 2014, have been realized by the People's Bank of China (PBOC) through its investment arm, i.e. the State Administration of Foreign Exchange (SAFE). The amount of investments has exceeded €3.2 billion and they include stakes of about 2% in eight of Italy's largest companies; the two most important ones are: (i) Fiat Chrysler Automobiles and (ii) the state-controlled Eni (oil and gas operator).[3] This has made the PBOC the 12th largest investor in Italy's stock exchange. Moreover, in May 2014 the Shanghai Electric Group bought a 40% stake in power engineering company Ansaldo Energia for €400 million. This was quickly followed by China's State Grid's acquisition of a 35% stake in the energy grid holding company CDP Reti for €2.1 billion. It must be noted that Italian media and public opinion showed mixed feelings toward these deals: on the one hand, the investments were welcomed as they demonstrated trust in the Italian industrial sector and provided fresh liquidity to the system; on the other hand, some media outlets and public opinion voiced concerns about China's acquiring stakes in strategic assets for the political implications that this may have.

Investment opportunities in Italy are abundant for Chinese investors; however, there is the need for a more orchestrated efforts between Chinese and Italian institutions in order to grasp those opportunities. It seems that both China and Italy have come to understand that coordinated actions are the right response in order to boost their trade relations. In fact, at the 12th Meeting of China–Italy Joint Commission for Economic and Trade Cooperation held in Rome in 2017, it seems that the two parties found new grounds to further develop their relationship and enhance economic and trade relations. The next section is dedicated to discussing the (programmatic) results of this meeting and the actions to be put in place to further advance cooperation.

7.1.2 *The 12th Meeting of China–Italy Joint Commission for Economic and Trade Cooperation held in Rome in 2017: Strengthening the Relations under the B&R Initiative*

The 12th meeting of China–Italy Joint Commission for Economic and Trade Cooperation was held in Rome on June 14, 2017. China International

---

[3] Due to the lack of reliable information on China's FDI, providing figures on how much investment has so far targeted Italy is a difficult task. According to the estimates by the Heritage Foundation, reported by the *Financial Times*, by the end of June 2014 Beijing had invested about €7 billion in Italy, half of which was recorded in the first half of 2014.

Trade Representative and Vice Minister of Commerce Fu Ziying and the Italian Vice Minister of Economic Development Ivan Stafaroto co-chaired the meeting. The two sides exchanged views on issues concerning implementing the leaders' consensus, strengthening trade and economic cooperation under the framework of B&R Initiative.

In particular, Fu Ziying during the meeting said that President Xi Jinping and Premier Li Keqiang have met with the visiting Italian Prime Minister Paolo Gentiloni during the Belt and Road Forum for International Cooperation held in May 2017 in Beijing, and the leaders of both sides have reached a major consensus on raising the China–Italy Comprehensive Strategic Partnership to a new level. In fact in recent years, China–Italy bilateral trade has made steady growth; two-way investment has grown rapidly, and fruitful achievements have been made in energy conservation and environmental protection, medical health, sustainable urbanization, agriculture modernization and aeronautical and space cooperation. "China is Italy's largest trading partner in Asia and Italy is China's 5th largest trading partner in EU. To further strengthen bilateral trade and economic cooperation under the framework of B&R Initiative and step up common development, Fu Ziying suggested: 1. We should strengthen the docking of bilateral economic development strategies, expand cooperation in infrastructure areas and the third party market; 2. We should lead local and SMEs cooperation through China-Italy industrial cooperation zones; 3. We should fully play the double tracks' role of China–Italy Joint Commission for Economic and Trade Cooperation and China–Italy Entrepreneurs Committee and continue to expand the size of trade and investment; 4. We hope Italy to play a more important and positive role in EU, jointly uphold trade liberalization and promote China-EU Investment Treaty negotiations."[4]

7.1.2.1 Reinforced Cooperation Under the B&R Initiative

"Stafaroto first expressed congratulations to China for the successful Belt and Road Forum for International Cooperation held in Beijing. Leaders of

---

[4] MOFCOM, press release, *Meeting of China–Italy Joint Commission for Economic and Trade Cooperation held in Rome*, June 19, 2017, the document is available at the following website: http://english.mofcom.gov.cn/article/newsrelease/significantnews/201706/20170 602595743.shtml.

both sides made frequent visits at present, which has created new room for the development of bilateral trade and economic relations. China–Italy trade and economic relations are satisfying; areas of cooperation have been becoming wider and deeper. China is Italy's third largest source of imports and fifth largest destination of exports. The bilateral trade and investment grew rapidly with great potential. Italy would like to strengthen cooperation with China in sea transport, aviation and infrastructure areas under the framework of B&R Initiative and increase exports of farm products to China. He hoped that China could actively help with e Italy's specific concern and Italy would like to continue to play its role in EU, jointly uphold trade liberalization with China and step up the China–EU Investment Treaty negotiations as soon as possible."[5]

It is worthy of mention that "after the meeting, China International Trade Representative and Vice Minister of Commerce Fu Ziying and Italian Vice Minister of Economic Development Ivan Stafaroto jointly signed the Minutes of the Meeting and MOU on Strengthening China–Italy Trade and Economic Cooperation in Medical Health Area."

7.1.2.2 Latest Diplomatic Developments: The Visit of President Sergio Mattarella in February 2017 to Strengthen Cooperation with China

Sergio Mattarella, President of the Italian Republic, met with his Chinese counterpart Xi Jinping during his state visit to Beijing from February 21 to 26, 2017.

The Italian president was accompanied by a delegation of entrepreneurs. The Italian Head of State presented the strengths of his country and encouraged Chinese companies to invest in Italy. During his visit, President Mattarella participated in the Italy–China Business Forum,[6]

---

[5] *Ibid.*

[6] The 2017 Business Forum Edition, held in Beijing, was organized to celebrate the high-level meeting between Italy's Republic President Sergio Mattarella and PRC President Xi Jingping. Over 250 Italian delegates attended the 4th Business Forum, representing 90 Italian enterprises. The Italian presence in China has widely developed in recent years and today the annual sales turnover of the 2.000 Italian enterprises based in China is over €5 billion. The 4th Business Forum Italy–China, hosted by China Chamber of Commerce for Import and Export of Machinery and Electronic Products (CCCME), Italian Trade Agency (ITA) and

whose two main themes were "Made in China 2025" and "B&R." In fact, the next stage now is to align China's B&R Initiative with Italy's national development strategies, integrate "Made in China 2025"[7] with Italy's "Industry 4.0,"[8] and connect China's "Internet plus" strategy with Italy's technological innovation plan.[9]

As far as cultural relations are concerned, China and Italy are carrying forward diversified programs of activities aimed to enhance mutual understanding and traditional friendship between the two peoples. Italy is a major EU country with worldwide influence, and China stands ready to heighten communication and coordination with Italy on the reform of the UN Security Council, climate change, sustainable development and other issues.

Regarding the "21st Century Maritime Silk Road," Italy boasts plenty of basic facilities and rich experiences in port operations and logistics, which enable it to play an important role in the project, in so doing promoting global economics, trade and cultural cooperation.

7.1.3 *Italy as the End-Point of China's 21st Century Maritime Silk Road*

The Maritime Silk Road is meant to connect China with the Mediterranean — at the center of which lies the Italian peninsula. This

---

Confindustria, sponsored by Ministry of Commerce of the People's Republic of China and Ministry of Economic Development of the Republic of Italy, was opened by Zhou Xiaoyan, Director of Ministry of Foreign Commerce of China who expressed the great efforts that the two countries are contributing to the development of the bilateral trade relationships and that today is represented by a trade exchange of US$43 billion.

[7] "Made in China 2025" is a concept derived from "Industry 4.0." The heart of "Industry 4.0" idea is intelligent manufacturing. Basically, it means using Internet to connect small and medium-sized companies in a more efficient way in global production and innovation networks. "Made in China 2025" is the first 10-year action plan designed to transform China from a manufacturing giant that relies on low-cost labor into a world manufacturing power. The plan is designed to increase national competitiveness and stimulate innovation rather than simply supporting a single industry.

[8] The Under-secretary of State of the Ministry of Economic Development of the Republic of Italy, On. Ivan Scalfarotto, presented the new program of industrial and commercial development (Industria 4.0) and invited China to "Do It With Italy" by using the advanced technologies developed through "Italy 4.0."

[9] See in this sense: http://www.oboreurope.com/en/mattarella-china/.

makes Italy particularly attractive. In fact, Italy is considered by Chinese leaders to be an important piece in the implementation of the B&R Initiative. Italian ports and rail connections to the markets in Central, Eastern and Northern Europe have become the focus of attention for the Italian government, and the Chinese are keen to exploit opportunities in the logistics and infrastructure sectors to promote the 21st Century Maritime Silk Road. Italy substantially represents the perfect entry point for Chinese goods destined to Central and Northern Europe. Chinese officials have declared on several occasions their interest for Italy as a gateway to the Mediterranean. For this reason, together with the fact that Italy is considered as an attractive destination to Chinese investors, there are great expectations that Chinese investments, related not only to the B&R Initiative, will surge in the near future. Furthermore, Italy is seen as a valuable source of those assets Chinese companies are very eager and thus willing to acquire, for example, companies in the food industry or operating in the fashion sector. However, the following sections will only cover B&R-related aspects and explain how the two countries are cooperating in order to render smoother development of this Initiative.

7.2 B&R and Italy: Strengthening the Southern Route of the Maritime Silk Road

Italy is deemed by Chinese leaders to be vital for the realization of B&R because of its position in the Mediterranean Sea. As underlined above, the Italian ports and rail connections to the markets in Central, Eastern and Northern Europe have become the Italian government's focus of attention and of course the reasons why China is so interested in developing synergies with Italy in developing this Initiative. The Chinese are eager to develop opportunities in the logistics and infrastructure sectors to promote the Maritime Silk Road, and existing Italian facilities perfectly fit Chinese plans.

It is clear that Chinese investments in Italy will not only continue targeting the most desired targets in the fashion and food industry and other industries (see next section) meeting the desires of Chinese investors, but also these investments will be directed to realize infrastructure projects, or acquiring infrastructure, to better serve the interests of China.

7.2.1 *Chinese Presence in Italy: A Brief Overview*

China has already invested heavily in Italy, and in different sectors. However, probably the most significant and redundant investment was the acquisition of Pirelli in 2015.[10]

When state-owned China National Chemical Corporation — or ChemChina, China's largest chemical company with a turnover of about €40 billion — bought Italy's premium tire maker, Pirelli, for US$ 7.7 billion in 2015, the deal was funded in part by the Silk Road Fund, which took a 25% stake in the ChemChina unit established to buy Pirelli's shares. This led some Italian business leaders, including personalities such as Marco Tronchetti Provera, Chief Executive Officer (CEO) of Pirelli — which is now effectively controlled by ChemChina — to mount a strong push to steer Italian foreign policy in a pro-China direction, prevailing over reservations in the Italian Ministry of Foreign Affairs. Today, the companies that are likely to benefit from B&R projects — and that are therefore lobbying the Italian government — are those operating in the logistics and infrastructure sectors.[11]

7.2.2 *Italy's Key B&R Project: The "Five-Port Alliance"*

In relation to the B&R Initiative, one particular project has attracted attention from Chinese and Italian business and political leaders since 2015, namely the five-port initiative, or "Five Ports Alliance" in the northern Adriatic Sea. The "Five Ports Alliance" consists of a major container

---

[10] A brief introduction soon after the acquisition was made in the book titled *Chinese Expansion in the EU — Strategies and Policies of the Two Blocks and the Role of the U.S.*, Cristiano Rizzi, Paolo Rizzi, Lex Smith and Li Guo, American Bar Association, August 2016. Chapter 1, §1.05 [B] Chinese investors and the four Fs: Fashion, Food, Furniture, and Ferrari, sub-paragraph [3.] The acquisition of Pirelli, p. 42, https://shop.americanbar.org/eBus/Store/ProductDetails.aspx?productId=255436382.

[11] In this sense, Frans-Paul van der Putten, John Seaman, Mikko Huotari, Alice EkmN and Miguel Otero-Iglesias, *Europe and China's New Silk Road*, ETNC Report, December 2016, Chapter 8: "OBOR and Italy: Strengthening the Southern Route of the Maritime Silk Road," Nicola Casarini, Head of Research for Asia, Istituto Affari Internazionali (IAI), Rome, October 2016. The document is available at: https://www.clingendael.nl/sites/default/files/Europe_and_Chinas_New_Silk_Roads_0.pdf.

terminal project by the Northern Adriatic Port Association (NAPA) that involves major ports in Italy including Venice, Trieste and Ravenna, and in Slovenia (Capodistria) and in Croazia (Fiume). "This initiative represents Italy's flagship B&R project. The project aims to create a docking system by building a giant offshore platform at the city port of Malamocco near Venice in order to allow the huge Chinese cargo ships coming via the Suez Canal to unload goods and send them by railway connections through Germany and Switzerland to markets in Central and Northern Europe. The project has received large interest from Italy and China and it will be financed by the Italian government, but it seems that there is also space for 'B&R capital' which should come from the Chinese government and Chinese SOEs (see Section 7.2.2.1).

Potentially, the 'Five Port Alliance' will challenge the position of Piraeus and Istanbul in South-East European and Rotterdam, Antwerp and Hamburg in Northern Europe."[12]

The "Five Ports Alliance" initiative received high-level support from Italian and Chinese authorities during the Forum of Cooperation of Silk Road Cities, [13] which was held in Venice on July 23, 2015,[14] and during a

---

[12] In this sense, Xieshu WANG, Joel Ruet and Xavier Richer, *One Belt One Road and the reconfiguration of China-EU Relations,* CEPN — Centre d'economie de l'Universite Paris Nord CNRS UMR n. 7234, Document de travail du CEPN, March 4, 2017, p. 13. Document is available at: https://cepn.univ-paris13.fr/wp-content/uploads/2017/03/DT-CEPN-2017-04.pdf.

[13] The Silk Road Cities Cooperation Forum is a project destined to "change the course of history and mark the future of the Eurasian continent," said Roberto Ciambetti, President of the Regional Council of Veneto region, of which Venice is the capital during the Forum which was held in Venice on July 23, 2015. "The most direct route between the entrance to the Suez Canal and the heart of manufacturing Europe is the Adriatic Sea, and Venice is a strategic point of the Adriatic. However, Costa went on saying, the Venice port is not equipped yet with the right infrastructures to serve the enormous movement of goods from China along the 'Belt and Road' route." Paolo Costa, Chairman of the Venice Port Authority, explained to Xinhua. http://news.xinhuanet.com/english/2015-07/26/c_134448483.htm.

[14] Hao Yaohua, President of Silk Road Cities Alliance, stressed the indispensable role of cities along the B&R in realizing the "five cooperation priorities," or policy coordination, facilities connectivity, unimpeded trade, financial integration and people-to-people bonds of the B&R. The Silk Road Cities Alliance, which aims to support cooperation between cities along the route, co-organized the forum with Priorita Cultura (Culture is Priority), an association promoting culture as a tool for international dialogue, chaired by former

follow-up event that was also held in Venice in July 2016.[15] Organizers included the Chinese Silk Road Cities Alliance and the Venice Port Authority,[16] while participants included policymakers and business leaders from both China and Italy.

---

culture minister of Italy Francesco Rutelli. The forum, attended by Italian Foreign Minister Paolo Gentiloni, was the second event of two days dedicated to the role of B&R and related "cultural diplomacy." See: http://europe.chinadaily.com.cn/business/2015-07/24/content_21395962.htm.

[15] The Venice Port Authority, together with the Foundation for Worldwide Cooperation and Nakai University (Center for the SILK ROAD STUDIES), with the support of the Binhai New Area (the Special Economic Zone in Tianjin), and in cooperation with TWAI, the Centre for Mediterranean Area Studies and Ca'Foscari University, has organized the International Conference 'Along the Silk Roads' in Venice. Introduced by President Romano Prodi and the President of the Venice Port Authority, Paolo Costa, the Conference was attended by Minister of Foreign Affairs Paolo Gentiloni, Minister of Infrastructure Graziano Delrio, Austrian Transport Minister JörgLeichtfried, the Russian Minister for Euro-Asian Integration, Ms Tatiana Valovaya, as well as by other representatives of various institutions and Think Tanks from China, Asia and Europe. https://www.port.venice.it/en/the-international-conference-along-the-silk-roads.html.

[16] During the event, two agreements have been signed for the development of the Venice (Marhera) and Tianjin Ports facilities and industrial areas and investments in infrastructure and technology for key ports along the 21st Century Silk Road, Venice, July 10, 2016 – During the International Conference 'Along the Silk Roads', organized by the Foundation for Worldwide Cooperation, the Venice Port Authority and Nankai University (Center for the Silk Road Studies), two important 'Memorandums of Understanding' have been signed between the ports that play a key role for the development of the new Silk Road — Venice and Tianjin — and between the two industrial and logistic areas of Porto Marghera and the Binhai New Area. These agreements turn into concrete results the vision identified in the Guidelines on the 'Silk Road Economic Belt and the 21st Century Maritime Silk Road' drafted by the National Development and Reform Commission and by the Ministries of Foreign Affairs and Commerce of the People's Republic of China. The aim of the Chinese Government is to invest jointly to build and integrate a maritime route and to facilitate a safe and efficient implementation of the port cities situated along the Silk Road. At the presence of Foreign Minister Paolo Gentiloni, the Mayor of Venice Luigi Brugnaro signed the cooperation agreement with Shan Zefeng (Deputy Governor of Tianjin Binhai) to jointly develop of projects in the fields of economy, science and technology but also culture and tourism. The two "twin" areas, Porto Marghera and Tianjin Binhai New Area, have a lot of aspects in common. Indeed, the aim of such cooperation is to promote and foster investment and the development of companies in the two countries by creating real partnerships. The infrastructural upgrade will increase the competitiveness in the logistics

7.2.2.1 Financing the Project

The project will cost around €2.2 billion. €350 million has already been budgeted by the Italian government to start work on the offshore docking platform near Venice and to build the initial infrastructure to service the mega-cargo ships in the five ports. Chinese investors have already shown interest in this project, particularly, the port authorities of Shanghai and Nongbo; the China Communications Construction Group (CCCG, the world's sixth largest infrastructure company); and the Industrial and Commercial Bank of China (ICBC). It is important to note that the ICBC has recently opened a few branches in Italy and has designed loan schemes to finance B&R projects that are open to both Chinese and Italian firms.[17]

---

and will strengthen the relationship between the EU and China. Indeed the route from China — via Venice — is the one that minimize the time and costs of maritime trip and of ground handling. So the maritime silk route will be the most efficient route for trade between the two continents. For this reason, the joint development of the ports, in both infrastructural and operational terms, and also through mutual assistance in the use of technological and organizational innovations, constitutes the main objective of the second agreement signed by the President of the Venice Port Authority, Paolo Costa and Lu Wei President from the Port of Tianjin, the largest Port in Northern China. This port — based on current forecasts — is expected to handle 20 million containers by the end of 2017. If — as forecast by the Shanghai International Shipping Institute — in 2030 the cargo handled at Chinese ports doubles, exceeding 25 billion tons, with container throughput reaching 505 million TEUs, and at least 40 million TEUs will travel along the maritime silk route to and from Europe. From now on the two ports will be working together at sea to strengthen the ties that bind the East and the West by exchanging information and through innovative plans and projects to consolidate the route followed by Marco Polo. Within this framework, the port of Venice, already identified as the Silk Road western terminal with the other Adriatic ports (Ravenna, Trieste, Koper and Rijeka), will in fact be playing a strategic role for historical and economic reasons, as well as for its potential as a link with the heart of the European manufacturing industry, which in the past 15 years has been increasingly shifting eastward. The entire Press release is available at the following website: https://www.port.venice.it/files/press_release/2016/160711apvcsen.pdf.

[17] In this sense, Frans-Paul van der Putten, John Seaman, Mikko Huotari, Alice EkmN and Miguel Otero-Iglesias (ed.), *Europe and China's New Silk Road*, ETNC Report, December 2016, Chapter 8: "OBOR and Italy: Strengthening the Southern Route of the Maritime Silk Road," Nicola Casarini, Head of Research for Asia, Istituto Affari Internazionali (IAI), Rome, October 2016. The document is available at: https://www.clingendael.nl/sites/default/files/Europe_and_Chinas_New_Silk_Roads_0.pdf.

7.2.2.2 Dimension of the Project

The five-port project involves the Italian ports of Venice, Trieste and Ravenna, plus Capodistria (in Slovenia, in the city of Koper) and Fiume (in Croatia), linked together in the North Adriatic Port Association (NAPA). This project is aimed at attracting, and thus providing services to, China's huge cargo ships that reach the Mediterranean Sea via the Suez Canal.[18] The NAPA alliance is supported by the Italian Ministry of Infrastructure and the Italian Ministry of Foreign Affairs. The plan is to create an offshore/onshore docking system by building a giant multimodal platform off the shore of the city-port of Malamocco, near Venice. The platform, eight miles from the coast where the sea is at least 20 m deep, is designed to allow the giant cargo ships to dock. Once operational, the platform is expected to handle between 1.8 and 3 million TEU per year. As a comparison, today all of the Italian ports combined can handle 6 million TEU.

7.2.2.3 Strategic Importance for China

The project, which all together includes building five terminals: three in Italy (i.e. Marghera, Ravenna and Trieste); one in Slovenia (Capodistria/Koper);[19] and one in Croatia (Fiume),[20] is of strategic importance for China. Once completed, this project will consist of a network of ports in the northern Adriatic Sea that is able to service the mega-ships coming from China and that will cut down shipping time to the markets in central,

---

[18] Chinese goods are currently shipped through the Suez Canal, then in a wide loop through the Mediterranean, the Bay of Biscay and the English Channel to ports on Europe's north-western coast, including Rotterdam, Antwerp and Hamburg, from where they are dispatched by road and rail to inland cities. China is investing large sums in the renovation, and upgrade, of rail systems in Southern and Eastern Europe. Once these projects are completed, Chinese products will go from the Suez Canal — which recently doubled its capacity — directly to Piraeus to be loaded on to trains, reaching the markets in Central and Northern Europe through the Balkan high-speed rail link, cutting transit times from roughly 30 to 20 days.

[19] Capodistria or "Koper" is a city that belonged to Italy before the First World War.

[20] Fiume also belonged to Italy before the Great War and where there is still a sizeable Italian community.

eastern and northern Europe. The journey from Shanghai to the northern Adriatic Sea is around 8,600 miles, compared to 11,000 miles from Shanghai to Hamburg — a route that requires eight more days of navigation.

The five-port initiative seeks to provide Chinese mega-ships with a parallel — and alternative — south–north route to the one running from Piraeus through the Balkans. To this end, the Italian government is upgrading rail connections between the Italian ports in the northern Adriatic Sea with the markets in central and northern Europe. There is now a new transalpine railway, which was inaugurated in June 2016 after completion of the San Gotthard tunnel between Italy and Switzerland. Another tunnel in Loetschberg is set to be completed by 2020, allowing trains to run from Zurich to Milan in two and a half hours. All this makes the project particularly attractive for China, but it also leads to the emergence of the necessity for a more in-depth dialogue with all the parties involved, in order to smoothly develop the project according to the Italian and EU legal framework concerning the realization of infrastructure projects.

It should be noted that Chinese shipping companies have a well-established presence in the Italian ports of Naples and Genoa, where both COSCO and the China Shipping Company have invested heavily. It is also interesting to note that the port of Gioia Tauro in southern Italy received some interest from Chinese investors before they decided to turn their focus to the Greek Port of Piraeus. With the five-port alliance in the northern Adriatic Sea, Italy thus hopes to regain some of the traffic that has been lost to the Greek port. However, the interest of China toward Italian ports infrastructures might be extended to other projects which are still at a preliminary stage (more information on these projects to be found in Section 5.3).

7.2.2.4 Potential Challenges and the Necessity to Abide with EU (and IT) Rules

It is necessary to underline that in Italy the B&R Initiative only with the efforts and propaganda of a few subjects, especially the business community, is being promoted. In fact, there is little discussion in the Italian media about the B&R and its implications especially at the economic level. Italy's public debate on the subject has so far focused on the opportunities that Silk Road projects could bring to the Italian economy, and only recently have more events and forum been dedicated to this subject. In particular, with regard to the "Five Ports" project, a few voices, mainly from local media and environmental NGOs, have raised concerns, particularly regarding the potential environmental risks that the five-port project — which involves the docking of giant cargo ships — could have for a city like Venice. So far, it seems that the business community's argument is winning over environmental concerns. However, it is possible, as the project enters its implementation phase, that groups of concerned citizens and associations will create difficulties and oppose the project. This is always possible as a consequence for projects with some impact on the environment. This scenario could pose some questions and put pressure on politicians, who will thus feel compelled to take action, leaving open the possibility of B&R's five-port initiative in the northern Adriatic Sea going through adjustments and/or being downsized, with potential implications for Sino-Italian relations.

While this possible scenario can always possibly accompany the development of a project like the Five Ports initiative, the main concern of the promoters should be respecting the rules in realizing such projects. In fact, one of the main obstacles that has impeded a faster development of the B&R Initiative, or better to say "of B&R-related projects" in the EU is the slow acceptance of the EU's role in shaping the rules for China's engagement with individual EU member states.

It must be underlined that the Chinese leadership clearly did not understand how the EU works. China while beginning to promote its B&R Initiative differentiated between the level of EU member states and the level of EU institutions and their respective roles in the China-led initiative. For example, Silk Road-related projects were quickly rolled out in Central Europe (under the 16+1 mechanism, which involves 11 EU member states from Central Europe and 5 western Balkan countries associated with the EU),[21] Greece (investments in the port of Piraeus) and Germany

---

[21] Reference must be made to 1.5.1, "How China is overcoming the situation: the "16+1 mechanism."

(the Chongqing–Duisburg train connection). When it comes to the realization of specific projects, Chinese parties involved in the project perceived the EU, and in particular the European Commission, with its emphasis on rules and regulations, as a potential problem. However, China quickly realized that the EU's rules on state aid and public procurement cannot be ignored, and these rules could represent an obstacle for the Chinese companies. In fact, the Chinese model of infrastructure financing, which involves state guarantees from the borrowing country and requires the direct award of a financed project to the Chinese companies, is completely different and without an open and competitive tender like it must be done in the EU.[22]

7.3 Infrastructures Related to the Maritime Silk Road to Be Developed in Italy

Italy, owing to its position in the Mediterranean, is at the center of Chinese attention. Under the umbrella of the EU,[23] Italy is developing its infrastructure facilities, in particular its ports, to better connect with the rest of the European market. This is one of the reasons why China is willing to cooperate with Italy in the realization of these infrastructures projects. In fact, China welcomes Italy to actively participate in building the "B&R" construction and support enterprises of the two countries to carry out cooperation in ports, shipbuilding and shipping. It is to be noted that

---

[22] See also: ETNC Report, December 2016. Chapter 16: *"The EU level: 'Belt and Road' Initiative Slowly Coming to Terms with the EU Rules-based Approach,"* Michal Makocki, Senior Visiting Academic Fellow, Mercator Institute for China Studies (MERICS), Berlin, September 2016: https://www.clingendael.nl/sites/default/files/Europe_and_Chinas_New_Silk_Roads_0.pdf.

[23] The EU is developing and financing several projects in Italy in order to enhance connectivity with the rest of the European market. The Venice port and the project to develop its capacity is connected to other EU initiatives such as the TEN-T program (Trans-European Transport Network and the Territorial Cooperation Programmes (Italy- Slovenia, IPA-Adriatic, Alpine Space, Central Europe, MED, South-East Europe; for further information visit: https://www.port.venice.it/en/european%20projects%201.html 2007–2013 European Projects: https://www.port.venice.it/en/2007-2013-european-projects.html; European projects 2014–2020: https://www.port.venice.it/en/2014-2020-european-projects.html.

Chinese President Xi Jinping has confirmed China's intention to include Italian ports on its investment list for this giant Silk Road Investment program. Thanks to Chinese investments, it will be possible in particular to develop the ports of Trieste[24] and Genoa, linked to the rail and highway system, and thus to reach the rich heart of Europe. These two projects together with the Venice project (VOOPS, see Section 7.3.1) and the Five-Ports Alliance, should allow Italy to regain a certain predominance and enable them to better compete with other EU ports and hubs. Also, these projects should integrate the China plans and become an important part of the Maritime Silk Road, together with the China-owned Greek Port of Piraeus. The next three sections aim at describing a little bit more in detail about these three Italian projects which are so important for the realization of the Maritime Silk Road.

7.3.1 *The Port of Venice in the B&R Strategy Framework and the VOOPS Project (Venice Offshore–Onshore Port System)*

Venice is situated at the top end of the Adriatic Sea, at the intersection of the main European transport corridors. The Port of Venice is in a position to act as the European gateway for trade flows to and from Asia.

The project of creating a Venice Offshore–Onshore Port System (VOOPS) is necessary to keep its competitiveness in the Mediterranean Sea, and it also perfectly responds to the interests of China in connection

---

[24]Trieste is the Italian port with the greatest tonnage of goods handled in 2016. Second place goes to Genoa, which on the other hand takes the top spot as a final destination for container traffic. La Spezia is second place on that front, while Gioia Tauro is the first port for Italian transhipment. For the second consecutive year, Trieste in the northern Friuli-Venezia Giulia region handled a record amount of goods: 59.2 million tons, up 3.68% compared to 2015. A large part of that was made up of liquid bulk goods (42.7 million tons), nevertheless solids also saw considerable growth, passing from 1.6 million to 1.9 million tons (+22.45%). On the other hand, container traffic declined from 501,000 TEUs (Twenty-Foot Equivalent Units) in 2015 to 486,000 in 2016 (−2.94%); traffic linked to the "highways of the sea" (that is those who travel with the ferry and roll-on/roll-off ships), was stable in terms of vehicles in transit (+0.29%). http://www.italy24.ilsole24ore.com/art/business-and-economy/2017-01-30/port-of-trieste-gets-prize-for-cargo-traffic-173748.php?uuid=AESKipK.

to the B&R. In addition, it seems that Venice and in general the North Adriatic ports are at the right place to make the Maritime Silk Road the greenest and with the best time/cost ratio:

➢ longest maritime leg with bigger and cleaner vessels (18,000 TEU and more);
➢ shortest land leg to "manufacturing Europe";
➢ innovative port and logistics handling of mega-cargoes.

It is interesting to note that the bureaucratic authorizations procedures started back in 2010, and the entire project was approved definitely on March 29, 2012.[25] The CIPE (Inter-ministerial Committee on Economic Programming) also approved the project which was inserted into the Budgetary National Laws of 2013 and 2014 that set bylaws to start "any activity related to the realization of the offshore Venice Platform (…)," in a public–private partnership (PPP) model.[26]

7.3.1.1 Cost of the Project

The estimated costs for the realization of the whole system lie at around €2.19 billion that are supposed to be earmarked with both public and private resources (PPP scheme) under project financing regime.[27] It is noteworthy that the promoter has applied for EU (EIB) financing.

---

[25] The entire project — consisting of the onshore terminal and the offshore platform — was approved by the Higher Council of Public Works (by its special section overlooking any project dealing with the safeguarding of Venice and its lagoon, under law May 5, 1907) on March 29, 2012. The project received the positive opinion of the Environmental Impact Assessment Committee of the Ministry for the Environment (opinion no. 1320) of August 2, 2013.

[26] http://offshore.port.venice.it/index.php/2016/02/venezia-il-voops-e-la-via-della-seta/?lang=en.

[27] In 2012, the Italian Financial Act for 2013 (Law 228/2012), as per Article 1, c.186, allocated €5 million funding to the VOOPS project's rump-up phase. In 2014, the Italian Financial Act for 2015 (Law 190/2014) allocated €100 million for the final design and first works. The €100 million approved were allocated as follows: 2016: €3 million; 2017: €30 million; 2018: €55 million, https://ec.europa.eu/eipp/desktop/en/projects/project-19.html.

However, this is not the only project involving Venice. The European Union approved the allocation of the funds to support European infrastructures. The port of Venice was awarded 2 projects out of 13 approved for Italy within the 2016 call for proposals of the Connecting Europe Facility (CEF), out of a total 349 projects submitted. Moreover, 35 projects of the 2016 call for proposals of the European "Adriatic-Ionian" Transnational Cooperation Programme (ADRION) were also selected, 2 of which concern the Port System Authority.[28]

7.3.1.2 Characteristics of the Project

The VOOPS project is seen and perceived as a necessary upgradation of Italian ports, in particular for the Port of Venice. With sea beds at 12-m depth, the port of Venice can today accommodate ships up to 7,000 TEUs, which is no longer enough to be competitive in the global shipping market that can count on ships up to 18,000 TEUs, already in operation, which will soon be overshadowed by 22,000-TEU ships, under construction. This perspective does not only place Venice, but also all the Italian ports, out of the market, based on the three parameters of nautical accessibility, port operating spaces and connecting infrastructures with port-related markets to serve. These three parameters can turn a modern port into an efficient hub of global logistic chains. The offshore terminal will be a strongly innovative,[29] future-oriented "port machinery," which will be able — also by virtue of its connection with multiple ports — to meet the market requirements of nautical accessibility and port-operating spaces. This is why it is strategic for the growth of Venice, of Italy and of Europe.[30]

---

[28] https://www.port.venice.it/files/press_release/2017/170629adspcsfondiue.pdf.

[29] Positioned 8 miles offshore, where the sea bottom is at least 20 m deep, the offshore platform will be protected by a 4.2 km long breakwater dam which will shelter an oil terminal and a container terminal able to accommodate up to three latest generation container ships at the same time. Along the quay with its modular development (1 km long in the first stage, which can be increased up to 2 km at a later stage) specially-made cranes and a highly automated system, able to ensure loading/unloading performances equal to those of the best worldwide terminals, will be accommodated.

[30] http://offshore.port.venice.it/index.php/progetto/?lang=en.

The VOOPS is a concrete project which also reduces the impact on environment and meets with the principles expressed at the Paris Convention on the climate change. In fact, the project expresses radical innovations in the transportation system to reduce global warming. These innovations should aim at constantly choosing the shortest and most efficient transportation paths. The port of Venice can significantly contribute to reducing greenhouse gases with its innovative VOOPS, ensuring the minimum transport cost on the maritime China–Europe maritime route. The port of Venice ensures the minimum transport cost on the inland-leg of the logistic chain as it is, geographically, the closest port to the center of European manufacturing industry.[31]

7.3.1.3 Synergies with Other Facilities

The project provides for a synergic connection with four onshore terminals: Montesyndial (Marghera), Chioggia, Mantua and Porto Levante. The transfer of containers from ocean ships will be performed on LASH vessels, the so-called "Mama Vessels," especially designed for Venice, which exploit the compressed-air technology of the British Royal Navy submarines and the Archimedes' principle to halve the travel time between the offshore platform and the onshore terminals.[32]

7.3.1.4 China Communication Constructions Company Group — The Winner of the Final Design of VOOPS

The final design of the new VOOPS has been awarded to the Italian–Chinese consortium 4C3, led by the China Communication Constructions Company Group (CCCC Group).[33] Although the solicitation for the new terminal was an international affair, only 4C3, which includes companies

---

[31] "(VOOPS) could serve as a model for ports worldwide struggling with accommodating massive container ships, protecting local environment, and maintaining port security." "Venice Offshore Onshore Port system: Building the Venice Offshore Port," Maritime Reporter and Engineering News, New York, September 2015.

[32] *Ibid.*

[33] See article at: http://www.maritimejournal.com/news101/marine-civils/port,-harbour-and-marine-construction/venice-port-system-design-awarded.

such as 3Ti Progetti Italia and E-Ambiente, passed the strict selection requirements of the solicitation and aimed at obtaining a high design standard. VOOPS includes the design for the offshore platform off the Malamocco district and the first container terminal to be established in the Montesyndial area at Porto Marghera.[34]

7.3.2 Port of Trieste

The port of Trieste also offers state-of-the-art maritime services in terms of accessibility, being one of the deepest ports in the Mediterranean Sea (18 m). All terminals are connected directly to the rail network, with inter-modal daily connections and direct to 12 destinations in central and eastern Europe, including Luxembourg, Hungary, Italy, Czech Republic, Germany, Austria, Northern Europe and the Baltic Sea.

The Trieste Port System Authority is committed to maximizing its excellent maritime accessibility through the further expansion of quays that, according to Italian law, may be granted in concession to private terminals or private navigators. Equally strong is also the commitment to enhance rail accessibility, based on an integrated infrastructure and logistic strategy, aimed at obtaining a better commercial optimization.

The aim of the project is, on the one hand, to create an optimal inter-modal system on the port terminals of Trieste and, on the other, two inter-modal internal systems in Cervignano and Opicina, thus creating an integrated intermodal logistic platform.

Trieste undoubtedly offers the possibility of becoming an inter-modal link hub for serving both Chinese and Italian interests, considering the presence of many well-connected airports which offer great potential.

7.3.3 Ports of Genoa and Savona/Vado

The port system of Genoa and Savona is one of the central ports, recognized at European level, and is the terminus of the Reno-Alps Corridor connecting Genoa to Rotterdam. The port system shall serve to supply the central European market through the Mediterranean provided that Genoa

---

[34] *Ibid.*

can accommodate large transoceanic vessel (18,000 TEUs and above), in service, particularly, on routes with the Far East. Moving and modifying the port protection works of Genoa represents the priority of the port. This priority is due to the need for the larger vessels to be able to operate with maximum safety. The proposed intervention on the dams of the port of Genoa is consistent with the land works already realized and under construction, such as the new Alpine passages, and the Third Railway Line on the Genoa–Milan–Turin which will be completed by 2021.

No doubt China is ready to participate in infrastructure constructions such as ports in Italy, in order to contribute to connectivity between China and Europe. Projects exist, but Chinese participation could become difficult because of the legal framework governing these projects. Section 7.4 will briefly examine the new Italian Public Procurement Code because it regulates the participation of companies in projects related to public work, and thus Chinese companies also should be aware of. However, before we discuss this, it is necessary to underline China's interests in the Mediterranean ports.

7.3.4 *Mediterranean: Final Destination of the Maritime Silk Road and Chinese Expanded Interests*

Officially, the ports of Piraeus in Greece and Venice in Italy are regarded as end points of the Maritime Silk Road. However, Chinese interests go behind these two ports. Greece is certainly a key terminus for the Maritime Silk Road. After finalizing the acquisition of the Greek port in August 2016, by COSCO, the port's capacity, infrastructure, operations and revenues have reportedly improved significantly due to the Chinese investment and management, and through an increased volume of imports from China passing through it.[35] However, the interests of China in the Mediterranean have further expanded; in fact, recently COSCO has acquired a 40% stake in the company which will operate two terminals in the Port of Vado in Italy. It seems the company has also registered an

---

[35]Yao Ling, "A New Chapter in Economic and Trade cooperation between China and Greece" (中国与希腊经贸合作掀开新篇章, zhongguo yu xila jingmao hezuo kai xin bianzhang), *Zhongguo yuanyang chuanwu*, 2016, (7): 15–15.

interest in leasing a terminal at the Algeciras port in the south of Spain, but details are currently scarce.[36]

A few years ago, China started implementing an expansion strategy which now appears to be connected to the B&R Initiative: "Over the last five years, China's interest in maritime infrastructure and inland ports in central and eastern Europe (CEE) has been reported only sporadically in local media, and has not yet led to any firm agreements. However, in 2015, during the China–CEE Summit in Suzhou, the Chinese premier, Li Keqiang, set out the concept of 'AdriaticBaltic–Black Sea Seaport Cooperation' (also referred to as the 'Three Seas Port Cooperation'), in which he envisioned 'establishing industrial cluster areas around ports with the right conditions'."[37] He specified that the approach should combine "China's equipment, European technology and central and eastern European markets on the way to achieving productive cooperation projects."[38] This idea is thus an embodiment of Li's signature concept of "industrial capacity cooperation." "The Three Seas initiative has since become an important part of the discussions taking place in the 16+1 framework."[39]

---

[36] "COSCO marine port acquisition 40 percent interest in Italy poly pier" (中远海运港口收购意大利瓦多码头 40% 权益, zhongyuan haiyun gangkou shougou yidali waduo matou 40% quanyi), *Xinhua*, 18 October 2016, available here http://news.xinhuanet.com/fortune/2016-10/18/c_1119740219.htm (hereafter Xinhua, "COSCO marine port acquisition 40 percent interest in Italy poly pier"); "COSCO intends to bid for Spain's largest container port" (中远海运有意竞购西班牙最大集装箱港码头, zhongyuan haiyun youyi jinggou xibanya zuida jizhuangxiang gang matou), *Caixin Online*, 28 August 2016, available here http://companies.caixin.com/2016-08-24/100981421.html.

[37] Yin Zhen, "Stand high, look far, go steady to promote Three Seas seaports cooperation" (推进三海港区合作要站得高、看得远、走得稳, tuijin sanhai gangqu hezuo yaozhan de gao, kan de yuan, zou de wen), Zhongguo yuanyang chuanwu, 2016 (3): 54–55 (hereafter, Yin Zhen, "Stand high, look far, go steady to promote Three Seas seaports cooperation").

[38] For capacity cooperation, please see: Qiu Zhibo, "The 'Triple Win': Beijing's Blueprint for International Industrial Capacity Cooperation," *China Brief*, Vol. 15, No. 18 (September 2015), available at https://jamestown.org/program/the-triple-win-beijingsblueprint-for-international-industrial-capacity-cooperation/#sthash.6PsUzf15.dpuf.

[39] European Council on Foreign Relations, China Analysis, *China and the Mediterranean: Open for Business?* Available at: http://www.ecfr.eu/publications/summary/china_and_the_mediterranean_open_for_business.

Furthermore it should be noticed that: "One recent article focusing on the French city of Marseille also illustrates how China's interest in ports in the Mediterranean extends beyond acquisitions or upgrades, as well as state-driven strategies.[40] An initiative called the Marseille International Trade City (MITC) is being established in the vicinity of the city's port. It aims to make Marseille the largest wholesale trade centre in the Mediterranean. Initiated and financed by Chinese private enterprises, the MITC is set to house more than 200 wholesalers and to provide a trading platform for small and medium-sized enterprises from France, Italy, eastern Europe, north Africa, and China."[41]

7.4 Participation of Chinese Companies in the Realization of Infrastructure Projects in Italy: An Overview on Public Procurement Regulations in Italy (Derived from the EU Legislation)

Chinese companies willing to participate in infrastructure projects in Italy should be aware of the new Italian Public Procurement Code (or "Public Contracts Code") which dictates the rules "on public procurement and awarding concession contracts, procurement by entities operating in the water, energy, transport and postal services sectors and on the reorganization of the Public Procurement Regulation" (Legislative Decree no. 50, April 18, 2016, "New Public Contracts Code" also known as the "New Code").[42] The New Code entered into force on April 19, 2016. The Code

---

[40] "Marseille builds links with the 'Belt and Road Initiative'" (法国马赛对接 "一带一路" 建设, faguo masai duijie "yi dai yi lu" jianshe), *Jingji Ribao*, February 21, 2017, it can be accessed here: http://china.chinadaily.com.cn/2017-02/21/content_28291376.htm (hereafter, Jingji Ribao, "Marseille builds links with the 'Belt and Road Initiative'").

[41] European Council on Foreign Relations, China Analysis, *China and the Mediterranean: Open for business?* Available at: http://www.ecfr.eu/publications/summary/china_and_ the_mediterranean_open_for_business.

[42] On April 18, 2016, the Italian Council of Ministers approved a new Legislative Decree reforming the Italian Public Procurement regulation. The Code has implemented the EU public procurement Directives, i.e. (i) Directive 2014/23/EU on the award of concession contracts, (ii) Directive 2014/24/EU on the public procurement, and (iii) Directive 2014/25/EU, coordinating the procurement procedures for the award of the same contracts

does not provide for a consolidated implementing regulation but for several secondary sources, such as Ministerial Decrees and guidelines issued by the National Anti-Corruption Authority ("ANAC"). Except for a limited number of ANAC guidelines, such secondary regulations have not been issued yet. Some of the guidelines to be issued by the ANAC are currently subject to discussion with the economic cooperators. Pending the issuance of such soft-law instruments, certain provisions implementing the previous Italian Public Procurement Code will continue to be valid.

This short section is only intended to introduce the main characteristics of the new Code and how contracts with public entities are regulated; in fact these rules apply to public work also, but the description does not pretend to give a complete picture on how to prepare an offer or to participate in the realization of infrastructure projects because an entire set of administrative laws and regulations are of relevance, thus the involvement of local law firms is necessary to assist Chinese investors wishing to participate in such projects.

7.4.1 *Brief Introduction of the New Italian Public Procurement Code*

The Code applies to public works, supply and service contracts and concessions awarded by contracting authorities and other awarding entities, as defined by the Code (e.g. state, regional or local authorities, bodies governed by public law and public companies).

With respect to the Government Procurement Agreement ("GPA"), its purpose is to open up as much of this business as possible to international competition. It is designed to make laws, regulations, procedures and practices regarding government procurement more transparent and to ensure that they do not protect domestic products or suppliers, or discriminate against foreign products or suppliers. Since the provisions of the EU

---

by entities operating in the water, energy, transport and postal services sectors. The scope of the Code is wider than the EU Directives, since it regulates all awarding procedures for contracts both above and below EU thresholds and it contains further rules that are not provided for by the EU Directives, although inspired by the same principles.

Directives and the GPA are closely aligned, compliance with the Code (which in turn implements the Directives) ensures *de facto* compliance by Italy with the GPA.[43]

The Code distinguishes between the ordinary and special sectors. Special sectors include: (i) gas and heat; (ii) electricity; (iii) water; (iv) transport services; (v) ports and airports; (vi) post services; and (vii) extraction of oil and gas and exploration for, or extraction of, coal or other solid fuels. The special sectors are subject to specific provisions, in particular with regard to the publicity of the tender documentation.

It is worth noting that in this context only point (v) might interest Chinese investors. Italian ports represent the natural end of the Maritime Silk Road; thus, these infrastructures are of great interest for Chinese to investors and companies willing to participate in public works aimed at enhancing those infrastructures.

7.4.1.1 Which Types of Contracts Are Covered?

The following types of contracts are covered by and are subject to public procurement legislation:

(a) public works contracts, meaning contracts the object of which is either the execution or both the design and execution of works indicated under Annex I of the Code or the realization, by whatever means, of a work corresponding to the requirements specified by the contracting authority;

(b) public service contracts;

(c) public supply contracts, the object of which is the purchase, lease, rental or hire purchase, with or without the option to buy, of products;

(d) public works contracted out by work concessionaires who are not awarding authorities;

(e) general contractor contracts;

(f) public–private partnership contracts;

(g) public works and public services concessions;

---

[43] Legislative Decree no. 50, April 18, 2016.

(h) availability contracts; and
(i) financial lease contracts of public works, the object of which is the provision of financial services and the realization of public works.

7.4.1.2 What Types of Award Procedures Are Available?

The Code distinguishes between ordinary and special procedures.
  Ordinary procedures include:

(a) open procedures: the contracting authority publishes a call for tender and any interested economic operator may submit a tender according to the conditions and timescales set forth by the call for tender; and
(b) restricted procedures: the contracting authority will solicit economic operators to submit a request to participate in the tender and, subsequently, only the operators invited by the contracting authority may submit a bid.

  The contracting authority is free to choose between open tender and restricted tender procedures.

  Special procedures include the following:

(a) competitive procedure with negotiation: the contracting authority publishes a tender notice open to all the economic operators. The potential bidders shall file their request of participation indicating the qualitative requirements listed under the tender notice. On the basis of such information, the contracting authority invites the qualified bidder to negotiate;
(b) negotiated procedure without previous publication of the call for tender: as a matter of fact, such procedure is similar to a private negotiation, except for the fact that the awarding authority will be required to apply the general principles of transparency, non-discrimination, equal treatment and proportionality; and
(c) competitive dialogue procedure: the contracting authority publishes a call for tender in which there is a list of both the requisites to be met by the competitors and the evaluation criteria of the bids. Any economic operator may request to participate in the tender procedure.

Then, the contracting authority conducts a dialogue with the candidates admitted to that procedure, with the aim of developing one or more suitable alternatives capable of meeting its requirements, and on the basis of which the candidates chosen are invited to tender.

7.4.1.3 What Are the Rules on Excluding/ Short-listing Tenderers?

There are three sets of requirements which must be met by the bidders in order to participate in a public procurement procedure, namely:

(a) general morality requirements;
(b) economic and financial capacity; and
(c) technical and professional skills.

Requirements under points (b) and (c) must be drawn up by the awarding authorities and proportionate to the subject matter of the public procurement.[44]

7.4.1.4 The Procurement Code Introduces a New Financial Guarantees System

With reference to works of a specific value, the "global financial guarantee" provided under the previous legal regime has been repealed and substituted by two different guarantees required under the New Code: (i) the "fair fulfill-ment guarantee" (in Italian: "Garanzia di buon adempimento"), which exists

---

[44] The Code aims to exclude from the tender: entities which have been convicted of certain types of crimes (such as participation in a criminal organization, corruption, bribery, fraud); entities facing bankruptcy (or entering into a proceeding for the declaration of bankruptcy); entities which failed to pay social security contributions or taxes; subjects who have been found guilty of material professional misconduct; and entities which rendered misrepresentations. The Code indicates a precise list of offences causing exclusion. Furthermore, the ANAC shall specify which evidence is appropriate to demonstrate such exclusions by means of guidelines not issued yet and that will be published on the ANAC website. Means of evidence referred to in the Code are imperative just for the awarding authorities. However, other means may be used by the competitors.

until the work is completed without any possibility of release and the (ii) "termination guarantee" ("Garanzia per la risoluzione") to cover costs (corresponding to the value of the damages suffered) incurred due to the need to conduct another public procurement procedure in order to re-enter into the relevant contract with a third party, in case the relationship with the original contractor cannot continue, and to cover costs for the new contractor.

7.4.1.5 Public Building Construction Planning Must be Organized According to Three Projects

The New Procurement Code furthers high quality standards for public works and attempts to limit excessive cost increases due to project variances in the execution of the works. Specifically, according to the New Code, the contracting authorities' public building construction planning must be organized according to three projects:

  (i) the new "technical and economic feasibility" project;
 (ii) the definitive project and
(iii) the executive project, which constitutes the planning standard for all bidders.

The technical and economic feasibility project is meant to increase the technical and economic quality of the project, since the technical and economic feasibility analysis will be drafted on the basis of geological and geotechnical surveys, and preventive archeological checks, with the cost–benefit analysis as the main objective.[45] A progressive introduction of open electronic modeling tools has also been provided, in order to enable a better definition of the projects starting from the first phase of planning.

7.4.1.6 Privatizations and PPPs: Brief Overview

Privatizations represent another way for Chinese investors to participate or to have a stake in infrastructure facilities if the local government allows

---

[45] In this sense see: Latham and Watkins, The New Italian Public Procurement Code (Client Alert commentary), Number 1971, May 18, 2016, document is available at: https://www.lw.com/thoughtLeadership/new-italian-public-procurement-code.

such investments. Privatizations do not fall within the scope of the Code. The disposal of participation held in state-controlled companies is governed by Law 474/1994, according to which the divestments of participations held by the state and the public entities, regardless of the value of the shares on sale, should take place through competitive tenders based on the general principles of transparency, non-discrimination, equal treatment and proportionality. The main issue to be faced is that the general criteria and the conditions of the disinvestment procedure shall be set forth by the Government. In addition, the privatization of companies operating in the sector of the services of general interest shall follow the setting up of independent regulatory bodies and the issuance of a prior opinion by the parliamentary committees. In this context, it is worth mentioning that the current regime provided by Law 474/1994 in relation to the so-called "golden share" (i.e. special powers reserved to the public authorities which disinvest their participation in companies operating in strategic sectors such as defense, energy, infrastructures, telecommunications) was amended by Law Decree 21/2012 and will be replaced following the adoption of specific regulations aimed at implementing the new regime set forth by Law Decree 21/2012.

The new Code has introduced a pivotal change in the Italian legislation on the PPP *(public–private partnership or "Partenariato Pubblico Privato")* as it expressly dedicates a section to PPPs.[46] Moreover, the new Code expressly implements the EU principles in the matter of PPP that were not recalled by the former legislation but nevertheless applied because of the direct effect of the European legislation.

The Code defines the PPP contracts[47] as a contract for pecuniary interest concluded in writing by means of which one or more awarding authorities entrust a set of activities consisting of the realization, transformation, maintenance and operational management of a work, the consideration for which consists in the availability or in the right to exploit the works that are the subject of the contract or in the performance of a service connected to such works. The duration of a PPP contract shall be

---

[46] Reference must be done to Article 179, and Articles 180–191 of the new Procurement Code.

[47] *Ibid.*, Article 180.

initially set depending on the amortization period of the investment and on the financing modalities of the same to one or more economic operators. A central point of the new PPP regulation is the correct allocation of the risk on the contractor. Moreover, the definition of PPP expressly recalls the application of the Eurostat decisions.

The Code specifies that the economic–financial balance is a key point in PPP contracts as it is the assumption for a correct risk allocation. The awarding authority can provide for a public contribution consisting of payments or in the transfer of real estate assets.

In order to ensure the effectiveness of the PPP system, the Code contains provisions aimed at ensuring the compliance of the PPP contracts with the needs of the financing entities. In particular, the PPP contract can be assessed by the awarding authority only provided that the contractor demonstrates the availability of a financing. The execution of the contract is subject to the financing of the works and the contract is terminated in the event that the financing agreement is not entered into by the contractor within 12 months from the execution of the PPP contract. Moreover, the PPP contractors are allowed (i) to issue project bonds also derogating from the provisions of the Italian Civil Code, and (ii) to strengthen the right of the financing entities to select the project company destined to step-in the concession in order to avoid the termination of the concession due to default of the concessionaire (so-called "step-in right").

This is how Italy has transposed the EU procurements rules into its system. However, it is necessary to give an overview about the European rules because these rules apply in all other EU member states.

7.4.2 *Introduction to the EU Procurement Legislation Which Has Modeled the Italian Law*

At the EU level, a set of rules regulating procurement activities does exist. The law applying to these activities deserves due attention. However, the scope of this section is limited to public works (infrastructures projects) which can be developed by Chinese construction enterprises together with the EU counterparts.

7.4.2.1 Applicability of EU Substantive Law — General Principles

Public procurement in the Europe is generally regulated by EU law, including principles that the ECJ held were flowing from the Treaty establishing the EC (EC Treaty).[48] These Public Procurement Directives[49] include: (i) Directive 2014/23/EU on the award of concession contracts, (ii) Directive 2014/24/EU on the public procurement, and (iii) Directive 2014/25/EU, coordinating the procurement procedures for the award of the same contracts by entities operating in the water, energy, transport and postal services sectors. It is worth noting that Directive 2014/24/EU of the European Parliament and of the Council has repealed Dir. 2004/18/EC and its contents now form part of the new framework regulating procurement activities in the EU.

Preliminarily, it is necessary to stress what the new EU legislation states: "Public procurement plays a key role in the Europe 2020 strategy, set out in the Commission Communication of 3 March 2010 entitled 'Europe 2020, a strategy for smart, sustainable and inclusive growth' ('Europe 2020 strategy for smart, sustainable and inclusive growth'), as one of the market-based instruments to be used to achieve smart, sustainable and inclusive growth while ensuring the most efficient use of public funds. For that purpose, the public procurement rules adopted pursuant to

---

[48] Consolidated Version of the Treaty Establishing the European Community (EC Treaty), OJ 2006 C 321/37.

[49] An EC Directive is binding on the EU member states as to the result to be achieved, but leaves to the national authorities the choice of form and methods. This means that the EU member states have the obligation to transpose the directives into their national legal system within a specified timeframe. However, an EU Directive is only binding on EU member states, and an international organization with a separate legal personality from its member states would therefore not have the obligation to implement it in its internal procedures, such as its public procurement rules, in principle. Therefore, as a matter of principles and without considering any exception contained in the directives or in relevant international law, there is a strong possibility that EU member states would have an obligation to implement applicable EC directives in the internal procurement rules and practices of international organizations of which they are members when they cannot be prevented to do so by non-EU member states. However, the international organizations themselves, being distinct legal persons under international law, would most likely not have such obligation.

Directive 2004/17/EC of the European Parliament and of the Council[50] and Directive 2004/18/EC of the European Parliament and of the Council[51] should be revised and modernized in order to increase the efficiency of public spending, facilitating in particular the participation of small and medium-sized enterprises (SMEs) in public procurement, and to enable procurers to make better use of public procurement in support of common societal goals. There is also a need to clarify basic notions and concepts to ensure legal certainty and to incorporate certain aspects of related well-established case-law of the Court of Justice of the European Union."[52]

Thus, it is necessary to ascertain how EU law applies to Chinese construction companies willing to realize infrastructure projects in cooperation with EU entities. In principle, international organizations created outside the EU were not subjected to EU law. According to this reasoning, legal subjects different from EU and not party to the EU cannot be bound by the EU legislation (or EC treaties). However, this is an application of the generic international law principle that treaties are only binding on their parties.[53] EU law can confer rights and obligations to individuals, and not just to EU member states,[54] and it seems widely accepted that the term "individual" in those rulings refers to both natural and legal persons.[55]

---

[50] Directive 2004/17/EC of the European Parliament and of the Council of March 31, 2004 coordinating the procurement procedures of entities operating in the water, energy, transport and postal services sectors (OJ L 134, 30.4.2004, p. 1).

[51] Directive 2004/18/EC of the European Parliament and of the Council of March 31, 2004 on the coordination of procedures for the award of public works contracts, public supply contracts and public service contracts (OJ L 134, 30.4.2004, p. 114).

[52] This is point n. 2 of the preamble of Dir. 2014/24/EU of the European Parliament and of the Council.

[53] Vienna Convention on the Law of Treaties of 1969, United Nations, Treaty Series, Vol. 1155, p. 331, Articles 26 and 34; A. Aust, *Modern Treaty Law and Practice* (2000), Chapter 14; C. Vincenzi and J. Fairhurst, *Law of the European Community*, 3rd Ed., 2002, at 180 et.seq.; A. Kaczorowska, *EU Law for Today's Lawyers*, 2000, Chapter 6; Alvarez, supra note 16, at 120.

[54] See, e.g. Case 26/62 van Gend en Loos; Joined Cases C-6/90 and C-9/90, *Francovich v Republic of Italy*, [1991] ECR I-5357; Kunoy and Dawes, 'Plate Tectonics in Luxembourg: The Ménage à Trois between EC Law, International law, and the European Convention of Human Rights following the UN Santions Cases', 46 CMLRev (2009) 73, at 80.

[55] Bosphorus Hava Yollari Turizm Ve Ticaret Anonim Şirketi v Ireland, Application no. 45036/98, ECHR (2005) Vol. VI, para 159.

An international organization operating in the EU, thus, in general terms, is subject to the EU legislation, and procurement activities fall in this ambit. However, the contents and scope of the EU substantive law is to be read in relation to the specific related case.

7.4.2.2 EU Public Procurement Rules: General Introduction

The EU only has the competence to improve the conditions for the establishment and functioning of the internal market, and it does not have a general competence to regulate "public procurement" where specific regulations are part of the internal market rules. Considering the fact that the EC Treaty does not even refer to public procurement and the "framework" of the Procurement Directive, it would seem that this still leaves sufficient freedom to EU member states, and that public procurement would currently not be an exclusive competence of the EU, but a shared competence between the EU and its member states. The latter would therefore not be prevented from concluding international agreements related to public procurement outside the framework of the EU.

7.4.2.3 The Public Sector Directive: Outline

The Public procurement Directive states that "Procurement within the meaning of this Directive is the acquisition by means of a public contract of works, supplies or services by one or more contracting authorities from economic operators chosen by those contracting authorities, whether or not the works, supplies or services are intended for a public purpose."[56]

The Directive in its Article 2 (Definitions) at point 6 specifies that "public works contracts" means public contracts having as their object one of the following:

(a) the execution, or both the design and execution, of works related to one of the activities within the meaning of Annex II;
(b) the execution, or both the design and execution, of a work;

---

[56] Article 1(2) of DIR. 2014/24/EU.

(c) the realization, by whatever means, of a work corresponding to the requirements specified by the contracting authority exercising a decisive influence on the type or design of the work;

And "a work" means the outcome of building or civil engineering works taken as a whole which is sufficient in itself to fulfill an economic or technical function.

These are the very basic elements concerning infrastructure projects. Naturally, a myriad of other details need to be taken into consideration; however, here we only want to stress some principles, and thus we are not going to expose the entire content of the Directive. The EU public procurement principles are discussed below.

7.4.2.4 EU Public Procurement Principles

The core EU public procurement principles include the following:

- The public procurement rules in each state apply to public sector "contracting authorities," including state, regional and local authorities, and bodies governed by public law.
- A contracting authority wishing to award a contract (other than one which is excluded from the rules) for "works," "supplies" or "services" will need to comply with the rules if its value exceeds a specific financial limit.
- The current threshold for public works contracts is €5,225,000.[57] Separate (lower) thresholds apply to supply and services contracts.[58]
- Contracting authorities must treat all suppliers equally and in a non-discriminatory way (e.g. not setting tender requirements which are easier for locally based contractors to comply) and act in a transparent manner.

---

[57] See the Thresholds Triggering EU-wide Rules, available at: http://europa.eu/youreurope/business/public-tenders/rules-procedures/index_en.htm.

[58] The EU Directive 2014/24 (Section 2 — Thresholds) at Article 2 states that: This Directive shall apply to procurements with a value net of value-added tax (VAT) estimated to be equal to or greater than the following thresholds: (a) EUR 5 186 000 for public works contracts.

- Contracting authorities must run a tender exercise following one of the specified procurement procedures in awarding its contracts — either the "open," "restricted," "competitive dialogue" or "negotiated" procedure — and follow certain minimum time limits in carrying out the tender exercise.

If a contracting authority breaches any of its duties and/or awards a contract without following a proper tender process, it will be at risk of a procurement challenge from unsuccessful suppliers or others within the market. Successful claims can result either in a contract being canceled, a fine and damage claims.

It is worth noting that a public authority can exclude a business from a call for tenders if it:

— is bankrupt or being wound up;
— has suspended its activities or its activities are administered by a court;
— has been found guilty of grave misconduct;
— has not paid taxes or social security contributions;
— has made false declarations to a public authority.

7.4.2.5 Award Criteria

Public authorities may use different criteria when evaluating tenders, such as the lowest price offered. In this case, each applicant should be informed of the different weighting given to the different criteria (i.e. price, technical characteristics and environmental aspects).

7.4.2.6 Transparency

Public authorities may only begin evaluating tenders after the deadline for submission has expired. If a business entity has submitted a tender, it has the right to be informed as soon as possible whether or not it has won the contract. If it has not been selected, it is entitled to a detailed explanation of why its tender was rejected. The public authority must observe strict confidentiality regarding the exchange and storage of the data concerning each case.

7.4.2.7 Technical Specification

Technical specifications define the characteristics of the service, supply or works that the public authority intends to buy. They may include aspects of environmental performance, design, safety, quality assurance or conformity assessment. For public works contracts they may also include tests, inspection and construction techniques.

7.4.2.8 Types of Public Procurement Procedures

The EU legislation specifically regulates the following types of procedures:

[a] Open procedure

In an open procedure, any business may submit a tender. The minimum time limit for submission of tenders is 35 days from the publication date of the contract notice. If a prior information notice was published, this time limit can be reduced to 15 days.

[b] Restricted procedure

Any business may ask to participate in a restricted procedure, but only those who are pre-selected will be invited to submit a tender. The time limit to request participation is 37 days from the publication of the contract notice. The public authority then selects at least five candidates with the required capabilities, who then have 40 days to submit a tender from the date when the invitation was sent. This time limit can be reduced to 36 days, if a prior information notice has been published.

[c] Negotiated procedure

In a negotiated procedure, the public authority invites at least three businesses with whom it will negotiate the terms of the contract.

Most contracting authorities can use this procedure only in a limited number of cases, for example, for supplies intended exclusively for research or testing purposes. The contracting authorities in sectors such as water, energy, transport or postal services may use it as a standard procedure.

The time limit to receive requests to participate is 37 days from the publication of the contract notice. This can be reduced to 15 days in extremely urgent cases, or 10 days if the notice is sent electronically.

[d] Competitive dialogue

This procedure is often used for **complex contracts** such as large infrastructure projects where the public authority cannot define the technical specifications at the start. After the publication of the contract notice, interested businesses have 37 days to request participation. The public authority must invite at least three candidates to a dialogue in which the final technical, legal and economic aspects are defined. After this dialogue, candidates submit their final tenders.

Competitive dialogue cannot be used by public services providers in the water, energy, transport and postal services sectors.

7.4.3 *Transposition of the Directive into the Italian Law* (*Reference*)

As mentioned in Section 7.4 the European Directives have been transposed into Italian law by Legislative Decree no. 50/2016 (the "New Public Contracts Code") published in the Italian Official Journal of Italian Republic ("Gazzetta Ufficiale della Repubblica Italiana") on April, 18, 2016. According to Article 220 of the Public Contracts Code, it is immediately in force and as a general rule, regulates the public tender procedures called after its entering into force.

Third parties interested in cooperating with Italian companies in realizing infrastructure projects in Italy should refer to this piece of legislation.

7.4.4 *European Single Procurement Document (ESPD): Brief Introduction*

Finally, a brief reference must be made to the European Single Procurement Document (ESPD). At the time of submission of tenders' requests to participate, contracting authorities must accept the European

Single Procurement Document (ESPD), which shall be provided exclusively in electronic form from April 18, 2018.

The ESPD consists of an updated self-certification confirming that the relevant economic operator fulfills the contracting authority's requirements and conditions in order to participate. This self-certification replaces — at a preliminary stage — all certificates issued by public authorities or third parties.

7.4.5 *Cooperation between Italy and China in Prospective and the Role of the EU*

In late February 2017, both the President of the Italian Republic, Sergio Mattarella, and French Prime Minister, Bernard Cazeneuve, paid state visits to China and met with Chinese President Xi Jinping and Premier Li Keqiang. During the separate meetings, all four leaders praised Sino-European cooperation and called for more exchanges between the two regions.

Mattarella and Cazeneuve are strong supporters of free trade, and their visits to China illustrate Europe's willingness to develop stronger ties with China. However, the lack of coordination between the two European neighbors is evident. Although the Italian president and the French premier visited China at the same time, no common meetings or shared events were held. Both countries presented their own assets for the completion of the new Silk Road. Mattarella emphasized the quality and locations of the Italian ports of Genoa and Trieste to reach the core of Europe, and Cazeneuve attended the arrival in Wuhan of a freight train coming from Lyon, France.[59] The French and Italian heads of state and government were focused on a bilateral approach of relations with China, but the success of the B&R Initiative largely depends on the participants' ability to manage multilateral projects. It is worth noting that Italy's

---

[59] In the city of Wuhan in the center of the country, Cazeneuve saw the arrival of a goods train from Lyon in France. The line was opened in April as part of China's project to build modern transport links to Europe, echoing the historical Silk Roads trading routes. (January 23, 2017). http://en.rfi.fr/france/20170223-french-prime-minister-wuhan-china-promote-made-france.

participation in China's Initiative, not just for projects in Italy, will certainly improve bilateral relationships, and Italian companies equipped with competitive strength in the infrastructure sector working together with Chinese companies would help Chinese operators to participate in the open and fair international bids (for infrastructure works) in third countries.

Furthermore, it is necessary to stress that President Xi, at the World Economic Forum in Davos (January 2017), firmly supported European integration and called on Europe and China to fight against trade protectionism.[60] The Chinese "B&R" Initiative may bring together the two blocs, but both China and European countries need to slightly redefine their approaches to the "B&R" Initiative in order to increase not only their (trade) exchanges, but also opportunities to cooperate and grow together. Naturally, enhancing infrastructures in the EU will help to bring near China and the EU.

---

[60] During his speech at Davos, in January 2017, Chinese President Xi Jinping urged global business and political elites to reject trade wars and protectionism. See: https://www.bloomberg.com/news/articles/2017-01-17/china-s-xi-urges-davos-elite-to-solve-excesses-of-globalization.

CHAPTER 8

The Impact of the B&R Initiative on the Development of International Law, Particularly of the Law of Carriage of Goods and of "International Business"

Fabio E. Ziccardi

It may appear obvious to note that the implementation of the Belt and Road (B&R) Initiative will have a highly remarkable, and — if an anticipation is proper — highly positive impact on the development of both the international law in strict sense and the international business law.

Some introductory notes on these statements are elucidated in the following sections.

8.1 The International Law as the *Law of Nations*

Whichever may be its real origin, it is a fact that, since the earliest times known in history, the political entities equivalent to states treated their mutual relations, as harsh and violent as they were, as subject to rules, sometimes in the form of interpersonal relations among the local Gods, anyhow subject to what was by then a law. It is widely known that the Kingdoms of Egypt and of the Hittites ended their long-lasting wars with a peace treaty, entered into by 1259 BC in Qades,[1] which is a clear evidence that a general system of law of nations was by that time in full force.

Since those times, the law of nations spread through the world, the peoples, the different political systems, any kind of war, and such a law, though it had neither code nor courts, was existing, basically respected, being the basis of treaties. And those treaties marked the great steps of each nation's life, both when they were equal (the Westphalia Treaties of 1640 and the Vienna Treaties of 1815, in Europe, the Shimonoseki Treaty of 1895 in the Far East) or unequal, as they could be.

The end of the Cold War,[2] and the resulting globalization, have, in a certain way, left behind the development of the law of nations, as if, today, the international laws were just the result of the United Nations General Assembly's resolutions, and this organization were a World Parliament.

Now, UN remains a masterwork of the human civilization and a powerful protector of the world peace. However, it is the effect of a treaty which rests on the solid basis of the law of nations — the great pillars of which remain the basis for nations' behaviors. However, these behaviors, in the last 30 years or so appear to have existed through, more than governed, the events of international politics, sometimes — as in Europe — apparently relying on the principle that "local" international organizations, such as the European Communities and now the Union, may be enough for maintaining a quiet path of the international law.

It is not so.

The "globalized" world still, and more — possibly — than in the previous decades, needs the development of an international law based on the nations' new approaches, and B&R Initiative appears to be the first new one, since just the European Communities creation in 1952–1956.

Stemming from long-standing traditions (the Silk Road), and based on the end of the world political "great divider," which made difficult, in some cases impossible, even the basic trade between the different "parties," B&R Initiative aims to come back to a set of inter-state relations

---

[1] Today, at ca. 30 km. southwest from Homs, Syria.
[2] The author, as an ex-officer of NATO Air Force, witnessed that, e.g. in the Sixties, "war" was quite cold, but very seriously "ready to go."

finding their foundations on mutual advantages, with no hegemonic power, creating a link or a way, but never a bar.

One might note that this is already the mission of a fundamental global entity, the WTO, and it is a fact that China's access to WTO was a powerful sign of the new Chinese vision of the international trade.

But, as the Latin saying goes, "WTO is a friend, truth is a closer friend,"[3] and the effects of this organization's operations, as powerful as it is, are in fact limited by a long set of reasons, possibly even in part good reasons, but it is also a fact that the world is marching faster than the pace set by WTO may allow.

If one thinks of the duration of each "round" and the results merely in terms of lower import duties (which in fact each country may lower in few days, as China did just at the end November 2017), alternative steps for the development of the international economic, political and legal relations may be better found elsewhere, namely in states' initiatives, as in the case of B&R Initiative.

8.2 The Progress of the Law of International Transportation

It may appear obvious that a political move for making easier the international trade on long *"roads"* will deeply involve the international transportation, and thus — from a legal point of view — the several instruments, which a millennial experience has created for regulating this class of human activities,[4] through Rules, then treaties, in this area denominated the Conventions.

---

[3] The Latin proverb read: *"Amicus Plato, magis amica veritas,"* meaning that truth shall be preferred even "against" the opinion of the philosophy apex, well represented by Plato.

[4] It is noteworthy that such millennial rules were set at the borders between Europe and Asia, not far from the sea routes, which will be a part of the southern, maritime part of the new Silk Road. The Roman *Lex Rhodia de iactu*, providing rules on salvage and general average, was based on customs followed primarily by Rhodes seamen, of course. And similarly, the oldest known rules on negotiable instruments, *syngraphae* and *chirografa*, were based on the trade customs of the Egyptian Alexandria, where today the Suez Channel flows into the Mediterranean: "roads" are perennial.

Each kind of transportation, in today's world, benefits from specific International Conventions, although with quite different weight and frequency of use.

(a) The modern law of transportation by road, albeit the means are now so different from those uses by the Polo family in the late 13th century, is governed by a set of United Nations Conventions.

The most diffuse is the 1975 one, on the International Transport of Goods Under Cover of TIR Carnets, or TIR Convention[5]; it is in fact mainly a Custom Convention, namely an agreement for facilitating the crossing of borders from a customs point of view.

The Convention on the Contract for the International Carriage of Goods by Road, or CMR Convention, of 1956[6] is still less diffuse, but of much wider scope. This text, the equivalent for the road transportation of the historical rules developed for sea trade, may be described as a part of a "global" civil code for this type of agreement, ideally used along with the Vienna Convention on the International Sale of Goods.

In fact, the Convention governs the formation of a carriage by road agreement (Articles 4–16), in its form and its minimal necessary contents — and this is a powerful instrument of uniformity — and in detail the carrier's liability (Articles 17–29). This latter legal issue is the core of all the international and domestic regulations of any carriage, a liability based an equally long tradition,[7] making it much wider than

---

[5]This Convention is described as follows in its home website (https://www.unece.org/tir/welcome.html): "To date, it has 71 Contracting Parties, including the European Union. It covers the whole of Europe and reaches out to North Africa and the Near and Middle East. More than 33,000 operators are authorized to use the TIR system and around 1.5 million TIR transports are carried out per year." The countries fundamental for the implementation of the B&R Initiative are now a party to this Convention: India is a party with effect from December 15, 2017.

[6]Fifty-five countries are presently parties (www.unece.org/trans/conventn/legalinst_25_OLIRT_CMR.html), including Mongolia, Iran and the Central Asia Republics; China, India and Pakistan are not; possibly, under the B&R auspices, the accession of the said Countries to the CMR system might be verified.

[7]This kind of liability, found even if no carrier negligence occurs, is frequently described with the Latin phrase *ex recepto*, meaning that the carrier is liable because he just

the usual one under an agreement, therefore — ironically — quite "strict," according to the English way of describing liability, albeit in the different area of the law of torts.

On the other hand, such a "strict" liability is limited in its amount: under Article 23.3 of this Convention, "Compensation shall not, however, exceed 8.33 units account per kilogram of gross weight short," where the said "units of account" are the International Monetary Fund Special Drawing Rights (with exceptions). A quite material limitation, which might be tolled formally "declaring" the value of the goods or "a special interest in delivery" (Article 23.6), but this "declaration" — which of course involve a remarkable increase of the freight — is quite seldom made, and the liability limits do largely apply.

Equally important are the rules on the foreclosure of claims after the delivery (Article 30),[8] and those on the "successive carriers" liability (Articles 34–40). The one and only one on jurisdiction over judicial claims based on carriage by road (Article 31) is however too "soft," in the sense that it leaves too many options to claimant, and is possibly one of the grounds of the comparatively limited acceptance of this Convention, as fundamental as it is. The particular issue of "carriage litigation" will be re-examined at the end of this section.

(b) The law of international railway transportation is authoritatively controlled by the 1980 Convention concerning the International Carriage by Rail (COTIF), which applies in Europe (including Russia), the Maghreb and in the Middle East (including Pakistan).[9]

"received" the cargo, or the passengers (a part of the law of carriage which developed certainly much later than the other!). Consistently, one of the few defenses available to a carrier is to claim the occurrence of a *vis maior*, in Latin, or *force majeure* (which surely describes the class of events so meant better than the English's somewhat excessive *Act of God!*): old words for never-lasting legal principles.

[8] Possibly, a better coordination between these rules and those concerning the foreclosure to claim the non-conformity of sold goods (Articles 38–39 of the Vienna Convention) would be proper, and this of course applies to the rules of similar content in the further Conventions on carriage of goods.

[9] A very clear picture of the somehow exoteric world of the law of international transportation by rail may be found in the COTIF's site http://www.cit-rail.org/en/rail-transport-law/cotif/.

This Convention, updated and modified up to 2010, is in fact merely a treaty instituting the Organization for International Carriage by Rail.

The uniform rules of law actually governing this kind of transportation in Europe and Maghreb are contained in a set of seven "Appendices" to the same Convention[10]; many of them pre-existed the same COTIF, one is brand new, and very important (the one on the Carriage of Dangerous Goods by Rail, of 2015), while some are of limited acceptance.

The great importance of the COTIF "Code"[11] in the B&R Initiative environment is self-explanatory, and is supported by actual examples, too: just during late Fall 2017 (28 November), the first direct trains connecting Northern Italy and Central China began to run, along the Silk Road.[12]

In view of this, the access of China, India and the Central Asian Republics to the COTIF system (possibly, if it were felt as necessary, excluding some "Appendices"[13]) might be a fine sign of expansion of

---

[10]Their acronyms, and contents, are: (1) CIV, on the *Carriage of Passengers*. (2) CIM, on the *Carriage of Goods by Rail*. (3) RID, a *Regulation concerning the International Carriage of Dangerous Goods by Rail*. (4) CUV, on the *Contracts of Use of Vehicles in International Rail Traffic*. (5) CUI, on the *Contract of Use of Infrastructure in International Rail Traffic*. (6) APTU, on the *Adoption of Uniform Technical Prescriptions applicable to Railway Material intended to be used in International Traffic*. (7) ATMF, namely the *Rules concerning the Technical Admission of Railway Material used in International Traffic*.

[11]No official source describes this set of Rules as a Code, but technically, and scientifically, it should be classified as such, and — just as such — it is a good example of a move toward the creation of uniform rules of the international trade, when this is proper, which might be adopted in many further areas.

[12]See A. Amighini, in http://www.ispionline.it/it/pubblicazione/italia-multimodale-nelle-future-vie-della-seta-19082; and G. Santevecchi, in *Corriere della Sera*, 25 November 2017, p. 5. The Italian starting station is in Mortara, equally distant from Milan, Genoa and Turin, and in straight connection with the Simplon and Gotthard railway lines; the Chinese arrival (and *vice-versa*!) is in Chengdu. A few days after (mid-December 2017), a major Korean operator announced the creation of a sea, then rail, link between South Korea ports and Chengdu.

[13]Russia, e.g. accepted only the CIM!

the uniform system, starting just from the now-quoted CIM, the more important and more productive agreement (passengers railway traffic from — say — Beijing to Venice is possibly not for tomorrow).

As an alternative, the countries involved in the B&R Initiative might enter into a special treaty, making a direct reference to some "Appendices," modified, if proper, in accordance with the special needs of the Silk Railway, special needs that the compiler of these Notes would find difficult to detail.

As far as the content of these many "Appendices" is concerned, the scheme of the CIM is similar to the CMR, as previously examined: rules on the formation of the contract (Articles 6–22), then the liabilities and their limits (Articles 23–41; the limit is set at 17 SDR per kilo by Article 30.2), rules on litigations, if any (with the same multiplicity of choice, Articles 42–48), relations between "successive" railway carriers (Articles 49–52).

(c) The law of maritime transportation, as noted, is the source of a major part of the legal principles on international carriage, especially of goods. Ironically, this has led to a major difficulty in updating the international instruments regulating this fundamental aspect of sea trade.

  The basis of the present law is embodied in the Hague Rules, the short name of the "historical" International Convention for the Unification of Certain Rules of Law relating to Bills of Lading of August 1924; this Convention is presently ratified by 74 countries, while its important amendments added in 1986, known as the Hague–Visby Rules (formally, the Brussels Protocol), are presently "in force" only in 22 countries.

  An equally modest success was a new effort by the United Nations for further amending and widening the scope of these international rules on sea transportation: the United Nations Convention on the Carriage of Goods by Sea 1978, or Hamburg Rules, presently in force in 24 countries.

  The number is still low, but in any case the Hamburg Rules demonstrated a better result than the one reached by the next UN attempt in the field, the Convention on Contracts for the International Carriage of Goods Wholly or Partly by Sea, or Rotterdam Rules, approved by the UN General Assembly on December 12, 2008. This Convention has gathered to date only 4 ratifications, while 20 are needed for its entry into force: it is presently a hope, not a law.[14]

The contents — here very summarily described — of those instruments, which are, as noted, the historical and cultural basis of the whole law of international carriage of goods, must take into account, of course, the many peculiarities of sea travels.

Among them, e.g. are the inherent risks and the resulting deviations for saving goods and human lives,[15] the sharing of such risks and salvage,[16] and the likely carriage on the deck.[17] Apart from these "legal specialties," the other main elements of the issue of liability in transportation by sea, under a bill of lading,[18] are of course in the same areas as those already listed:

— the formation of the contract, thus the above-mentioned issuance of a bill of lading, with a legally mandatory content;

---

[14]The United Nations Convention on International Multimodal Transport of Goods, signed in Geneva on May 24, 1980, is also meeting the same fate; it is not yet in force, under its Article 36, which requests 30 ratifications or similar countries' decisions, and they have not (yet?) been expressed.

[15]See, e.g. the exemptions from liability in Article IV(4) of the Hague–Visby Rules.

[16]An issue so fundamental, to be governed by the quoted "very first" set of rules on the sea trade, the *Lex Rhodia de Iactu*, today embodied in the York–Antwerp Rules, lastly updated in 2004, rules which apply to any event verified at sea, not only if under a transportation agreement, and thus a bill of lading. The same remark applies to salvage: see the International Maritime Organization International Convention on Salvage, 1989.

[17]Deck cargo is governed by Article 9 of the Hamburg Rules, but not by any Hague–Visby Rule, as decided in the English case *Sideridraulic Systems SpA and Anr v. BBC Chartering & Logistic GmbH & Co KG, The BBC GREENLAND* [2011] EWHC 3106 (Comm): a clear example of the problems posed by the uneven "geographic distribution" of the applying Rules!

[18]The issuance of a bill of lading is mandatory if requested by the shipper (Article III(3) of the Hague–Visby Rules, and Part IV, Articles 14–18 of the Hamburg Rules).

— the liabilities and their limits (Article IV of the Hague–Visby Rules and Articles 6–8 of the Hamburg Rules, having, however, quite different limits);
— rules on litigations, only in the Hamburg Rules (Part V, Articles 19–22[19]).

It is easy to note that, presently, the situation of the law of sea is by far largely less "clear" than those of the other classes of transportation. The countries involved in the B&R Initiative might usefully "enter" into this arena, accepting — those which have not yet so done — the Hamburg Rules, which are surely more adequate to global sea traffic than the Hague–Visby ones, with their decidedly European flavor, as if they were decided within a "Club of Happy Few."[20]

And, within this partly new B&R maritime law, remarkable importance should be given to the arbitration: international transportation needs uniformity of rules, and of their application in case of disputes. A net of arbitration centers (many already well operating, e.g. the one in Singapore, and others), having a common coordination, e.g. at the Paris CCI Arbitration Court, the oldest and still the most effective one, would be very helpful. In addition, starting from maritime law, where arbitration is fostered — as noted — by the most recent and operating international Convention, the practice of arbitration might well find its way along the roads and the rails of the Belt and of the Silk.

---

[19]Article 22 provides an express "invitation" to the parties of a carriage by sea to include and accept an arbitration clause in the bills of lading, a further remarkable difference from the Hague–Visby Rules.

[20]A factual globalization of the Hamburg Rules could even lead the UN and its special Agency UNCITRAL to take quite a simple decision, and yet a sign of courage (but unlikely, it must be admitted; see the UNCITRAL's position in www.uncitral.org/pdf/english/texts/transport/rotterdam_rules/ICS_PositionPaper.pdf): to "revoke" the Rotterdam Rules, setting them aside, a destiny already verified to some "Hague" Convention on matters of Family Law, approved at the beginning of the 20th century, and remained in the drawers.

(d) Finally, even air law shall be mentioned, although the B&R Initiative's impact on it will be smaller, as aircrafts fly over the Belts and the Roads, but at quite higher costs.

Be it enough, therefore, to recall that the law of air transportation is presently embodied in the Montréal Convention, a text comparatively recent (1999), but rooted in the long experience of the 1929 Warsaw Convention, adapted as it was to the sharp increase of the air traffic by the Hague Protocol of 1955 and the Guatemala City Protocol 1971. A total of 118 countries and the European Union "personally" ratified the Montreal Convention; among them, many are involved in the B&R Initiative.[21]

Its content is, on one hand, less influenced by the "peculiarities" of the fluid through which the goods are carried (no deck cargo, no salvage), on the other hand updated to the best practices followed by professional carriers, insurers and forwarder: an effective tool, although it needs competence. There is no need here to repeat the classes of provisions; it is noteworthy, however, that the Montreal Convention has canceled the traditional tolling of the liability limits in case of "*gross negligence*," for the carriage of goods only, limiting the scope of litigations.

On the other hand, no "invitation to arbitrate" is included, while avoiding ordinary Courts would cause a clear progress in this area of the law, because sea law cases are dealt with — almost with no exception — in Courts located in maritime towns,[22] where specialized judges do operate. Nothing alike, however, verifies in many case of air law, which is less difficult, but not that much less. Developing an arbitration chambers' net might improve the application of this branch of the law of international transportation as well: B&R may also help aircraft transport.

---

[21] China, Kazakhstan, Mongolia and Russia did ratify (Russia in August 2017!), but no country is totally out of the scheme: Kyrgyzstan and Uzbekistan ratified the Hague Protocol, Turkmenistan the original Warsaw Convention. Only Tajikistan is not a party to any International instrument.

[22] The author of this chapter, in his 51 years in the legal profession, has dealt with air law cases almost everywhere, but never with maritime law cases but in Port cities: Genoa, Leghorn, Trieste and the like.

8.3 The Impact on Other Institutes of International Business Law

One may wonder whether a similar impact might verify in further areas of international business law, such as the law of trade entities (companies, partnerships, joint ventures and the like), and of further types of contracts. Among them, the constructions and procurement agreements, the financial agreements (loans, and alternatives), the commercial agency and brokerage agreements, the insurance agreements, while the sale of goods, thanks to the Vienna Convention of 1980, ratified by 88 countries,[23] is a branch of the law updated and operating (albeit still sometime overlooked by the practitioners).

In certain areas, something already exists: the WTO has submitted a standard Convention text on public procurements, in 1994, amended in 2012, and the accessions to date are 47.[24]

However, this Convention, exactly as the European Union Directives and the NAFTA rule on the same issue, does not provides a uniform law, but just public law provisions, aiming to ensure the opening of this particular market to competitors also coming from abroad. The Convention contains not one rule on the right and obligations of the parties to a construction agreement, but a set of rules which is badly needed, if civil works are to be performed in view of building roads and railways, as smooth as silk, of course. On the other hand, no uniform law on this exists within the European Union, and constructors going abroad for performing works go, as far as the legal environment is concerned, toward the unknown — it is not effective.

The international practice and their "private" organizations have obviously powerfully helped in circulating and diffusing standard texts

---

[23]Among the countries which remain out of the Vienna CISG, there is the United Kingdom, and, among the countries involved in the B&R project, India, Pakistan, Iran, Kazakhstan, Kyrgyzstan and Tajikistan.

[24]"The Agreement on Government Procurement (GPA) consists of 19 parties covering 47 WTO members (counting the European Union and its 28 member states, all of which are covered by the Agreement, as one party). Another 31 WTO members and four international organizations participate in the GPA Committee as observers. 10 of these members with observer status are in the process of acceding to the Agreement": www.wto.org/english/tratop_e/gproc_e/memobs_e.htm.

(the same sociological proceeding which led to the "birth" of the maritime law "Rules"), but important differences remain, and a move toward a wave of formal, worldwide texts, following the Vienna CISG example, is highly advisable.

As noted before, in connection with the issue of proper additions to the Conventions on transportation, the B&R Initiative might effectively promote the adoption of uniform rules on each of the listed items between the countries directly involved in its implementation.

As an example, and coming back to the construction and procurement agreements, a standard text, embodied as an appendix to a multilateral Convention, would be an excellent tool for attracting investments on the needed infrastructure for re-building the "roads." Assuming that several contractors shall perform such works, it would be an oddity if different substantial rules would apply to the construction of the many parts of the long road.

Remaining within this hypothesis, the text might be authored by the representatives of the countries directly involved in the "physical" implementation of the B&R Initiative, then "proposed" to further countries, or unions. This is what verified with the existing uniform law Conventions, sometimes successfully (it is the quoted Montreal and Vienna Sale of Goods Conventions case); but any single success would be a further addition, brought by the B&R Initiative, to the building of a renewed international community, based on the law, and thus on peace.

Conclusion

China finds itself in the middle of a delicate transition from a planned economy toward a more market-oriented model, and in order to reach its goals China needs to engage in a new round of opening to the world. President Xi Jinping, at the beginning of his first mandate, affirmed that China needs to accelerate the construction of a new economic model based on openness, and the Belt and Road (B&R) Initiative seems to be expressly designed to help China develop this new model of growth and not just to connect more efficiently with the rest of the world, and in particular with the EU, which represents the natural end of both the land Silk Road and the Maritime Silk Road.

As it emerges from the analysis we have conducted, clearly this Initiative is not predominantly about transportation infrastructures, but about a better economic integration among countries in the Eurasian region. This is the main goal. In fact, China has become the new paladin of globalization, and another aim of this ambitious Initiative should be to help in building sustainable and inter-operable cross-border infrastructure networks in countries and regions between the EU and China. The Maritime Silk Road is meant to adapt sea transportation to new patterns of global trade, and to complement the land routes.

In order for this Initiative to be successful and produce the effects, which Xi Jinping has in mind, all the countries along the Belt and Road should fully coordinate their economic development strategies and policies, work out plans and measures for regional cooperation, negotiate to solve cooperation-related issues and jointly provide policy support for the implementation of practical cooperation and large-scale projects connected to the B&R. Only if the international community, especially those countries directly involved in the B&R Initiative, is able to coordinate their efforts will it be possible to realize this project.

It is true that the B&R Initiative is a Chinese Initiative primarily, aimed at serving Chinese interests; however, it has profound international and domestic implications. In developing its own internal regions, China aims also at enhancing economic relations with all the other countries somehow connected with China. In particular, it seems that the B&R Initiative will further stimulate and strengthen trade relations with the EU. The fact that the initial focus of the Belt and Road is on China's immediate interests should not blind observers to the fact that Europe is its final destination.

Another aspect to keep in mind is that the B&R Initiative attempts to change the rules organizing the global economy, primarily by granting China a set of tools (e.g. AIIB, Silk Road Fund) with which it can re-order global value chains, or at least with these tools China will have a greater influence on adopting a different approach financing investment projects related to the development of the Eurasian region, and stamp its imprint on the rules governing the global economy.

The B&R Initiative represents an incredible opportunity for the EU in order to further stimulate its economy, but it is a Chinese project aimed to respond to the Chinese needs primarily. Moreover, the EU feels uncomfortable letting China invest freely in the continent's infrastructure. At the end of the day, Europe and China have similar aims and concerns, that is to say, preserving jobs, fueling economic growth and maintaining social stability. It is consequently necessary to find the best way to cooperate and create a win–win compromise which will allow all players involved in developing this Initiative in reaching their respective goals and creating the globalized world envisioned by the Chinese leadership but based on more harmonious and equal parameters.

Appendix and Extra Contributions on the Belt and Road Initiative by UBS

A.1 Appendix: Contribution by UBS on the Belt and Road Initiative (Interview with UBS Conducted by Mario Tettamanti)

Question 1

> - *The concept of "Label" is important for the fundraising of private capital. Is the B&R Initiative Label sufficiently known today to attract private capital in different forms into this initiative?*

The concept of the Belt and Road (B&R) Initiative today is widely known in Asia-Pacific, and also well-recognized globally. Following the launch of the Initiative in 2013, China has been more actively and successfully promoting the B&R Initiative since the beginning of 2017, including via the Belt and Road Forum for International Cooperation hosted in Beijing in May 2017 by President Xi Jinping. This forum was attended by 29 foreign heads of state and government as well as representatives from more than 130 countries and 70 international organizations. These efforts have generated greater awareness of the BRI among the relevant stakeholders, and as a result we are starting to receive an increasing number of inquiries from our European clients and counterparties.

However, while the name and concept of the Belt and Road is known and is beginning to gain attention and interest from many stakeholders, this is not in itself a sufficient condition for attracting private capital to the related projects. A number of additional conditions, in particular those related to the "bankability" of projects, are required to drive private capital, as will be further discussed.

Nonetheless, as the B&R Initiative Label becomes more popular across markets, we expect that our clients will increasingly inquire about it and want to better understand its practical implications and the ways to selectively gain exposure to it. During 2017, we have started to see more Chinese investors including B&R Initiative as one of their most important considerations when making investments.

Question 2

> • *What are the necessary conditions for the private financial sector to become involved in the financing of the B&R Initiative? Pension funds, insurance companies and investment funds are important sources for private sector funding. To what extent will they be attracted in the near future by the B&R Initiative?*

While the conditions will vary depending on the type of private sector involvement, for the private sector to invest in projects related to the B&R Initiative, in particular in infrastructure, the projects will need to have an adequate risk/return profile.

• On the return side, this implies that there must be an underlying commercial need, economic profitability and clear cash flows for the project so that it can generate the appropriate financial returns.

• On the risk side, this implies an appropriate management and sharing of the risks involved in the project, including political risks, currency risks and legal/enforcement risks. It is important that the right risks are well understood and allocated to the stakeholders (e.g. government, multilateral institution, insurance, private sector financial institution) that are best able to assess and manage these risks.

Large institutions, which would still constitute the main source of funding compared to individual investors, may be interested in investing in B&R Initiative projects as a way to increase exposure to BRI economies/sectors, diversify their portfolios and gain some illiquidity premium.

At an individual project level, the amount of interest from the institutional investors will need to be assessed on a case by case basis, according to the nature of the projects and types of investors. But in general, the most important factors that will be taken into consideration would be:

- *Returns*: The return metrics will vary, and can be internal rate of return (IRR), dividend yield, capital gain or ongoing dividend distribution. However, the project needs to meet a certain hurdle defined by the investor. It is also important to be able to reasonably forecast the revenue flows, e.g. the ability to make a solid projection of the throughput/traffic is often a prerequisite in deciding whether to invest in a highway project or not.
- *Stage of project lifecycle*: Depending on the forms of participation, different types of institutional investors may prefer getting involved in different stages — planning, development, construction or operation. Whether they want to participate as a financial investor or a strategic investor also matters. In general, they tend not to get involved in the early stages, but rather at a later phase — when projects are being constructed or have started operation.
- *Contractual structure/arrangement*: This could include, for example, the detailed concessional arrangement, exit terms, tariff/subsidy framework (e.g. in power projects), adjustment mechanism (e.g. inflation-linked income). At this stage of B&R Initiative, there is a strong emphasis on connecting transportation links to and between countries. From an investment perspective, the risks associated with investing into greenfield (development/construction stage) transport projects such as rail, roads, airport and seaports are inherently high, as the patronage of these projects is relatively hard to predict. Therefore, certain government guarantee mechanisms may be required for these types of greenfield projects.

- *Size of the holding/other shareholders*: The absolute amount of investment has to be sizable. Share of the equity investment also needs to be significant enough to ensure a meaningful governance position in the project (a board seat normally requires 10%). In addition, the nature of the shareholder base will affect the appetite for such projects.
- *Duration*: In certain cases, some institutional investors would prefer shorter-duration (<10 years) projects.
- *Currency*: Depending on the country, the stability of the currency will be an important consideration, along with the availability and cost of currency hedging.
- *Political and regulatory risk*: Countries with more transparent and stable regimes will be preferred by investors. Assessment of this will be based on the historical track record of these regimes.

Question 3

> - *What would be the most appropriate approach to finance the B&R Initiative by international banks? Are bonds the most appropriate products? What about other products related to equity financing?*

The optimal type of financing will need to be tailored to the specific project and also depends on the nature of the financial institution.

The debt component of infrastructure projects may be financed in a variety of ways, including bank loans, corporate bonds via both private placement and public offering in the capital markets, project bonds, collateralized loan/debt obligations (CLO/CDOs), securitized mortgages and other forms of infrastructure assets in tranches to meet different investor appetite. These instruments have different features and may be more or less suitable for any particular infrastructure project.

The corporates who own or participate in the projects can also raise funding from the equity capital markets, for example, via initial public offerings, or follow-ons if already listed.

There can also be infrastructure mandates offered to institutional investors (insurers, SWFs, pension funds) and individual investors (wealthy individuals) via either direct investment (mostly equity) or portfolio investment through a fund product (equities and/or bonds).

In the case of an M&A transaction, the international banks could also help with the financing, whether that is through a bridge loan, project finance or permanent funding, by syndication or by assembling banks and other institutional investors.

Question 4

> • *What is the role of public institutional investors/multilateral investors in co-financing projects with the private sector? How can public institutional investors (such as for example the Silk Road Fund, the Asian Infrastructure Investment Bank (AIIB)) help attract and protect the private sector to subscribe bonds or other financial instruments dedicated to B&R Initiative financing?*

Private sector investors would invest into the B&R Initiative projects once the projects become bankable with attractive risk-adjusted returns. To get these projects to the bankable stage, multi-lateral investors may provide initial incubation funding for projects with better business potential to enable these projects to have sufficient capital and get past the initial development/construction stage.

After the project has been de-risked and the operation has stabilized, the multilateral investors could fully or partially sell down their investments and recycle this capital to incubate other projects with promising potential. While a full sell-down would result in more capital being recycled, a partial sell-down also has its merits as some private investors may gain much comfort in investing alongside public institutional investors, thereby increasing the chances of getting private investors to buy into these projects.

Question 5

> • *Will Hong Kong become the major financial hub for the B&R Initiative?*
> *How can other financial places also play a role in the B&R Initiative?*

Hong Kong is a leading international financial center with well-developed capital markets, and it remains the main gateway to China. In 2004, Hong Kong was the first offshore market to launch a renminbi business, and since then Hong Kong has become the main global hub for renminbi trade settlement, financing and asset management.

As a result, Hong Kong is very well positioned to play a key role in the B&R Initiative in the following areas:

• *Financing*: As an international financial center, with a well-developed infrastructure, a vast and diverse investor base, and proximity to Mainland China, it can act as the gateway to facilitate cross-border flows.
• *Professional services:* With its excellent pool of well-educated labor and business professionals, Hong Kong is well positioned to provide related professional services, including risk management, dispute resolution and legal services, which are critical components of successful infrastructure projects. Hong Kong could also become a center for legal arbitration related to the B&R Initiative.

The Hong Kong authorities are actively supporting the initiative, including via the Infrastructure Financing Facilitation Office (IFFO) under the Hong Kong Monetary Authority (HKMA), and the Hong Kong Trade Development Council (HKTDC), a statutory body serving as the international market arm for Hong Kong-based import/export traders, manufacturers and service providers. Both have been actively promoting Hong Kong's role as the infrastructure financing center, leveraging the city's unique proximity and close ties to the Mainland, to provide platforms for relevant partners to share information, experience and best practices and bridge the gap between infrastructure financing and investment.

However, the market is very large. UBS research estimates total overseas direct investment (ODI) of between US$90–160 billion in B&R nations over the next five years (up to US$30 billion per annum), compared with investment of just US$14 billion per annum from 2014 to 2016. According to other estimates from UBS, B&R Initiative-related infrastructure, investments will range between US$312 billion and US$581 billion over the next five years. In this context, a number of other financial centers are also expected to play an important role in the B&R Initiative, including Singapore, London and potentially also Switzerland.

The enablers for a financial center to play a key role in B&R Initiative will likely include the following:

- *Geographic location*: The financial institutions should be located in a prominent position along the B&R Initiative markets and therefore be able to promote the connectivity along the corridors where the trades flow through.
- *Institutional development*: Housing global/local financial institutions (e.g. multilaterals, banks, funds) which will be the key force in facilitating the funding and investment to B&R Initiative.
- *Financial infrastructure*: Having a well-developed financial infrastructure, including deep and liquid foreign exchange and money markets, diversified capital market instruments, stable and free exchange rates.
- *Legal infrastructure*: Having a robust law system to support becoming a center for legal arbitration and dispute resolution.
- *Political support*: Having the necessary national and local governments' support for the B&R Initiative.
- *Professionals/talent*: Having high-quality professionals with the right profile and skillset that are critical components of successful infrastructure projects, for example, in project management, logistics, risk management and legal services.

Question 6

> • *How does UBS intend to make use of its strong presence in China, APAC and globally to participate in the funding of the B&R Initiative?*

We believe that the B&R Initiative has the potential to enhance prosperity along the Belt and Road routes and to increase connectivity between the Asian and European continents. UBS has a presence and market know-how in 28 B&R Initiative countries across Asia-Pacific (ASEAN, South Asia, Central Asia) and Europe (Central and Eastern Europe). Through our strong market understanding, global capabilities and reach, UBS is well positioned to play a role supporting and "bridging" our Chinese and global clients in their BRI endeavors. We see opportunities to support and collaborate with leading corporations when they are actively pursuing B&R Initiative investments or providing services to B&R Initiative projects, such as Chinese sovereign wealth funds and leading transport, construction and infrastructure companies.

More specifically, we think that UBS can play a role in the following areas:

- Capital markets financing advisory and bond/equity underwriting, to address the financing needs of corporate/institutional clients who are involved in B&R Initiative.
- M&A financing and advisory services, as Chinese companies expand into B&R Initiative markets.
- Trade finance and FX solutions, for both Swiss and international corporates.
- Infrastructure investment mandates, for our Asset Management and Wealth Management clients.

We will be monitoring the evolution of the B&R Initiative and will continue to identify new attractive opportunities to work with our clients and counterparties on the B&R Initiative projects.

Question 7

> • *Do you think that a UBS engagement might also be interesting for Swiss infrastructure companies?*

UBS is committed to contributing to the further strengthening of connectivity under the B&R Initiative between China, which is a strategic priority for the firm, and Switzerland, which is our home market. We have a leading corporate and investment banking platform in Switzerland with strong relationships with Swiss companies across infrastructure-related sectors.

We believe that B&R Initiative projects will trigger the needs for our clients in the areas of trade finance and financing through capital markets. This would include those from core infrastructure sectors (e.g. energy supply, distribution and storage), as well as subcontractors or suppliers (e.g. equipment, technology and logistics) and we will maintain close dialogues with our clients and partners in China and the other B&R Initiative nations to gain insights into local project components and provide project ideas to Swiss corporates where they can play a role and bring in expertise, e.g. as a technology provider, engineer or designer.

In addition, in our view, infrastructure will be only part of the equation, and we see B&R Initiative as a broader driver of economic growth and integration across many of the countries it will affect. In the longer run, this will expand to developing modern retail, commercial real estate, healthcare and education among the B&R Initiative nations. With our broad sector coverage and country network, as well as global client franchise and distribution capabilities, we believe we could support the needs of not only the Swiss infrastructure companies but also those in other sectors and from other markets.

UBS — A First Mover in China

China represents one of the most important sources of new business opportunities for UBS across its businesses anywhere in the world. In 1964, it was the first Swiss-based bank to establish a presence in the Asia-Pacific region, primarily through its wealth-management business, and has provided corporate finance advice to Chinese enterprises since 1985.

The firm invested early in Mainland China and, since 1989, has expanded to establish a multi-entity domestic platform made up of multiple entities with a broad range of licenses, which aim to capture opportunities arising from ongoing wealth creation, market opening and globalization.

UBS' China strategy is centered on bolstering its leadership position in the investment bank and expanding the wealth and asset-management businesses. The firm expects to double headcount in China over the next few years.

The Investment Bank business focuses on maintaining its leading position among the foreign players, while pursuing onshore expansion via its securities JV platform (primarily in Equities and Corporate Client Solutions) to capture China market reform and globalization opportunities. UBS Securities Co. Ltd., with 24.99% owned by UBS, is the first foreign-invested fully-licensed securities firm in China. It offers solutions for Chinese corporate and institutional clients looking for advice with respect to capital markets financing and M&A. It provides equities and fixed-income trading and execution services to both domestic institutions as well as QFII/RQFII clients. The research team offers not only differentiated independent content but also the most comprehensive coverage of any joint-venture companies in China.

The firm aspires to pursue wealth-management business expansion amid the continued, strong market growth. This will be enabled by leveraging the two existing domestic entities, the securities JV and the wholly foreign-owned bank UBS (China) Ltd., as well as the firm's top-notch offshore platform. The strategic vision is to develop capabilities and deliver over time the firm's full wealth-management value proposition, providing clients' access to advisory and investment solutions underpinned by UBS' scale and global resources.

UBS aims to become a leading player in asset-management business in China for both onshore and offshore investors, and a strong partner to Chinese clients investing overseas. To achieve the goal, the firm has built up a multi-entity platform with requisite licenses, which consists of UBS SDIC Fund Management Co. Ltd., 49% owned joint venture, offering onshore mutual funds; wholly-owned UBS Asset Management (Shanghai) Ltd., providing institutional and high net-worth investors in China with private funds, investing both onshore and overseas under the Qualified Domestic Limited Partner (QDLP) scheme; and wholly owned UBS Asset Management (China) Ltd., offering investment management and advisory services for alternative assets.

The firm has also established its service center in China, UBS Business Solutions (China) Co. Ltd., which provides exclusive services to UBS businesses domestically, regionally and globally, maximizing cost and process efficiencies across the firm. It has now expanded its footprint to three locations across China — Shanghai, Beijing and Wuxi — with over 500 employees from the local talent pool.

In addition to onshore China, Hong Kong has always been a hub for UBS in the Asia-Pacific and a headquarters for its investment bank and wealth and asset-management business in the region. UBS Wealth Management is the leading manager of wealth in Asia-Pacific with an excess of CHF 345 billion of assets under management. The Corporate Client Solution (CCS), Equities and Fixed Income, Rates & Currencies (FRC) businesses provide clients with market-leading advice and intermediation, and high-quality solutions via best-in-class technology and infrastructure platforms. The Equities and FRC businesses are focused on providing pricing transparency and sales efficiency.

UBS milestones

1964 — Opens first office in Asia-Pacific in Hong Kong

1985 — Begins to provide corporate finance advice to Chinese companies

1989 — Opens representative offices in Beijing and Shanghai

2003 — Becomes the first international institution to receive Qualified Foreign Institutional Investor (QFII) status

2004 — Opens UBS AG Beijing Branch

2005 — Establishes a joint venture with the State Development Investment Corporation and becomes the first international institution to hold a maximum 49% stake in a Chinese fund management company

2006 — Incorporates UBS Securities Co. Ltd. and becomes the first international bank to invest directly in a fully licensed domestic securities firm

2011 — Establishes UBS Global Asset Management (China) Ltd.

2012 — Converts UBS AG Beijing Branch into UBS (China) Ltd. and becomes the first Swiss bank to establish a wholly foreign-owned bank in China

2014 — Establishes UBS (China) Ltd. Beijing Huamao sub-branch, UBS' first ground-floor presence in Asia-Pacific

2015 — UBS Asset Management launches QDLP (Qualified Domestic Limited Partner) business

2016 — Opens Wuxi Branch of UBS Business Solutions (China) Co. Ltd.; Opens UBS (China) Ltd. Shanghai Branch

2017 — UBS Asset Management receives Private Fund Management License

Bibliography

Textbooks

— Cristiano Rizzi, Paolo Rizzi, Lex Smith and Li Guo, *Chinese Expansion in the EU — Strategies and Policies of the Two Blocks and the Role of the U.S.*, American Bar Association, August 2016.

— Brian Edward Banner, Yee Wah Chin, Drew Foerster, Trevor Gates, Daniel J. Gervais, Fuxiao Jiang, LLD, Jiancheng Jiang, C. Frederick Koenig III, Cristiano Rizzi, Yin Shao, Lex Smith, Kate Spelman, Donna Suchy, Xianjin Tian, Mark Wittrow, Jessica Xu, Hu Yuzhang and Stephen Yang, *IP Protection in China*, American Bar Association, Donna Suchy, Editor, published by the IP Section of the American Bar Association, June, 2015.

— Cristiano Rizzi, *E-Commerce Law in China — The Functioning of E-commerce in China and the Influence of the EU Model*, Wolters Kluwer, Law & Business, September, 2013.

— Cristiano Rizzi, Li Guo and Joseph Christian, *Mergers and Acquisitions and Takeovers in China — A Legal and Cultural Guide to New Forms of Investment*, Wolters Kluwer Law & Business, 2012.

— Shan Wenhua, *The Legal Framework of EU–China Investment Relations: A Critical Appraisal*, Hart Publishing, 2005.

— V. Io Lo and X. Tian, *Law and Investment in China — The Legal and Business Environments After WTO Accession*, Routledge Curzon Abingdon, 2005.

— Wolff, Lutz-Christian, Zhang Xian-Chu and Charles Zhen Qu, *Chinese Business Laws*, CCH Hong Kong Limited, 2008.

— Maria Weber, C. Berbatelli, R. Cavalieri, V. Gattai, S. Sideri, W. R. Vanhonacker and S. Vettori, *La Cina non è per tutti: Rischi e opportunità del più grande mercato del mondo*, Olivares Milano 2005.

Other Sources: Reports, Pieces of Legislation and Articles (English and Chinese)

— Abu Dhabi fund takes 9.9% stake in Thames Water. The document is available at http://www.arabianbusiness.com/abu-dhabi-fund-takes-9-9-stake-in-thames-water-434970.html (last accessed on October 12, 2014).

— Agreement between the European Communities and the Government of the United States of America regarding the application of their competition laws, September 23, 1991, reprinted in 4 Trade Reg. Rpt. (CCH) 13, 504, and OJ L95 (27 Apr. 1995) corrected at OJ L131/38 (June 15, 1995).

— 'Along the Silk Roads', the Venice Port Authority, together with the Foundation for Worldwide Cooperation and Nakai University (Center for the SILK ROAD STUDIES), with the support of the Binhai New Area (the Special Economic Zone in Tianjin), and in cooperation with TWAI, the Centre for Mediterranean Area Studies and Ca'Foscari University, has organized the International Conference 'Along the Silk Roads' in Venice. Introduced by President Romano Prodi and the President of the Venice Port Authority, Paolo Costa, the Conference was attended by Minister of Foreign Affairs Paolo Gentiloni, Minister of Infrastructure Graziano Delrio, Austrian Transport Minister Jörg Leichtfried, the Russian Minister for Euro-Asian Integration, Tatiana Valovaya, as well as by other representatives of various institutions and Think Tanks from China, Asia and Europe. https://www.port.venice.it/en/the-international-conference-along-the-silk-roads.html.

— All the legislation concerning QFII is available at: http://www.csrc.gov.cn/pub/csrc_en/OpeningUp/RelatedPolices/QFII/ (last accessed on March 21, 2018).

— American Law Institute, *Principles of Corporate Governance: Analysis and Recommendations*, trans. by LOU Jianbo *et al.*, Law Press, 2006, p. 13 (美国法律研究院: 《公司治理原则: 分析与建议》, 楼建波等译, 法律出版社 2006 年版, 第 13 页).

— *BBC News*, "China wealth fund buys nearly 9% of Thames Water". The document is available at http://www.bbc.co.uk/news/business-16643989 (last accessed on October 12, 2014).

— *ChemChina to Buy Controlling Stake in Pirelli*, http://www.wsj.com/articles/china-national-chemical-corp-to-buy-controlling-stake-in-pirelli-1427065364.

— China Business Update, *Outward FDI Chapter: How to 'Go Out' Smoothly?* April 24, 2013.

— Chris V. Nicholson, "CIC Approved to Buy Stake in Apax Partners". The document is available at http://dealbook.blogs.nytimes.com/2010/02/04/cic-approved-to-buy-stake-in-apax-partners/ (last accessed on October 12, 2014).

— Christopher Cox, "The Rise of Sovereign Business", Gauer Distinguished Lecture in Law & Policy at the American Enterprise Institute. The document is available at http://www.sec.gov/news/speech/2007/spch120507cc.htm (last accessed on last October 12, 2014).

— Dan Milmo and Gwyn Topham, "China takes 10% stake in Heathrow", *The Guardian*, available at http://www.theguardian.com/business/2012/oct/31/china-takes-stake-heathrow (last accessed on October 12, 2014).

— Daniel H. Ronen, *Avoiding the Blind Alley: China's Economic Overhaul and Its Global Implications*, Asa Society Policy Institute, 2014.

— Daniel H. Rosen and Thilo Hanemann, *New Realities in the US–China Investment Relationship*, Rhodium Group and the U.S. Chamber of Commerce, April 2014.

— David Dollar, *United States-China Two-way Direct Investment: Opportunities and Challenges*, Brookings Institution, December 2014.

— David M. Smick, *The World is Curved: Hidden Dangers to the Global Economy*, CITIC Press, 2009.

— *Europe 2020 — A Strategy for Smart, Sustainable and Inclusive Growth* (COM (2010)) 2020 final, Brussels, 3.3.2010. The document is available at: http://eur-lex.europa.eu/LexUriServ/LexUriServ.do?uri=COM:2010:2020:FIN:EN:PDF (last accessed on March 21, 2018).

— European Commission, Report From the Commission, Report on Competition Policy 2012, COM(2013) 257 final.

— European Commission, Antitrust — Manual of Procedures, Internal DG Competition working documents an procedures for the application of Articles 101 and 102 TFEU, March 2012. The document is available at: http://ec.europa.eu/competition/antitrust/antitrust_manproc_3_2012_en.pdf (last accessed on March 21, 2018).

— European Council on Foreign Relations, China Analysis, *China and the Mediterranean: Open for Business?* This document is available at: http://www.ecfr.eu/publications/summary/china_and_the_mediterranean_open_for_business (last accessed on March 21, 2018).

— EU Commission Staff Working Document — Impact Assessment Report on the EU–China Investment Relations, COM (2013) 297 final, and SWD (2013) 184 final (last accessed on March 21, 2018).

— EU–China 2020 Strategic Agenda for Cooperation, November 2013. This document is available at: http://eeas.europa.eu/delegations/china/documents/news/20131123.pdf.

— EU–China BIT negotiations. The document is available at: http://www.euro-biz.com.cn/eu-china-bit-negotiations/ (last accessed on March 21, 2018).

— Frans-Paul van der Putten, John Seaman, Mikko Huotari, Alice Ekman and Miguel Otero-Iglesias (eds.), *Europe and China's New Silk Road*, ETNC Report, December 2016. The document is available at: https://www.clingendael.nl/sites/default/files/Europe_and_Chinas_New_Silk_Roads_0.pdf.

— Feng Zhongping, Xi's Initiatives for EU Partnership, *China Daily*, April 3, 2014.

— GAO Chen, "CIC entered into British Real Estates Industry through investment in Songbird Estates", *Beijing Times*, September 2, 2009 (高晨: "入股英国歌鸟公司 中投进军英国房地产市场",《京华时报》2009 年 9 月 2日).

— GAO Xiaozhen and JIANG Xinghui, "Britain's Financial Big Bang and the Revival of City of London", Research Center Report of China Securities Regulatory Commission, 2006.

— George Friedman and Mauldin Economics, July 19, 2017, *One Belt One Road Doomed to Failure*. This document is available at: https://amp.businessinsider.com/one-belt-one-road-doomed-to-failure-2017-7 (last accessed on March 21, 2018).

— George Parker, "Brown Urges China Fund to Use City as Hub", *Financial Times*. The document is available at: http://www.ftchinese.com/story/001016852/en (last accessed on October 12, 2014).

— Graham Ruddick, "Qatar Investment Authority backs UK", *The Telegraph*, available at http://www.telegraph.co.uk/finance/newsbysector/retailandconsumer/10630475/Qatar-Investment-Authority-backs-UK.html (last accessed on October 12, 2014).

— Guo Li, "China Investment Corporation: A Financial Holding Company Supervising the Sovereign Wealth Fund", *Peking University Law Journal*, 2009, Vol. 21, No. 4, pp. 533–544.

— Guo Li, "Demystifying the Chinese Sovereign Wealth Fund Amidst U.S. Financial Regulation", *Tsinghua China Law Review*, 2010, Vol. 2, No. 2, p. 353.

— Initial appraisal of the European Commission Impact Assessment — European Commission proposal on EU-China Investment Relations — Impact Assessment (SWD (2013) 185, SWD (2013) 184 (summary)) for a Recommendation for a Council Decision authorising the opening of negotiations on an investment agreement between the European Union and the People's Republic of China. This document is available at: http://www.

europarl.europa.eu/RegData/etudes/note/join/2013/514077/IPOL-JOIN_NT(2013)514077_EN.pdf (last accessed on March 21, 2018).

— IMF International Working Group of Sovereign Wealth Funds", Press Release No. 08/06(c). The document is available at: http://www.iwg-swf.org/pr/swfpr0806.htm (last accessed on October 12, 2014).

— International financial analysis team of People's Bank of China Shanghai Head Office, "International Financial Market Report of 2007". The document is available at http://finance.sina.com.cn/china/hgjj/20080319/15544642368.shtml (last accessed on October 12, 2014).

— International Monetary Fund, Country Report No. 13/211, People's Republic of China, July 2013.

— Jeremy Clegg and Hinrich Voss, *Chinese Overseas Direct Investment in the European Union*, Europe China Research and Advice Network, 2012.

— Jonathan Braude, "New German Foreign Investment Law Faces Challenges", *The Deal*, September 8, 2008.

— Kabita Kumari Sahu, "Does Urbanisation Promote Foreign Direct Investment? Lessons and Evidences from China and India", *International Journal of Arts and Commerce*, 2013, Vol. 3, No. 2, pp. 17–26.

— Karl P. Sauvant and Victor Zitian Chen, "China's Regulatory Framework for Outward Foreign Direct Investment," *China Economic Journal*, 2014, Vol. 7, No. 1, pp. 141–163.

— LI Liming, "CIC Has Decided Its Entrusted Private Equity Fund Partner for a USD 4 Billion Investment", *The Economic Observer*, April 6, 2008 (李利明: "中投选定 40 亿美元私募股权基金合伙人",《经济观察报》, 2008 年 4 月 6 日).

— LV Ming and YE Mei, "Thesis on Transparency of SWFs", *Journal of Finance and Economics*, 2008, Vol. 5, pp. 106–113 (吕明、叶眉: "主权财富基金信息透明度问题研究",《广东金融学院学报》, 2008 年第5期, 第106–113 页.

— Lynia Lau, *China: Approval and Regulatory Requirements For Chinese Foreign Direct Investment*, May 2014 (mondaq).

— Matthew Saxon, "It's Just Business, Or Is It?: How Business and Politics Collide With Sovereign Wealth Funds", *Hastings International & Comparative Law Review*, 2009, 32, p. 693.

— "Marseille Builds Links with the 'Belt and Road Initiative'" (法国马赛对接"一带一路" 建设, faguo masai duijie "yi dai yi lu" jianshe), *Jingji Ribao*, February 21, 2017. The document is available at: http://china.chinadaily.com.cn/2017-02/21/content_28291376.htm (hereafter, Jingji Ribao, "Marseille builds links with the 'Belt and Road Initiative'").

— MA Jianguo, "Lou Jiwei: CIC Would be Better off without Being Too Transparent and Emphasize on Long-term Investment Return", *Xinhua Net* (马建国,《楼继伟: 中投不宜太透明 强调长期投资收益》, 新华网). The document is available at http://news.xinhuanet.com/fortune/2007-12/12/content_7232132.htm (last accessed on last October 12, 2014).

— Mei Xinyu, "Growing Influence — China Takes on Greater Global Responsibilities", *Beijing Review*, February 2017, Vol. 60, No. 5–6.

— NDRC, June 19, 2012, Notice on Guiding and Encouraging Private Enterprises to Conduct Foreign Investment (unofficial translation by the European Chamber of Commerce in China).

— ODI Set to Become more Diverse, *China Daily*, October 16, 2013.

— OUYANG Xiaohong, "Will CIC Invest in Italy? Gao Xiqing Secretly Negotiated Investment Portfolio in Rome", *Economic Observer*, February 6, 2010. 欧阳晓红: "中投看上意大利? 高西庆赴罗马密洽组合投资",《经济观察报》, 2010 年 2 月 6 日.

— *Paris 2015 — Getting a Global Agreement on Climate Change.* The document is available at: http://www.green-alliance.org.uk/resources/Paris%20 2015-getting%20a%20global%20agreement%20on%20climate%20change. pdf (last accessed on March 21, 2018).

— Philip Schellekens, *A Changing China: Implications for Developing Countries*, May 2013.

— *Provisions on the Foreign Exchange Administration of the Overseas Direct Investment of Domestic Institutions* issued by the State Administration of Foreign Exchange ("SAFE"), 2013.

— Report by the European Chamber of Commerce in China, "*Chinese Outbound Investment in the European Union*, European Chamber, January 2013.

— Report by the World Bank and the Development Research Center of the State Council, "*China 2030 — Building a Modern, Harmonious, and Creative High-Income Society,*" 2013.

— Richard McGregor and Jenny Wiggins, "CIC's 1.1% Diageo Stake Fits Emerging Strategy", *Financial Times*, July 21, 2009.

— Ronald J. Gilson and Curtis J. Milhaupt, "Sovereign Wealth Funds and Corporate Governance: A Minimalist Response to the New Mercantilism", *Stanford Law Review*, 2008, Vol. 60, No. 5, pp. 1345–1369.

— Stephen J. Choi and Jill E. Fisch, "On Beyond CalPERS: Survey Evidence on the Developing Role of Public Pension Funds in Corporate Governance", NYU Law and Economics Research Paper No. 07-30, 2007.

— Study by Ernst & Young, *China Going Global*, 2013. The document is available at the following website: http://personal.vu.nl/p.j.peverelli/Ernst YoungReport.pdf (last accessed on March 21, 2018).

— Report by EIAS, *The EU–China Investment Agreement: Projections, Expectations and Hurdles,* December, 2013.

— Rhodium Group, *China Invests in Europe — Patterns, Impacts and Policy Implications,* June 2012.

— SHENG Xuejun (ed.), *Survey of EU Securities Regulation*, Law Press, 2005, p. 362 (盛学军编:《欧盟证券法研究》, 法律出版社, 2005 年版, 第 362页).

— Steffen Kern, *SWFs and Foreign Investment Policies — An Update*, Deutsche Bank Research, October 22, 2008.

— SUN Ke and KUANG Ye, "SWFs Actively Engages in Financial Markets While CIC is Determining Its Investment Strategy", *21st Century Business Herald*, May 12, 2008 (孙轲、旷野: "主权财富基金积极进入金融市场, 中投定投资策略",《21 世纪经济报道》2008 年 5 月 12 日).

— Terms of Reference of the EU–China Competition Policy Dialogue, is available at: http://ec.europa.eu/competition/international/bilateral/cn2b_en.pdf (last accessed on March 21, 2018).

— The Comprehensive EU–China Investment Agreement. The document is available at: http://trade.ec.europa.eu/doclib/press/index.cfm?id=1013 (last accessed on March 21, 2018).

— *The Indian Express, China Companies Plan to Step up Europe Investment,* 2013. http://www.indianexpress.com/news/china-companies-plan-to-step-up-europe-investment/1067277/1 (last accessed on March 21, 2018).

— The EU Commission, Best Practices on the Conduct of EC Merger Control Proceedings. The document is available at: http://ec.europa.eu/competition/mergers/legislation/proceedings.pdf (last accessed on March 21, 2018).

— *The EU–China Investment Agreement: Projections, Expectations and Hurdles*, European Institute for Asian Studies (EIAS), 2013.

— Thilio Hanemann, *How Europe Should Respond to Growing Chinese Investment*, September 2012.

— Thilo Hanemann, *Chinese Investment: Europe vs. the United States*, February 25, 2013.

— Thilo Hanemann and Cassie Gao, Chinese FDI in the US: 2013 Recap and 2014 Outlook, Rhodium Group, January 7, 2014. The document is available at: http://rhg.com/notes/hinese-fdi-in-the-us-2013-recap-and-2014-outlook.

— Thilo Hanemann and Adam Lysenko, *Chinese Investment: Europe vs. the United States*, Rhodium Group, February 25, 2013.

— Thilo Hanemann and Daniel H. Rosen, *China Invests in Europe — Patterns, Impacts and Policy Implication*, Rhodium Group, 2012.

— Tian Yun and Ouyang Xiaohong, "Detailed List of CIC Overseas Mergers and Acquisitions", *The Economic Observer*, March 22, 2010 (田芸、欧阳晓红: "中投海外并购明细单", 《经济观察报》 2010 年 3 月 22 日第 1 版).

— Towards a Comprehensive European International Investment Policy (COM (2010)342 final), Brussels, 7.7.2010. The document is available at: http://trade. ec.europa.eu/doclib/docs/2011/may/tradoc_147884.pdf (last accessed on March 21, 2018).

— U.S. and Chinese Delegations Conclude 25th Session of the U.S. — China Joint Commission on Commerce and Trade. Visit: http://www.commerce. gov/news/press-releases/2014/12/18/us-and-chinese-delegations-conclude-25th-session-us-china-joint-commi (last accessed on March 21, 2018).

— WANG Xia and WANG Shuguang, "SWFs and Investment Protections of Western Countries", *On Economic Problems*, 2008, Vol. 6, pp. 110–112. (王霞、王曙光: "谈主权财富基金与西方投资保护措施", 《经济问题》, 2008年第6期, 第110–112页) Wayne M. Morrison, *China–U.S. Trade issues*, Congressional Research Service, March 2015.

— Wayne M. Morrison, Congressional Research Service, *China–U.S. Trade Issues*, July 10, 2014.

— Why foreign funds thirst for UK water, *The Telegraph*. The document is available at http://www.telegraph.co.uk/finance/newsbysector/utilities/10093391/Why-foreign-funds-thirst-for-UK-water.htm (last accessed on October 12, 2014).

— World Bank, *Country Partnership Strategy for the Period FY13–FY16*, 2012.

— World Bank, Report No. 67566–CN, *International Bank for Reconstruction and Development International Finance Corporation and Multilateral Investment Guarantee Agency Country Partnership Strategy for the People's Republic of China for the Period FY2013–FY2016* (last accessed on October 11, 2012).

— Wu Jiangang, On the Right Road to Acquisition in Europe, *China Daily*, October 14, 2013, p. 20.

— Wu Yiyao, PBOC Boss Sheds Light on Yuan Exchange Rate, *China Daily*, April 12, 2014.

— *Financial reform 'one of China's easiest'*, article by Liu Chang and Cai Chunying, China Daily, April 12, 2014.

— Xian Guoyi, Upgrade Outbound Investment, *China Daily*, November 8, 2013.

— XIANG Jing and WANG Susheng, "Thesis on International Comparison and Transforming Trend of SWFs", *Academic Research*, 2009, Vol. 5, pp. 75–80

(向静、王苏生: "主权财富基金的国际比较和变化趋势研究", 《学术研究》2009年第5期, 第75–80页).

— XIE Ping and CHEN Chao, "The Theoretical Logic of Sovereign Wealth Funds", *Economic Research Journal*, 2009, No. 2, pp. 4–17(谢平、陈超: "论主权财富基金的理论逻辑", 《经济研究》, 2009年第2期, 第 4–17 页.

— YE Tan, "CIC Invested in Songbird Estates: Another Stupid Business?" (叶檀, "中投投资歌鸟: 又一笔愚蠢生意? ", 财华网). The document is available at: http://caihuanet.com/zhuanlan/geren/yetan/200909/t20090902_984076.shtml (last accessed on October 12, 2014).

— Yin Zhen, "Stand High, Look Far, Go Steady To Promote Three Seas Seaports Cooperation" (推进三海港区合作要站得高、看得远、走得稳, tuijin sanhai gangqu hezuo yaozhan de gao, kan de yuan, zou de wen), *Zhongguo yuanyang chuanwu*, 2016, 3: pp. 54–55.

— ZHANG Lijuan, "The Direct Effect of Directives", ZHAO Haifeng and LU Jianping (eds.), *European Law Review*, Vol. 2, Law Press, 2001, p. 76 (张丽娟: "共同体指令的直接效力", 载赵海峰、卢建平主编: 《欧洲法通讯》, 第2辑, 法律出版社, 2001年版, 第76页).

— Zhong Nan, Top Officials: Boost B&R Finance Links, *China Daily*, June 29, 2017. This document is available at: http://www.chinadaily.com.cn/business/2017-06/29/content_29926835.htm (last accessed on March 21, 2018).

— ZHONG Wei and WANG Tianlong, "Controversy around SWFs: Do We Need an International Regulatory Framework?", *Foreign Exchange*, January 19, 2009 (钟伟、王天龙: "围绕主权财富基金的争议: 是否需要一个国际监管框架? ", 《中国外汇》, 2009 年1月19日).

— Zhu Ruixue, Liu Xiuling and Cai Li, "Background and Strategic Significance of the Belt and Road Initiative of China", *Journal of Behavioural Economics, Finance, Entrepreneurship, Accounting and Transport*, 2016, Vol. 4, No. 3.

Official Documents Related to the Belt and Road Initiative Are as Follows:

• Education Action Plan for the Belt and Road Initiative, Belt and Road Portal, https://eng.yidaiyilu.gov.cn (last accessed on March 21, 2018).

• Vision for Maritime Cooperation under the Belt and Road Initiative (Seven language versions), Belt and Road Portal, https://eng.yidaiyilu.gov.cn (last accessed on March 21, 2018).

- Initiative on Promoting Unimpeded Trade Cooperation along the Belt and Road, Belt and Road Portal, https://eng.yidaiyilu.gov.cn (last accessed on March 21, 2018).
- China Outbound Investment Report, Belt and Road Portal, https://eng.yidaiyilu.gov.cn (last accessed on March 21, 2018).
- Vision and Actions on Energy Cooperation in Jointly Building Silk Road Economic Belt and 21st — Century Maritime Silk Road, Belt and Road Portal, https://eng.yidaiyilu.gov.cn (last accessed on March 21, 2018).
- Guiding Principles on Financing the Development of the Belt and Road, Belt and Road Portal, https://eng.yidaiyilu.gov.cn (last accessed on March 21, 2018).
- Joint communique of leaders roundtable of Belt and Road forum, Belt and Road Portal, https://eng.yidaiyilu.gov.cn (last accessed on March 21, 2018).
- The Belt and Road Ecological and Environmental Cooperation Plan, Belt and Road Portal, https://eng.yidaiyilu.gov.cn (last accessed on March 21, 2018).
- Vision And Actions On Jointly Building Silk Road Economic Belt And 21st-Century Maritime Silk Road, Belt and Road Portal, https://eng.yidaiyilu.gov.cn (last accessed on March 21, 2018).
- Report on Development of China's Outward Investment and Economic Cooperation (2016), Belt and Road Portal, https://eng.yidaiyilu.gov.cn (last accessed on March 21, 2018).
- Ministry of Culture's Action Plan on Belt and Road Culture Development (2016–20), Belt and Road Portal, https://eng.yidaiyilu.gov.cn (last accessed on March 21, 2018).
- Guidance on Promoting Green Belt and Road, Belt and Road Portal, https://eng.yidaiyilu.gov.cn (last accessed on March 21, 2018).
- Building the Belt and Road: Concept, Practice and China's Contribution (Seven language versions), Belt and Road Portal, https://eng.yidaiyilu.gov.cn (last accessed on March 21, 2018).
- Vision and Action on Jointly Promoting Agricultural Cooperation on the Belt and Road, Belt and Road Portal, https://eng.yidaiyilu.gov.cn (last accessed on March 21, 2018).
- Action Plan on Belt and Road Standard Connectivity (2015–17), Belt and Road Portal, https://eng.yidaiyilu.gov.cn (last accessed on March 21, 2018).
- Development Plan of China-Europe Freight Train Construction (2016–20), Belt and Road Portal, https://eng.yidaiyilu.gov.cn (last accessed on March 21, 2018).

- Action Plan on Development of Belt and Road Sports Tourism (2017–20), Belt and Road Portal, https://eng.yidaiyilu.gov.cn (last accessed on March 21, 2018).
- Guidelines on Construction of China-Mongolia-Russia Economic Corridor, Belt and Road Portal, https://eng.yidaiyilu.gov.cn (last accessed on March 21, 2018).
- 'The Belt and Road' Vision and Actions for Cooperation in Metrology, Belt and Road Portal, https://eng.yidaiyilu.gov.cn (last accessed on March 21, 2018).
- Asian Infrastructure Investment Bank Articles of Agreement, Belt and Road Portal, https://eng.yidaiyilu.gov.cn (last accessed on March 21, 2018).
  More documents are available at https://eng.yidaiyilu.gov.cn (last accessed on March 21, 2018).

Internet Sources:

— Belt and Road Portal, https://eng.yidaiyilu.gov.cn/info (last accessed on March 21, 2018).
— Asian Infrastructure Investment Bank (AIIB), https://www.aiib.org/en/index.html (last accessed on March 21, 2018).
— Asian Development Bank, www.adb.org (last accessed on March 21, 2018).
— Silk Road Fund, http://www.silkroadfund.com.cn/enweb/23775/23767/index.html (last accessed on March 21, 2018).
— European Investment Bank, http://www.eib.org/ (last accessed on March 21, 2018).
— International Monetary Fund, http://www.imf.org/en/About (last accessed on March 21, 2018).
— European Commission: Trade policies, http://ec.europa.eu/trade/policy/countries-and-regions/countries/china/ (last accessed on March 21, 2018).
— European Centre for International Political Economy (ECIPE), http://www.ecipe.org/about-us/ (last accessed on March 21, 2018).
— European Investment Bank, http://europa.eu/about-eu/institutions-bodies/eib/index_en.htm (last accessed on March 21, 2018).
— Delegation of the European Union to China, http://eeas.europa.eu/delegations/china/eu_china/political_relations/index_en.htm (last accessed on March 21, 2018).
— State Council Opinions on Further Improving the Utilization of Foreign Investment (2010), http://www.uschina.org/members/documents/2010/04/sc_opinions_foreign_investment.pdf (last accessed on March 21, 2018).

The Consolidated Versions of the Treaty on European Union and the Treaty on the Functioning of the European Union Can be Downloaded at the Following Website:

— http://www.consilium.europa.eu/documents/treaty-of-lisbon?lang=en (last accessed on March 21, 2018).
— The Treaty of Lisbon: http://eur-lex.europa.eu/LexUriServ/LexUriServ.do?uri=OJ:C:2007:306:FULL:EN:PDF (last accessed on March 21, 2018).
— National Development and Reform Commission People's Republic of China (NDRC), http://en.ndrc.gov.cn//mfndrc/default.htm (last accessed on March 21, 2018).
— China Securities Regulatory Commission (CSRC), http://www.csrc.gov.cn/pub/csrc_en/ (last accessed on March 21, 2018).
— Information Centre of the Legislative Office of the State Council (last accessed on March 21, 2018).
— www.chinalaw.gov.cn (last accessed on March 21, 2018).
— Invest in China: www.fdi.org.cn (last accessed on March 21, 2018).
— State Administration Foreign Exchange, www.safe.gov.cn (last accessed on March 21, 2018).
— State Administration for Industry and Commerce, www.saic.gov.cn (last accessed on March 21, 2018).
— State Administration of Taxation, www.chinatax.gov.cn (last accessed on March 21, 2018).
— Ministry of Commerce, www.mofcom.gov.cn (last accessed on March 21, 2018).
— Ministry of Labor and Social Security, www.molss.gov.cn (last accessed on March 21, 2018).
— Supreme People's Court, www.court.gov.cn (last accessed on March 21, 2018).
— China Council for the Promotion of International Trade (CCPIT), www.ccpit.org/ (last accessed on March 21, 2018).
— China Foreign Investment Registration, www.wzj.gov.cn (last accessed on March 21, 2018).
— China Association of Enterprise with Foreign Investment (CAEFI), http:caefi2.mofcom.gov.cn/ (last accessed on March 21, 2018).
— China Internet Information Center, www.china.org.cn (last accessed on March 21, 2018).
— People's Bank of China, www.pbc.gov.cn (last accessed on March 21, 2018).

— World Bank, http://www.worldbank.org/en/country/china/overview (last accessed on March 21, 2018).
— World Trade Organization (WTO), http://wto.org (last accessed on March 21, 2018).
— World Intellectual Property Organization (WIPO), http://www.wipo.int/about-wipo/en/index.html (last accessed on March 21, 2018).
— International Centre for the Settlement of Investment Disputes (ICSID), www.worldbank.org/org/icsid (last accessed on March 21, 2018).
— Organisation of Economic Co-operation and Development (OECD), www.oecd.org/home (last accessed on March 21, 2018).
— DG Trade of the European Commission, http://europa.eu.int/comm/trade/index_en.htm (last accessed on March 21, 2018).
— DG External Relations of the European Commission, http://europa.eu.int/comm/dgs/external_relations/index_en.htm (last accessed on March 21, 2018).
— EU Delegation in China, www.delchn.cec.eu.int/ (last accessed on March 21, 2018).
— European Chamber of Commerce in China (EUCCC), www.euccc.com.cn/ (last accessed on March 21, 2018).
— Asia Invest, http://europa.eu.int/comm/europeaid/projects/asia-invest/ (last accessed on March 21, 2018).
— International Court of Justice (ICJ), www.icj-cij.org/ (last accessed on March 21, 2018).
— Asian Pacific Economic Co-operation (APEC), www.apecsec.org.sg/ (last accessed on March 21, 2018).

Other Internet Sources:

— OBOR Europe, http://www.oboreurope.com/en/about-us/ (last accessed on March 21, 2018).
— Mediterranean Dialogues (MED), https://rome-med.org/ (last accessed on March 21, 2018).
— The European TEN-T Network. https://ec.europa.eu/transport/themes/infra-structure/about-ten-t_en (last accessed on March 21, 2018).
— *China invests in Europe*, http://www.hsbc.com/news-and-insight/2015/china-invests-in-europe (last accessed on March 21, 2018).
— China Investment Corporation (CIC), http://www.china-inv.cn (last accessed on March 21, 2018).
— China-Britain Business Council (CBBC), http://www.cbbc.org/who_we_are/ (last accessed on March 21, 2018).

— World Association of Investment Promotion Agencies (WAIPA), http://www2.waipa.org/cms/Waipa/ (last accessed on March 21, 2018).
— Bureau of Economic Analysis. 1960–2014. "U.S. International Transactions, 1960– Present", http://www.bea.gov/international/index.htm (last accessed on March 21, 2018).
— Framework Plan for the China (Shanghai) Pilot Free Trade Zone, http://en.SFTZ.gov.cn/FrameworkPlan.html (last accessed on March 21, 2018).
— Special Administrative Measures (Negative List) on Foreign Investment, http://en.SFTZ.gov.cn/Special.html (last accessed on March 21, 2018).
— Administrative Measures for the China (Shanghai) Pilot Free Trade Zone, http://en.SFTZ.gov.cn/Administrative%20Measures.html (last accessed on March 21, 2018).
— Filing Administrative Measures for Outbound Investment in Setting up Enterprises, http://en.SFTZ.gov.cn/Investment.html (last accessed on March 21, 2018).
— Filing Administrative Measures for Outbound Investment Projects, http://en.SFTZ.gov.cn/Enterprises.html (last accessed on March 21, 2018).
— Polices and Measures on Capital Market for Supporting and Promoting SFTZ, http://en.SFTZ.gov.cn/Polices.html (last accessed on March 21, 2018).
— Silk Road Fund, http://www.silkroadfund.com.cn/enweb/23775/23767/index.html (last accessed on March 21, 2018).

Printed in the United States
By Bookmasters